Dedicated to 'the thousands who toiled with utmost devotion, confident in their abilities to overcome' by the authors Arvind Pande and Sanjay Kumar, 'Making The Elephant Dance' is a must-read for not only corporate leaders and managers, but also for research scholars, policymakers, consultants, teachers and management students or in fact for any individual who aspires to become a successful leader and bring about a miraculous transformation steering through all odds.

—*IRON & STEEL REVIEW, 2021*

The book 'Making the Elephant Dance' by Mr. Arvind Pande and Mr. Sanjay Kumar is a valuable contribution to the Management Literature. The insights from this book can be leveraged not only by the future managers of SAIL, but also managers across the Indian and global steel industry. I had been closely associated as a Management Advisor in a previous turnaround of SAIL in 1985-88 with the then Chairman Mr. V Krishnamurthy. His main message to the workers was: *let us together raise the production, productivity, and profits of SAIL, so that we can deserve a modernization investment of Rs. 15,000 crores from the Government of India*. The whole team marched towards this goal and SAIL rose from a loss of Rs. 350 Crores per annum to a profit of Rs. 1,000 Crores. A similar tune was echoed when 1991 Economic Reforms of India created a new and highly competitive environment. By 1997, SAIL needed another turnaround effort and this time the company was ably led under the captainship of Mr. Pande, who was Chairman from 1997 to 2002. Mr. Pande comes in the tradition of a Civil Servant, turned Manager, Corporate Leader, and writer. The book can be used creatively in MBA and Executive Training Programs. Each of the fifteen chapters can be seen as a case study with lessons in some of the key management issues. I commend this book to policy makers, business leaders, managers, teachers, and consultants.

—**Dr. M.B. Athreya (Padma Bhushan),**
Management Advisor,
One of the founders and pioneers of Indian Management Movement, Education and Executive Training

MAKING THE ELEPHANT DANCE

The Turnaround Story of SAIL

Arvind Pande | Sanjay Kumar

AF520682

ATLANTIC
PUBLISHERS & DISTRIBUTORS (P) LTD

ATLANTIC
PUBLISHERS & DISTRIBUTORS (P) LTD
7/22, Ansari Road, Darya Ganj, New Delhi
Tel.: +91-11-4077 5252, 2327 3880
E-mail: orders@atlanticbooks.com
Web: www.atlanticbooks.com

Published by Atlantic Publishers & Distributors (P) Ltd 2024

Previously Published by SAGE Publications in 2021

Printed & bound in India by Atlantic Print Services

Advance Praise

Shri Pande was at the helm of SAIL during some of its most difficu
years towards the end of the last century. Vagaries of a cyclical indu
try, SE Asia's economic meltdown, high capital charges, inadequ
competitive capabilities, etc., had pulled down the financial positio
India's largest steel company. Restructuring of the business, enhan
service parameters, improving product mix, downsizing manpo
etc., were some areas where complex decisions were taken. The e
organization was galvanized to bring about a remarkable turnar
in the fortunes of the company. As Chairman, Shri Pande had d
all and seen it all. This book portrays the journey of that transf
tion story. This book offers insights that can find resonance w
future practitioners in the steel industry. A great read!

—Soma M

Former Chairm

Making the Elephant Dance is a brilliant story of the exempl
round of SAIL, the pride of India, under the visionary le
its former Chairman Shri Arvind Pande who has penne
insight, his first-hand account of the restructuring and re
giant central PSU in the turbulent times by the turn of th
tury. This outstanding treatise is a must-read for corpo
research scholars, policymakers and management stude

—Prof.

Chairman, Centre of Corpor
CSR an
Indian Institute of Man

The book title 'Making the Elephant Dance' by Shri Arvind Pande and Shri Sanjay Kumar covers a crucial period in the chequered history of Steel Authority of India Ltd (SAIL). The book is a case study for management practitioners with several lessons. Most important is to never waste a crisis and use it as opportunity for structural improvements, which may otherwise be difficult to implement. The book is a valuable reference in the current season of privatisation and highly recommended for policy makers, managers, and academicians.

—K K Pahuja,
Former President,
Indian Stainless Steel Development Association (ISSDA)

Dedicated to the thousands who toiled with
utmost devotion, confident in their abilities to overcome.

Contents

Preface

The idea for this book has come from a shared perspective of how SAIL grappled with the economic reforms after 1991, the challenges it faced, the internal efforts by which these were tackled and the successful turnaround during 1997 to 2003. It is not intended to be either an academic exercise or an autobiographical effort but goes beyond the personal experiences of the authors to document an important part of India's corporate history.

The book is co-authored with Sanjay Kumar, who had joined SAIL in the mid-eighties as a young economist in the business planning department from where he has just superannuated as its head. He was closely associated with SAIL's Corporate Plan 2005 and has remained closely involved in all related actions in later years, including a close involvement with the entire exercise of turnaround and restructuring, which this book is about. He has also done all the painstaking research and data collection required to put this book together.

This book is a collaborative effort with some of my colleagues who were closely involved in the restructuring and turnaround of SAIL, which I had the privilege to lead, from January 1997 to September 2002. I had come to SAIL mid-career in 1986 after 21 years in the Indian Administrative Service (which had taken me to Madhya Pradesh, Government of India, the World Bank and the Prime Minister's Office), to join as a whole-time member of the Board. Many friends thought it was foolish to join what was then being seen as a sunset industry in India. I had come at the inspiration of Dr V. Krishnamurthy, who was then Chairman, SAIL and conceptualized and initiated the modernization of the older plants. SAIL culture began to change under his leadership.

Both SAIL and steel proved to be very resilient and fascinating and have continued to grow with a confident outlook towards the future. I went on to spend 16 years in SAIL, across different functions, the last six as Chairman and CEO. Those six years from January 1997 to September 2002 were, for me, the most challenging and satisfying years of my career. This started with a meeting with the then Prime Minister H. D. Deve Gowda before he approved my appointment as Chairman, SAIL. In those days and maybe even now, many looked at these jobs and these public sector companies as being used by political leaders for extractive purposes. I was apprehensive about this meeting but to the credit of then prime minister (PM) and my own relief, the meeting went off very cordially. His request was something that we ourselves, in SAIL, had been wanting to do. Visvesvaraya Iron and Steel Limited (VISL) at Bhadravati in Karnataka was an old steel company started by Sir Visvesvaraya and at that time SAIL owned 60 per cent of the company. The balance 40 per cent was owned by the Karnataka government. It was not doing too well and Shri Deve Gowda was keen that SAIL take over the Karnataka government's share and make it a 100 per cent subsidiary of SAIL. We had ourselves wanted to do this so that we could invest more time and resources in the company and improve its health. We, however, did not want to be saddled with the company's liabilities. The then PM immediately agreed to get the balance sheet cleaned up so that there would be no additional liability to SAIL. He not only agreed but over the next month personally called up ministers and secretaries in the finance, steel and relevant ministries to get this done. My memories of him are very pleasant.

This was a good start to the challenges we would have to face in the next few years and what this book is about—a company on the brink of being declared sick but being successfully turned around largely by the efforts of its own employees and leadership.

While the focus of the book is on SAIL's restructuring and turnaround from 1997 to 2003, some reference to the past may be useful to understand how the steel industry grew in India in the early years.

The pre-Independence period was dominated by Sir Jamshetji Tata at Jamshedpur, Sir Biren Mukherjee at Burnpur and Sir Visvesvaraya at Bhadravati in the south. Post-Independence growth of the public sector—Nehru's temples of modern India—happened mostly in the 1950s and 1960s at Rourkela, Bhilai, Durgapur and Bokaro and contributed to nation building. The 1970s saw a slowdown in the steel industry, when the emphasis of the government's Five-Year Plans shifted to poverty removal and the rural sector.

The 1980s were when this hugely technology-driven industry could not modernize. Even early in the decade, the Indian steel industry was far behind those in countries like Brazil, Korea and China, even though their plants did not even exist when the Indian steel plants were built in the 1950s.

Around the mid-1980s, realization dawned as regards the need to do something for this critical industry. Price controls were gradually relaxed and efforts were made to modernize the older steel plants.

Total delicensing and decontrol of the steel industry in India occurred in one stroke in the 1991–1992 fiscal and changed the dynamics of the industry. New players came in the market and began to fight for market share. The integrated steel plants of SAIL and TISCO (now Tata Steel) began to dominate the market less and less.

The home industry became increasingly vulnerable to international price fluctuations, as the liberalization package included a progressive cutback in excise and customs duties and the near captive home market was increasingly poached on by the steel mills of the Commonwealth of Independent States (CIS).

The euphoria over a free market proved short-lived, as steel makers in India learnt to cope with the backlash of global trends. After the Asian crisis of 1997 and the consequent slowdown in the world and India's economy, the demand for steel slumped. That was also when new capacities were coming up in the private sector. SAIL was completing a massive modernization programme of ₹12,000 crores (at the nineties' prices) in the Durgapur, Rourkela and Bokaro steel plants, which had begun in the late 1980s and early nineties. These investments were financed largely by market borrowings and internal resources, with no cash or budgetary support from the government or exposure to commercial banks.

Completion of this modernization programme and benefits therefrom happened in the late nineties. Meanwhile, SAIL was facing a heavy debt burden and lower price realizations affecting the bottom line. SAIL was also carrying a legacy of what was earlier considered our contribution towards nation building in terms of higher costs for manpower, townships, social amenities and other efforts to develop backward regions. In 1997–1998, it was close to being declared a sick company. In fact, in one of the Board meetings around that time, one of the Directors had predicted that we would soon be out on the streets. We were to prove him wrong.

In the next few years, however, through actions described in this book, it was able to turn around, leave the worst behind and become a very healthy company. It would have been very easy to allow SAIL to go to the Board of Industrial and Financial Reconstruction (BIFR) and be treated like a sick company—as many felt was inevitable—get protection from debt repayments and slowly try to revive. The SAIL collective refused to let this happen and stood together to face and overcome the challenges. This is the main story—the determination of the SAIL family to come together and take actions and decisions, which were unprecedented and, in a sense, unbelievable.

The SAIL spirit can be traced to the early years of the 1950s when the brightest of the country's engineers, metallurgists and managers joined the company to open up backward areas and build steel plants, which were not only massive in their size but also in their complexity—converting a piece of earth (iron ore) to the most complex and sophisticated steels used in advanced technologies like space and nuclear applications. They also built well laid-out townships, with schools, hospitals, community centres, stadia, etc., which enabled them to develop a strong sense of camaraderie. Families grew together, shared stories of successes and failures, achievements and breakdowns. This was a bond that built a group, which was not going to be set back by the circumstances faced by the company in 1997.

This book details the diagnosis of the situation in 1997, formulation of an action plan to revive the company and steps taken to successfully implement the required actions across the steel plants and various functions of the company like marketing, finance, operations, communications, law, personnel and human resources. Although we had help from consultants like IDBI and McKinsey, the major strategies were evolved through interaction with a large cross-section of management and employees at all levels.

While debt or financial restructuring was a major component, it was a comprehensive programme to reduce operational costs, improve productivity, reduce manpower through a well-designed voluntary retirement scheme (VRS), reduce procurement costs, divest some assets like captive power plants and surplus houses in plant townships, reorganize the marketing set-up and also review the organization structure. We were fully supported by Steel Ministers Navin Patnaik, Dilip Ray and B. K. Tripathi, Finance Minister Yashwant Sinha and then Steel Secretary, Ashok Basu. All of them intimately knew SAIL and the steel industry. Navin Patnaik had just returned from New York to take charge of the Biju Janta Dal and his first job was as Steel Minister. His father, the legendary Biju Patnaik, had been closely associated with SAIL, steel and mining industries as Union Steel Minister and Orissa Chief Minister. I remember meeting him in the late 1980s in Paradip with a Korean steel delegation, where he was keen to set up a second integrated steel plant. It did not work out then but SAIL is again toying with the idea.

Dilip Ray, during whose period our Restructuring and Turnaround Plan was finally approved, started his career in Rourkela. Yashwant Sinha, due to his constituency in Hazaribagh had been exposed to the Bokaro steel plant (BSL). Ashok Basu had spent many years with the steel industry as Iron and Steel Controller with the JPC and then as Joint Secretary and Secretary in the Ministry of Steel.

Involvement and support of our employees at all levels came through an intensive communication exercise at the shop floor, plant and company levels to initiate change and get support and commitment.

There was also excellent teamwork and inter-functional coordination in an integrated manner at the top leadership level, which enabled the management to better communicate the need to adopt a new approach. Many useful suggestions came from the employees themselves at different levels. The greatest strength for the success of the SAIL turnaround was this close involvement of the entire team. One of the major achievements was to change the mindset of employees across the company from looking only at production tonnages to becoming aware of the cost implications at each stage of the manufacturing cycle.

- SAIL and TISCO (now Tata Steel), representing in steel the first major large-scale manufacturing industry, attracted the best of trade union talent. We were dealing with a very mature leadership of different trade unions, who went on to become prominent nationally. To mention a few, Shri Gopeshwar, R. C. Arya, S. L. Passey of INTUC, Dr M. K. Pandhe and Mrinal Banerjee of CITU, Shri Gaya Singh of AITUC, Shri R. K. Samanthray and Dr Shanti Patel of HMS. They appreciated that it was necessary to take steps to overcome the adverse situation if the larger interest of employees was to be protected. It was this appreciation, which after much initial hesitation, discussions and negotiations, enabled us to get full support for contentious issues like a VRS, removal of restrictive practices, wage settlement, divestment and monetization of assets like captive power plants, houses, etc.

Divestment of power plants was initially opposed by the employees and it took effort to get them on board. While more details are given later, I recollect one incident about Durgapur. A proposal for modernization of one of the Blast Furnaces was pending with us. This was very much needed to improve the quality of iron being produced there. I had to tell the Managing Director that the investment would be approved only if he could overcome opposition from the employees for transferring the power plant to a joint venture (JV) with NTPC, for which discussions were then at an advanced stage. To his credit and to my surprise S. B. Singh was able to get the employees on board within days and get the blast furnace investment through. This is an example of the very close relations between top management and the rest of the employees and their mutual appreciation and concern for the growth and future of the company. In fact, it is this spirit which enabled successful implementation of what we were trying to do and the story we are telling in this book.

Equally important was the full support of the Steel Executives Federation of India (SEFI), who responded to all our concerns and helped resolve major issues relating to salary revision, incentives, etc. I believe that the strength of SAIL has been its very valuable human resource as became evident from the enthusiasm with which they accepted the challenges and responded to them. The SEFI leadership proved that 'when the going gets tough, the tough get going'.

A major change during this period was the induction of independent directors on the Board. SAIL came in the first list of disinvestment and sale of shares of PSUs in the early nineties, followed by the GDR issue in 1996 as a result of which, by 1997, government holding was down to about 86 per cent. SAIL was listed in the Stock Exchanges and SEBI regulations required independent directors on the Board. We were lucky to have a very eminent group like D. Basu ex-MD SBI, R. V. Gupta, former Deputy Governor RBI, economists Isher Ahluwalia, Ramprasad Sengupta, Atul Sarma and HRD consultant Y. V. Reddy. They brought a larger perspective to the discussions, which began to focus more on wider policy issues. Delegation of powers with SAIL being declared a Navratna company in 1997 gave the Board greater responsibility and freedom to approve many issues, like investment decisions, which earlier needed inter-ministerial consultation and approval within the government. These delegations and the changed nature of the Board brought a whole new dimension to decision-making in SAIL and helped us make many of the more difficult decisions needed to implement the Restructuring and Turnaround Plans.

The SAIL experience of turnaround during 1997–2003 was unique in many ways for all of us. This book recollects what we believe was a well and meaningfully considered and carefully designed range of interventions implemented in SAIL. Even though written many years after the events described, restructuring and turnaround are relevant even today, not only for the Public Sector but also for the industrial sector as a whole, both public and private—going by recent challenges of the kind that have been referred to the National Company Law Tribunal (NCLT) for resolution.

Acknowledgements

The contributors to the book had a first-hand experience in being a part of this transformation process.

Dr Sanak Mishra spent many years in the Research and Development Centre of SAIL and has many patents to his credit. He moved to the Corporate Office and headed the Business Planning Department of SAIL from 1998 to 2002 and was closely involved in all phases of diagnosing the problem, evolving strategies and implementing the restructuring and turnaround efforts. He was able to build on this as Managing Director of Rourkela with a new model and initiatives to turn the plant around between 2003 and 2005.

Ashok Shahi as the Chief Legal Adviser contributed significantly to resolving issues relating to the company's debt rescheduling, which involved negotiations with the government and fighting legal battles at the Calcutta High Court and then in the Supreme Court, eventually clearing the cloud on the nature of the Steel Development Fund (SDF). His wise counsel also helped resolve many of the contentious issues, which cropped up during the divestment of captive power plants and leasing of surplus houses to employees. His contribution to Indian industry in getting the legal controversy on absorption of contract labour in industrial establishments in India settled by the constitution Bench of the Supreme Court of India 2001 is widely acknowledged by Indian corporates. He is now an eminent advocate in the Supreme Court.

Dr Shoeb Ahmed supervised the Corporate Communications Group and developed a major structured and interactive communications platform, which enabled involvement and support of our employees at all levels, essential for supporting several decisions and initiatives needed for the turnaround exercise. He later superannuated as Director Commercial of SAIL.

Arti Luniya was a pillar of support in the Chairman's office and closely involved in all phases of this exercise, more particularly the reforms in the communications and the marketing set up. She later went on to head the Commercial and Coal Import Departments of SAIL.

Others who have provided some inputs are B. K. Singh, our dynamic Operations Director, later to head Bokaro and Bhilai steel plants, who visited all the plants and evolved an ambitious cost reduction programme, which initially most thought impossible but was soon achieved; G. Upadhyaya, who headed the HR function at Bhilai and was later at the Corporate office; Suresh Pandey Managing Director at Bokaro.

We also take this opportunity to thank K. K. Khanna, who was GM (Projects) at the time of restructuring and later held the position of Director (Technical) in SAIL, for his input. Of the many who shared their experience of the period, we would specifically like to mention, Dr Anil Dhawan, who handled international trade during the toughest times and later became Executive Director (LP, CMO), Ravinder Kumar Garg, Company Secretary, Devinder Kumar, Company Secretary and Executive Director (Finance) and Alok Sahay, who then was SEFI president and is currently Executive Director (Commercial) in SAIL.

Many others were involved in this exercise, but we have not been able to get all their inputs due to constraints of time and space. We acknowledge the efforts of all and believe that what we are presenting is a representative description.

We would like to place on record the support we received from Supriyo Gupta, who saw the restructuring initiatives in SAIL first hand as a professional from Rediff PR, an agency hired by SAIL in the area of Corporate Communications. Supriyo, currently Managing

Director, Torque Communications, allowed himself to be the sounding board and a generous critic as we developed the SAIL's turnaround story.

We also acknowledge the support extended by ex-Chairman SAIL, Shri Anil K. Chaudhary, in the publication of the book, which enabled sharing this extraordinary story with the wider audience.

CHAPTER 1

The Turbulent Nineties and Indian Steel

Steel is a versatile metal and a universal intermediary. Over the years, it has been the most abundantly used metal and faced competition only from materials such as aluminium and plastics. It has its usages in a variety of applications covering construction, machinery and equipment, transport, household goods, etc., and is the material of choice for engineers and architects.

Modern steel combines high strength with low weight, which has revolutionized its application. Although steel is made through a highly energy intensive process, it has the great advantage of recyclability. With a global recovery rate of around 70 per cent, it is the most recycled material ever used.

The dominance of steel as a metal can be seen by its global production, which in 2019 was 1870 million tonnes in contrast to the next most-consumed metal aluminum with a worldwide production of around 64 million tonnes during the same year.

Steel was the facilitator of the industrial revolution. Its mass production, which started in the mid-19th century made it affordable, enabling its wide application in the construction of bridges, buildings, railways, shipping, machinery and machine components, turbines and generators, pipes for transmission of water and steam, as well as defence equipment, which enabled rapid industrialization and urbanization of economies. Steel intensity of GDP can, in most cases, provide a fair measure of the development stage of an economy.

Historically, steel was known in India and China several thousand years ago. Smelting of iron in India can be traced back to around 1800 BCE. The craftsmen in India as early as 3rd century BCE were smelting wrought iron with charcoal in crucibles to produce 'wootz' steel, which was used for making the world-famous Damascus swords, known for their excellent quality. The industrial production of steel, however, started only in the middle of the 19th century after the invention of the Bessemer converter process.

Steel: A Metal of Choice

Steel is an alloy of iron and carbon, where the percentage of carbon in the alloy is reduced to around 2 per cent or lower. This imparts to the alloy hardness, strength as well as ductility. In the modern integrated process of steel production, iron ore is smelted to make molten iron (hot metal), which is then processed into steel by an oxidation process. Once steel is made, it is shaped for final application in the rolling mills based on the end-use requirement.

The finished steel obtained from the rolling mills are categorized under two broad headings depending upon their shape. The steel categorized as long products comprise—bars and rods, structurals (angles, channels and joists) and rails, while the flat products include plates, coils and sheets, which are hot rolled or cold rolled and further coated or left uncoated depending on their end use. The flat products consist of HR and CR coils and sheets, plates, galvanized coils and sheets, electrical steel sheets, tin plates, etc.

Long products are mostly used in construction, engineering and fabrication industries. Flat steel products are used in manufacturing pipes and tubes, construction, fabrication, electric machinery and components, automotive vehicles, wagons and coaches, cylinders, drums and barrels, ship building, etc., as well as for manufacturing household goods such as refrigerators, air conditioners, coolers, steel almirah, etc.

While the long products are mostly used for construction purposes and consumed in the local markets, the flat products dominate the product-mix internationally traded. As an economy matures, the product mix switches from longs categories towards flats categories. This is so because with maturing of construction and infrastructure building in an economy, the incremental steel volumes flow towards sectors such as automobile, white goods, consumer durables, etc., where the requirement of flat products is higher.

An important distinction between longs and flats also emerges from the supply side. Long products are preferred by small manufacturing units, operating within scales ranging anything between a few thousand tonnes to about a million tonnes; the flat products however have an economic size of more than a million tonnes and its mills are highly capital intensive.

Evolution of Steel Production Process

Iron, which was traditionally made for centuries by smelting iron ore with charcoal, started being made in the blast furnaces using coking coal, as the world faced shortage of wood in the 18th century. The Bessemer process invented in the 1850s led to the industrial production of steel, whereby molten iron received from the blast furnace was converted into steel in just around 30 minutes. The Bessemer process however was overtaken by producing steel through open hearth furnaces, which although had a much longer processing time, provided better process control and improved quality of steel.

From the beginning of the 20th century up to the 1950s, the process of steel making did not undergo any significant change. However, in the 1950s, a new process of steel making called the LD process was introduced, which involved blowing oxygen to convert hot metal into steel. The LD process, which was a refined concept of the Bessemer Converter process, reduced the time for converting hot metal to steel from 10 to 12 hours in the open-hearth furnaces to just around 40 minutes.

Changes also came in the steel casting technology. Earlier the liquid steel was cast into steel blocks called ingots and then shaped first in an intermediary mill into blooms, billet or slabs and then further rolled into the final shapes in the finishing mills.

This process underwent a change when the need of the intermediary mills—blooming and billet or slabbing mill—was done away with by casting steel into the shapes obtained in the intermediary mill, at the casting stage itself. Called continuous casting, this process was instrumental in greatly reducing the energy consumption and improving the yield and quality of the steel cast.

Another production process that gained ascendancy from the 1960s was to produce steel through electric furnaces. Electric arc furnaces were being used earlier only for making alloy and special quality steels. However, with the abundant availability of steel scrap, it became economical to produce carbon steel by making use of steel scrap and power. The electric arc furnaces use the power supplied through graphite electrodes to produce an arc in the steel scrap charged in the furnace. The heat generated through the process is sufficient to melt the scrap to produce liquid steel, which is then refined to obtain the desired quality.

The electric arc furnace (EAF) route has an advantage over the LD route as it requires less capital, enables greater customization of production and is less land, energy and material intensive. Companies such as Nucor emerged using the EAF route of production and with the passage of time introduced innovative technologies, such as compact strip production, which enabled the EAF producers to enter the lucrative market of flat products, which earlier was outside its reach.

After the Energy Crisis of 1973, the steel industry underwent extensive restructuring, the open-hearth furnaces were phased out and technology switched to LD and continuously cast route of steel production, which had the added advantage of being more eco-friendly.

Today, the Blast-Furnace BOF (LD) route, where steel is made using iron ore and coking coal, dominates the steel production process. The EAF route, which uses steel scrap, hot briquetted iron/sponge iron and power as the key inputs, has gradually been improving its share and accounts for nearly 30 per cent of the global production. The integration of EAF route with furnaces producing direct reduced iron/sponge iron has allowed it greater flexibility and economy of operations wherever the advantage of cheap iron ore exists.

Vigour and Languor of the World of Steel

The industrial revolution found a wide range of applications for steel as a universal intermediary. Extensively used for railways and shipping, it also was useful in agriculture as the steel-tipped ploughs were very effective in tilling virgin lands and later in manufacturing of the farm equipment. By the turn of the 20th century, steel was used for constructing high-rise buildings, which changed the landscape of the coastal cities of the USA and for making transformers and turbines, which enabled the world to switch from steam-based systems to electricity-based power systems.

Global steel production rose sharply in the first decade of the 20th century, registering an average growth of 9 per cent per annum. However, its journey thereafter was characterized by huge swings and cyclicality. Impacted by events such as the world wars as well as the great depression, a great surge in steel production came only after the Second World War was over.

The world wars also saw nationalization of steel companies, as steel was a vital input for manufacturing war equipment and also for railways and shipping, which were essential for transporting men and material during the war years.

The steel industry had its golden period in the 1950s and the 1960s led by the post-war construction boom. Global crude steel production nearly tripled during the two decades to 1970; from around 200 million tonnes in 1950 to around 600 million tonnes by 1970, registering an average annual rate of 6 to7 per cent per annum. However, there was a huge shift in its fortunes in the subsequent decades.

The oil crisis in 1973 signalled a sharp deceleration in steel demand worldwide and the industry was left holding a large excess capacity. As the steel production process was highly capital intensive, lower capacity utilization made it extremely difficult to cover high fixed costs, spelling doom for the industry.

The growth in the steel industry in the decades of the 1970s and 1980s was very meagre—at an average of around 1 to 2 per cent per annum, earning it the name of a sunset industry.

Indian Steel Industry, Evolution and the Era of Controls

At a crude steel production of 111 million tonnes in 2019, India today is the second-largest producer and consumer of steel in the world after China.

The growth of steel in India saw phases of upswings and deceleration, as, from a modest presence in 1947, the steel sector in India grew to become the tenth largest in the world by 1997. The supply of crude steel in India during this period increased from a level of around 1.2 million tonnes in 1948 to around 24 million tonnes by 1996–1997.

The history of the modern steel industry in India, however, goes back to 1907 when the house of Tatas floated the Tata Iron and Steel Company (TISCO). Located at Jamshedpur, TISCO (now named Tata Steel) produced its first hot metal by 1911 and tapped steel in early 1912. Mysore State in 1923 set up a much smaller unit called the Mysore Iron and Steel Works Limited (MISW). In 1936, the Steel

Corporation of Bengal set up a steel plant near Asansol and three years later tapped its first tonnes of steel. This plant later amalgamated with the Indian Iron and Steel Company (IISCO). Thus, India at the time of Independence had three integrated steel plants—TISCO, MISW and IISCO.

The industrial policy at the time of Independence was to foster rapid industrialization of the economy, by gaining self-sufficiency in capital goods. Given the export pessimism prevalent in those times, rapid investment in the core and infrastructure sector appeared to provide the only means of telescoping the growth process. India possessed the basic input materials for steelmaking—iron ore, coking coal, etc., and steel was the basic material required for manufacturing capital goods and for large infrastructure projects. Recognizing the importance of the steel sector in economic development, the Second Five Year Plan stated, 'The expansion of [the] iron and steel industry has the highest priority since more than any other industrial product, the level of production of these materials determine the tempo of progress of the economy.'

In line with the economic philosophy of those times, the Industrial Policy Resolution of 1956 stated that the state would assume exclusive responsibility for the iron and steel industry. Other than the objective of gaining commanding heights of the economy, the policy was driven by considerations such as lack of a developed capital market to finance the lumpy investments and containment of monopoly power in the steel industry.

Given its strategic significance, the government decided to exercise a tight control over the steel sector; a policy that persisted till the economic reforms of 1991.

Setting up integrated steel plants is a highly complex task. Its majesty is striking for visitors seeing it for the first time. Spread over thousands of acres of land, its size and scale of operations are striking. The sight of liquid metal being tapped into ladles and the red hot steel blocks being shaped in the rolling mills, leave an everlasting imprint in the memory of the viewers. Larger than life, the steel plants are an exhibition of the grandeur of industrialization and human ingenuity.

As a part of the economic vision of the Government of India, three public sector integrated steel plants were set up under the erstwhile Hindustan Steel Limited (HSL) in the early 1960s. Subsequently, two more integrated steel plants were added at Bokaro and Vizag. While BSL along with the integrated steel plants at Bhilai, Durgapur and Rourkela became a part of the Steel Authority of India Limited (SAIL) in 1973, Vizag commissioned in 1992 came up under a newly formed public sector company—Rashtriya Ispat Nigam Limited (RINL).

The steel sector, which experienced a high growth phase during the Second and Third Five Year plans, at an average rate of around 8 per cent per annum, saw a deceleration between 1970 and 1980 when the growth in crude steel production dropped to a range of 4 to 5 per cent.

Steel was amongst the most controlled sectors up to 1990. The integrated route of steel production using blast furnaces was reserved for the government sector. Additionally, products such as HR coils were also kept exclusively for the government-owned companies. To make cheap steel available to the consuming segments, the integrated steel producers operated within the ambit of administered pricing and distribution controls.

The low administered prices for steel, however, resulted in a lack of investible funds for the integrated steel producers. This constrained not only their ability to expand capacity but also technological upgradation of the units. To overcome this constraint, the government introduced the concept of SDF, which allowed a small element in the price of steel towards a fund, from which the integrated steel producers could borrow to meet their investment needs.

The other controls for the integrated steel producers came in the form of the freight equalization fund (FEF), which subsidized consumers at distant locations by charging the nearby customers higher!

In addition to SDF and FEF, the steel prices also had the Engineering Goods Export Assistance Fund (EGEAF) to subsidize engineering goods exporters and a Joint Plant Committee (JPC) cess to take care of the administrative cost of JPC, which looked into administered prices and distribution control.

Steel was subject to trade controls, similar to numerous other products and materials, where quota and tariff created an effective wall of protection, and canalization was the means of importing or exporting. Further, the setting up of steel capacity in the private sector or expansion of capacity in the existing steel mills were subject to licensing policy and clearances from agencies such as Monopoly and Restrictive Trade Practices (MRTP) Commission and Directorate General of Technical Development (DGTD). Indeed, the steel sector controls appeared straight out of a Kafkaesque imagination!

The non-integrated route of steel production called the 'secondary producers' in India was dominated by the private sector, which used EAF technology, which in 1997 accounted for slightly more than 10 million tonnes in capacity. Electric arc furnace units, also called mini steel plants, were allowed to come up in the private sector during the late fifties. A chronic shortage of steel and relatively easy availability of scrap led to the quick growth of the mini steel plants during early 1970, whereby their estimated capacity increased from 0.5 million tonnes per annum during 1967–1968, to around 3 million tonnes per annum by 1973–1974.

However, from the mid-1970s the electric arc furnace sector started facing problems due to an acute shortage of power from the grid and escalation in the price of steel scrap. Fragmentation in the capacities of the units also did not lend it to technological improvements or gaining economies of scale. The capacity utilization of the electric arc furnace sector, hence, continued to be affected by the problems of rising input cost, lack of power availability and obsolete technology.

A third segment of the Indian steel industry comprised the re-rolling sector. At the time of Independence, there were about

32 re-rolling units with a capacity of around 140,000 tonnes per annum. The shortage of finished steel in the late 1950s had forced the government to encourage the growth of the re-rolling units. These units took semi-processed steel (semis) in the form of blooms, billets, slabs from the integrated steel plants, or pencil ingots from the mini steel plants to roll in their finishing mills. Operating mostly in the long products category, the re-rollers catered to dispersed local demand. Later, bigger units with cold rolling mills were also set up to meet the requirement of cold-rolled or galvanized products. The capacity of the re-rolling sector by the mid-nineties increased to around 21 million tonnes.

The Economic Reforms of the Nineties

The nineties was an extraordinary decade for the Indian steel industry. Beginning July 1991, within a span of a few years, the steel sector transformed from being the most protected to the most open. In a slew of reforms, the sector was de-licensed, pricing and distribution controls disbanded, restrictions on steel imports abolished and the sector opened to FDI. Also abolished were levies such as Freight Equalization Fund, the SDF and the Engineering Goods Export Assistance Fund.

Customs duty on steel product which in 1991 ranged from 40 to 50 per cent ad-valorem in addition to a specific duty ranging between ₹1,100 to ₹6,600 for the flat products and 105 per cent for bars and rods was progressively reduced to a range of 25 to 30 per cent by 1996–1997 for both flats as well as long products categories.

Private entrepreneurs entered the field earlier reserved only for the government companies. TATA steel set up capacity in hot rolled coils and new players such as Ispat, Essar, Jindal and Lloyds emerged, targeting the flats product segment. Also, a new route using the induction furnaces (IF) emerged in the secondary sector. So dramatic was the rise of the induction furnaces that from a negligible presence in 1990, these galloped to 16 per cent of the domestic crude steel production in 1997–1998.

The induction furnaces operate on the principle of generating heat through electromagnetic induction. These furnaces are cylindrical, open-topped, tiltable refractory crucibles with a water-cooled induction coil installed on the outside. The coil, powered by alternating current, induces eddy currents in the metallic charge that generate heat and melts the charge in the furnace. The induction furnaces have an advantage over the EAF as they can be operated in much smaller sizes, leading to further reduction of space and capital cost. Also, technologically induction furnaces are easier to operate and give better material productivity. There are limitations in the induction furnaces in producing superior grades but this factor did not inhibit the explosive growth of the IF route for India.

The Surge and the Great Decline

Following the economic reforms unleashed in 1991, the business associations such as CII and FICCI by the mid-nineties started holding seminars and conferences on the prospect of India's GDP growth breaching 8 per cent—a figure unimaginable in the pre-reform era. It in a way captured the upbeat mood of industry, which after being unshackled wanted to test the heights it could soar to.

Unprecedented growth in the mild steel consumption, estimated at 22 per cent in 1994–1995 and 14 per cent in 1995–1996 appeared to redefine the growth trajectory. Some of the consultancy firms started predicting that 6 to 7 per cent CAGR—the traditional long-term growth associated with steel consumption in India was a thing of the past and the consumption growth henceforth would range between 10 to 12 per cent.

However, the picture turned dramatically in 1996–1997, when the growth in finished steel consumption plummeted to 4 per cent. A further deceleration followed in 1997–1998 when the growth in steel consumption collapsed to 2 per cent.

The steep decline in the growth of steel consumption was but a reflection of what was happening in the economy. The GDP growth of 8 per cent in 1996–1997, buoyed on account of high growth rate in agriculture and services, hid the slump in the industry where the growth dropped by more than 40 per cent to 6.4 per cent. A slowdown engulfed all major steel-consuming segments. As if to underline that it was not a blip in an otherwise robust trend, the growth rate for industry never crossed 7 per cent for the next 5 years!

Like the overall GDP, the overall consumption growth for finished steel also did not truly reflect what was happening in the sector. Consumption growth for flat steel was negative during 1996–1997 and nil for 1997–1998. This was the segment targeting, where most of the new players had set up fresh capacities. Ending up with significant excess capacity vis-à-vis domestic demand, the new steel companies were in choppy waters immediately after committing huge funds. Given the faltering domestic demand, exports appeared to provide an outlet to cushion the impact.

A Globalized World

In contrast to the sanguinity with which the Indian steel industry perceived the future at the onset of the nineties, a sense of foreboding loomed large for the steel manufacturers in the developed world.

The genesis of this lay in the collapse of the Soviet Union in 1991. Prior to its collapse, the Soviet Union was the largest producer of crude steel in the world. After 1991, its crude steel production, which had peaked at 163 million tonnes in 1988, experienced a precipitous fall and shrank to less than 100 million tonnes by 1993. Even more dramatic was the collapse in its domestic demand, which fell from a level of 125 million tonnes of finished steel in 1988 to a mere 35 million tonnes by 1994!

Given the collapse in domestic demand, CIS countries led by Russia and Ukraine entered the export market like never before. Commonwealth of Independent States (CIS) nations, whose annual export volume was less than 10 million tonnes prior to 1990, left the traditional exporters Japan and Germany far behind as their combined exports reached a volume of 40 million tonnes per annum in 1994.

Within a span of 5 years, a region that was more or less self-sufficient transformed to the biggest net steel exporter in the world.

The surge in steel imports from the erstwhile Soviet Block hit the developed nations immediately at the onset of globalization. At the beginning of the 1980s, the world had seen progressive dismantling of trade barriers, reduction in ocean freight, falling cost of communication and emergence of global private capital, all of which had given a wing to international trade. Under its impact, the steel sector where the aggregate finished steel production had remained stagnant saw an intensification in the trade component as the worldwide exports measured as a percentage of finished steel increased from a level of 26 per cent in 1990 to more than 40 per cent by 1995.

The European steel industry had faced very tough times during the seventies. Having experienced a growth in capacity, production and labour force from 1950 up to 1970, the oil shock of 1973 was the harbinger of an unprecedented misery for the sector. After unsuccessful interventions and support programmes for the industry, the member countries of the European Union agreed on a series of measures to deal with the manifest crisis. These interventions took the form of production quotas, minimum price mechanisms, plant closures as well as social support measures.

Support of 36 billion European Currency Unit (ECU) was given by the member countries to oversee closure of uneconomic capacities in the steel sector. It helped retain the steel capacities which were most efficient, effected a reduction of around 48 per cent in the steel labour force between 1977 and 1990 and led to an overall capacity rationalization of more than 40 million tonnes. However, the fall of the USSR brought back the spectre of overcapacity.

Asian Currency Crisis

The turmoil caused by the fall of the USSR was a mega phenomenon but fell in the realm of a disruption anticipated at the beginning of the nineties. The misery of the sector immediately after was compounded by an unexpected event—the Asian Currency Crisis. Starting July 1997, Baht, the currency of Thailand, came under acute speculative pressure, which forced the Thai government to float the currency, as it could no longer support its peg to the dollar. The contagion soon spread to Indonesia, Malaysia and South Korea, raising fear of a worldwide financial meltdown. The South-East Asian tiger economies were bailed out by the IMF and coerced to take corrective measures.

For the steel industry, the Asian Currency Crisis resulted in a net steel-importing region turning overnight into a net steel exporting region. The domestic demand collapsed and the capacities set up to meet the domestic demand were deployed to export steel, supported by highly devalued home currencies.

Consumption of finished steel in Thailand, Malaysia, Indonesia and South Korea crashed from a level of around 60 million tonnes in 1997 to 36 million tonnes in 1998. Steel exports from the region increased sharply and were maintained at a high level.

In search of safer heavens, some of the global funds were diverted to Russia, where the depreciation of the rouble due to a poorly performing economy provided no respite. Soon enough Russia and Brazil were also engulfed by the contagion. All this resulted in the acute volatility of steel prices and starting of trade disputes, as the domestic steel companies scrambled to protect their home turf.

The price collapse was so severe that cost competitiveness did not have much meaning. Almost all companies suffered. In Korea, the steel demand fell from around 40 million tonnes in 1997 to around 25 million tonnes in 1998. The Korean currency, which had traded at 850 won to a dollar before devaluation, crashed to 2,000 won to a dollar in 1998. The world spot price for HR coils fell by 40 per cent from US $310 per tonne in January 1998 to US $185 per tonne in December 1998.

The virtual 'death spiral' of steel prices in 1998 and 2001 led to worldwide bankruptcies. It is believed that in the years 1998 and 2001, steel prices fell the lowest relative to the cost in the history of the industry and were below the marginal cost for two-third of the industry!

As it happens in a crisis, the economic devastation for the sector provided opportunities for consolidation in a highly fragmented industry. The steel companies tried to avail business synergies through mergers and acquisition and use it to gain requisite scale to tide over the crisis.

Mergers and Acquisitions and Survival of the Fittest

The distress caused by the downward spiral in steel prices led to a massive restructuring of the sector resulting in the privatization of the government companies, a large reduction in surplus capacities and labour force and an across-border consolidation.

The highly fragmented structure of the global steel industry over the years had resulted in a lack of pricing power and a lack of regulation of production even when the industry faced a demand collapse. The key input-supplying industry such as iron ore and coking coal, on the other hand, were much more consolidated. The consequence of the interplay of this market structure resulted in a cost-price margin squeeze for the steel industry; as, despite a collapse of the end product price, the input prices tended to hold relatively firm.

The privatization of state-owned enterprises after 1990 and the unprecedented downturn following the Asian Currency Crisis led to a consolidation of capacities and restructuring of the steel industry. As a consequence, the share of the top ten global companies in the world in steel production for the decade 1994 to 2004, increased from a level of 20 to 27 per cent.

Several new entities emerged, the most significant amongst which was Mittal Steel. Set up in 1978 as Ispat International, the company went on an acquisition spree. It acquired the Iron and Steel Company of Trinidad and Tobago in 1989, Sibalsa in Mexico in 1992, followed by Sidbec-Dosco in Canada in 1994. In 1995, it acquired Hamburger Stahlwerke and formed Ispat International Ltd and Ispat Shipping and also bought Karmet Steel of Temirtau, Kazakhstan. In 1997, it took over Thyssen Duisberg in Germany and acquired Inland Steel in the USA in 1998. It took over Unimetal, France in 1999 and followed it up with purchase of Sidex Galati in Romania and Alfasid in Algeria in 2001 and thereafter acquired majority stakes in Iscor South Africa in 2002.

Mittal Steel blazed a trail of acquisitions never witnessed before in any industry. From a global rank of 17 and crude steel production of 8 million tonnes in 1996, it became the second-largest steel company in the world in 2002, with a production of 35 million tonnes. After waiting for just another four years, Mittal Steel merged with Arcelor to create the biggest steel company ever—ArcelorMittal, whose crude steel production during 2006 was a whopping 117 million tonnes!

Arcelor was created in 2001 through the merger of Arcelia (Spain), Usinor (France) and Arbed (Luxembourg). It was the biggest steel company when formed and had a crude steel production of over 40 million tonnes. Arcelor merged with Mittal Steel in 2006.

The other notable mergers and acquisitions included ThyssenKrupp, which emerged in 1999 as a result of the merger of the German companies Thyssen AG and Krupp; Corus, which was formed by the merger of Hoogovens, a Dutch steel company with British Steel, which had been privatized in 1988; and the Riva Group, which emerged amongst the largest steel companies by the acquisition of Ilva in April 1995, Italsider in 1997 and SAM in 2000. In Japan, NKK merged with Kawasaki Steel to form JFE Holding in 2002.

Thus, within a span of seven years from 1995 to 2002, five of the top ten global steel companies morphed into entirely new entities.

The opportunities for mergers and acquisitions in the steel sector had been facilitated significantly by the privatization of state-owned companies in Europe and the erstwhile CIS countries and Eastern

Europe. *The Hindu* on 8 November 2001 carried a new item of Mr L. N. Mittal calling for privatization of India's steel industry. The newspaper reported that while speaking to the journalists after signing an agreement with the Romanian Prime Minister for the privatization of SIDEX-SA, Romania's integrated steelworks, Mr Mittal said that his heart was still in India and 'would be there' as and when the Indian government decided to privatize the steel industry.

Mr Mittal believed that producing steel was not the government's business and privatizing steel production was becoming a global trend. 'If everything else is privatized why not steel?' *The Hindu* quoted him saying.

Defeat of the Free Trade

The Asian currency crisis redirected the flow of steel from the previously fast-growing regions of Southeast Asia, to the markets of the USA and Europe. Furthermore, the appreciation of the dollar made the already low price of imported steel, even more competitive relative to the domestic steel manufacturers. Consequently, in 1998, the steel imports in the USA hit an all-time high of 41.5 million tonnes.

To protect the domestic industry, which faced falling revenue and operating income, the USA imposed anti-dumping duty cases against Brazil, Russia and Japan. As the situation worsened, more cases were filed; and Europe and Canada also followed the suit to protect their home markets from exports, which faced trade barriers in the USA.

Despite the protective measures, 40 companies in the USA alone faced bankruptcy. Companies operating under Chapter 11 of the bankruptcy code included Bethlehem Steel, National Steel, Wheeling Pittsburgh and Weirton Steel. LTV, the third largest integrated producer in the USA, was liquidated.

US policymakers, under pressure from Congress, workers and the industry, took recourse under Section 201 of US Trade Law. Under the law, the President could implement temporary relief to the domestic industry, after an independent finding established the injury to the industry by a surge in imports. The USA in 2002 announced a series of three-year remedy tariffs on a selected range of steel products.

The Hindu on 7 March 2002, reported that the USA had slapped tariffs up to 30 per cent on the imported steel to help the struggling home industry. This move set the stage for trade wars overseas as it affected many countries in Asia, Americas and Europe. In Asia India, South Korea, Japan and China were most affected.

The newspaper reported in May 2002 an announcement by the USA that it was considering levying 153.65 per cent anti-dumping margin on Indian cold-rolled steel exports to the USA. The final determination on anti-dumping cases was expected in July and the ruling of the US International Trade Commission, mandatory for imposing dumping duties, in August 2002. Besides India, anti-dumping probes were also initiated against 18 other countries including Australia, France, Japan, Korea, the Netherlands, China, Russia, Sweden, Spain, Thailand and Turkey.

The Hindu quoted William Lash, the US Assistant Secretary of Commerce, speaking in New Delhi that the US steel industry was facing a problem of excess capacity of nearly 120 million tonnes of rolled steel and more than 30 companies were virtually bankrupt. Although a decision had been taken to phase out part of steel capacity, some excess remained.

Many anti-dumping cases were initiated in countries all over the world against steel imports. The maximum number of cases involved products such as HR coils, plates, CR coils, etc. In the US anti-dumping investigations were initiated against 21 countries, in the EU against 14 countries, while Canada and Thailand filed cases against 17 and 10 countries, respectively.

Exports of steel from SAIL faced anti-dumping and countervailing duty imposed on HR coils and plates in the USA, EU, Canada and Thailand. The total duty imposed ranged from 15 per cent for plates exported to Canada to 41.2 per cent for HR coils exports to the USA.

Indian Steel: From Shortage to Excess

The year 1996–1997 had witnessed a drastic transformation in the Indian steel scenario. A slowdown in the economic activity led to a steep drop in the growth of steel consumption.

A major factor for the adverse market situation was the continued slowdown in the major steel-intensive segments, particularly the capital goods where average growth of more than 20 per cent during 1994–1995 and 1995–1996 turned negative in 1997–1998. This was accentuated by a reduced investment by the government in the infrastructure development projects, which could not be compensated by equivalent private sector participation.

The domestic availability, particularly in the flats categories, exceeded demand by large volumes and the prices experienced a downward pressure due to cheap imports, particularly from CIS and some European countries precluding any increase despite rising input costs.

The opening up of the steel sector in 1991 had evoked a strong interest from several entrepreneurs who wanted to seize the opportunity. In fact, such was the enthusiasm that a famous company which was in the business of selling ice cream visited SAIL to gain an understanding of the prospects of venturing into steel; also, a shoe-manufacturing company evinced interest in setting up a steel plant! By the mid-nineties, there were many greenfield projects under various stages of approval/implementation.

The greenfield steel projects announced included Ispat Industries, Dolvi (3 mtpa), Usha Ispat, Maharashtra (1.5 mtpa), Mideast Integrated Steel (1.2 mtpa), Jindal Strips, Raigarh (0.6 mtpa), Malvika Steel (0.6 Mtpa), Jindal Vijaynagar (1.6 mtpa), Bellary Steel and Alloys (0.5 mtpa), Neelachal Ispat (1 mtpa), Mukund Steel (2 mtpa), Nagarjuna Group (2 mtpa), MESCO, Kalinga (2.25 mtpa), TISCO, Gopalpur (2.5 mtpa) and Orissa industries (1 mtpa) amongst others.

The private sector manufacturers who entered the arena and built up capacity received financial support from institutions such as IDBI,

IFCI, ICICI, in raising the capital. With the benefit of hindsight, it could be said that the assumptions made by the financial institutions at the time of approval of project financing were over-optimistic and did not factor cyclical downturn.

The Hindu (2003, January 10), in an article, cited World Steel Dynamics, which in its report on India said, 'The huge debt of most of the companies is a double-edged sword. The debt is a major problem because it is not being repaid. However, without it, some of the industry's newest and best steel plants would not be in existence.'

When the recession hit the global and Indian steel industry, large scale dumping by CIS and South-East Asian countries forced many of the new entrants to shelve their new projects. Some projects which were discontinued included TISCO's Gopalpur project, Mesco Kalinga, Mukand and L&T's project.

According to *the Minerals and Metals Review*, December 2002, following the decontrol, 19 new projects with a capacity of 13 million tonnes at an investment of ₹32,000 crore were planned. Of the 19 projects, nine were commissioned with an annual capacity of 5.75 million tonnes. Of the nine, one shut down while three with a capacity of 2.2 million tpa were partially commissioned of which two were closed and one was in production.

In fact, the mismatch between demand and supply of steel in India was such that its status of a traditional net importer transformed to that of a net exporter of finished steel. India's modest net exports (exports less imports) of finished steel of around 30,000 tonnes in 1996–1997, rose year after year to cross 1 million tonne in 1999–2000 and attained a high of 3.4 million tonnes in 2003–2004.

The export orientation of the industry enabled a higher utilization of the capital assets but did not prevent the industry from financial devastation. The Centre for Monitoring India Economy (CMIE) estimated that from 1998–1999 to 2001–2002, the Indian industry on aggregate lost more than ₹13,500 crore. The losses in the industry were all-pervasive and did not spare even the largest steel manufacturers.

S. Rohini, in her performance analysis of the steel industry in the *Economic & Political Weekly* (17 April 2004), wrote that although from 1996–1997 to 2001–2002 there was a decline in the manufacturing sector as a whole in India, the decline in steel, both in sales and profitability was much steeper. She analysed the performance of the big seven players in the steel industry—SAIL, RINL, TISCO, Ispat, Essar, JSW and Lloyds and found that heavy borrowings and the resultant interest outgo was a big burden on the industry. All the big players had resorted to borrowings, be it for modernization in case of SAIL or greenfield projects for the new entrants. The large-scale borrowings affected the debt-equity structure of the steel companies, which ended up being much higher than the average for the manufacturing sector as a whole. Older steel companies such as SAIL and TISCO also had to bear a high manpower cost compared to the new entrants.

The borrowings for the steel sector, which was financed by the banks and the financial institutions (FI) resulted in them having a huge exposure in the industry. Project delays led to an accumulation of about a one-third of the interest accrued and every tonne of steel shipped had an interest cost of US $35 per tonne, the highest in the world. The ratio of operating income (profit before depreciation, interest and taxes) to sales was not bad but was wiped out at the net profit level, because of the huge interest cost. It was estimated that around 20 per cent of the overall non-performing assets of the FIs were on account of the steel sector.

The respite for the industry came only in 2003 when the markets recovered. *The Hindu* on 23 January 2003 carried a news item—'Steel companies get new lease of life'. It reported that the steel industry had been thrown another lifeline by the financial institutions who cleared a package aimed at reducing the debt burden for some major steel companies. The package aimed largely for the three defaulting hot rolled coil (HRC) manufacturers—Essar Steel, Jindal Vijaynagar

Steel and Ispat Metallics and Ispat Industries—was in the form of a mix of conversion of debt into equity, conversion into preference shares, a moratorium on repayment, repayment of unsecured foreign debt at discounts and personal guarantees from the promoters of steel companies.

The newspaper (2003, January 23) quoted Seshagiri Rao, Director, Finance, Jindal Vijayanagar Steel Limited (JVSL), saying, 'This move has happened at the right time when the market is picking up. Effectively now, there are several windows of opportunity which open up for us. There is the refinance opportunity, interest rate swaps and the like. It is definitely a positive step.'

Although the declining trends were visible, the events that were to mark the steel industry could not have been fathomed, when Arvind Pande took over charge as Chairman SAIL, the largest steel company in India, on 3 January 1997.

In his opening address to SAIL collective, Arvind Pande urged the workforce to find a way of working so that everyone was involved in the fortunes of the company, had a sense of pride in the company, its systems, values, and products which represented it in the marketplace.

To the managers, he appealed for a sense of purpose and dedication with an emotional ingredient. Being a vital part of the personality of a manager, their resolution was more important than anything, as in its absence the promises would remain promises and the goals unattainable, he added.

Pointing to the challenging times he said, 'We have no choice but to be decisive, daring and different, take calculated risks and not seek refuge in conventional alibis. The trouble is if we do not risk anything, we risk even more.'

CHAPTER 2

Being Prescient Makes One Proactive

With a capacity of nearly 20 million tonnes of crude steel, SAIL today is the leading steel producer in India. The story of SAIL over the years, in a way, has mirrored the story of industrial evolution in independent India. It has seen its periods of vicissitude; there were crests when it was an unquestionable leader in the industry; also, there were troughs when its very existence was threatened. What has stood out in the journey of SAIL is its ability to resurrect itself from the deep recesses of crisis, exhibiting a resilience not commonly observed.

The company has recently come back to profits after being in the red for three years starting 2015–2016. However, what it experienced in recent times pales in comparison to the crisis it confronted in the second half of the nineties. The combined impact of an unprecedented downturn in the steel market and its weaknesses had brought the steel behemoth down to its knees. Its losses had skyrocketed and its net worth eroded in a manner to make it a potentially sick enterprise. Under such a scenario, SAIL scripted an unparalleled turnaround to emerge as a transformed organization. The years of crisis were used not only to keep the organization afloat but make it stronger and more robust than ever before.

The tumultuous period during 1997–2003 imbued the company with resilience and confidence that had a long-lasting impact. The case in point is the severe crisis that SAIL faced 2015–2016 onwards. On the strength of learning from experience, braving all the obstacles and chalking out and implementing suitable strategies, SAIL once again could make a turnaround and posted a profit before tax of more than ₹3000 crore in FY 2018–2019 as well as FY 2019–2020 from the staggering losses incurred in the three previous years.

Every organization is like a living organism, which continuously learns throughout its lifespan. Mr Anil Kumar Chaudhary, ex-Chairman, SAIL, reflected,

> Passing through a hard time makes the organization more mature and confident to surmount the future challenges. The 1997–2003 period was an enormously challenging time and became the case study of a corporate turnaround. Along with this, it gave extensive learning to the organization and created organizational confidence to face any challenges in the future. It had its positive impact in staging the turnaround in 2018–2019 and remaining so thereafter. (ex-Chairman, SAIL, Personal Interview)

The foreboding crisis was the last thing on the agenda of Arvind Pande as he took the reins of the company in January 1997. There was little reason for it. SAIL's performance had been impressive in the immediate past, and its financial parameters post liberalization displayed a significant improvement over the pre-reform years. A comparison of the quinquennial 1987–1988 to 1991–1992 and 1992–1993 to 1996–1997 showed the average saleable steel production increasing from 7.0 million tonnes to 8.8 million tonnes, average turnover increasing from ₹7,325 crore to ₹12,911 crore and average profit (after tax) shooting up to ₹782 crore compared to ₹233 crore for the earlier period. It appeared that SAIL had made a smooth transition from the era of controls to that of a competitive market economy.

The government had announced that under the new economic policy, its investments would focus mainly on the areas of strategic importance, high technology and certain infrastructure projects.

Consequently, the government started the process of disinvestment of its holding in major PSUs in 1992, where SAIL was one of the first PSUs taken up for disinvestment. After disinvestment of part equity held by the Government of India, SAIL shares were listed in all major stock exchanges of India, viz., Mumbai, Delhi, Calcutta, Madras, Ahmedabad and the National Stock Exchange, Mumbai.

Taking advantage of its position in the domestic and global markets, SAIL was able to raise resources in the international market. During March 1996, SAIL became one of the first PSUs to successfully raise equity through the issuance of Global Depository Receipts (GDRs), as it raised US $125 million by issuing 14.45 crore equity shares of ₹10 at a premium of ₹19.55 per share. SAIL GDRs were listed on the London Stock Exchange. The issuance of GDRs gave the company recognition in the international market, enabling it to mobilize resources from the foreign market through other instruments as well. The disinvestment of the equity of the GoI and raising additional equity through GDR, reduced the equity of GoI in SAIL to around 86 per cent by 1996, which further reduced to 75 per cent in 2015 following subsequent disinvestments undertaken by the GoI.

The tenth-largest steel company in the world in 1996, SAIL was soon to face the worst crisis ever in the history of the global steel industry. So acute was the crisis that many companies that featured amongst the top ten steel companies in the world in 1996, ceased to exist by the time normalcy returned in the sector in 2003.

SAIL, the domestic leader in India in steel, accounted for 45 per cent of domestic crude steel production during the fiscal 1996–1997. It had four integrated steel plants at Bhilai, Durgapur, Rourkela and Bokaro, two special steel units at Durgapur and Salem and three subsidiaries—IISCO, MEL and VISL, all of which later merged with the parent company.

The genesis of SAIL could be traced to Hindustan Steel Limited, set up in 1954 to manage a one-million-tonne plant at Rourkela with German collaboration. In 1955, the Government of India signed agreements to set up two other one-million-tonne plants at Bhilai and Durgapur with Russian and British collaboration respectively. The location for setting up the steel plants was based on the proximity of key raw materials such as iron ore and coking coal. Also set up within the folds of HSL was Alloy Steels Plant (ASP) at Durgapur, which was commissioned in 1965.

Bokaro Steel Plant (BSL), which later became a part of SAIL, was formed as a company in 1964. The project, however, was fraught with delays. Initially conceived with technical assistance and funding from the USA, BSL came up with the assistance of the USSR after the USA backed out. There were major changes in technical specifications and the plant started iron production only in 1972.

HSL and SAIL were fortunate to have leadership of many eminent professionals and bureaucrats at the helm and as well as on their Board. Mr S. Bhoothalingam, Mr G. Pande, Mr K. T. Chandy, Mr Hiten Bhaya, Mr Wadood Khan, Mr R. P. Billimoria, Dr P. L. Agrawal, Mr K. C. Khanna, Mr V. Krishnamurthy, were a few of the many eminent persons, who led HSL and SAIL over the years. The Boards of HSL and SAIL also benefited by having eminent professionals such as Mr K. C. Mahindra, Mr P. L. Tandon, Prof. P. N. Dhar, Mr Mantosh Sondhi, Prof. K. N. Raj and Mr M. P. Wadhawan, among others.

Hindustan Steel Limited

HSL was a manifestation of the vision of the founding fathers of India, for whom economic freedom formed an integral part of political freedom. The steel plants were to form the base for rapid industrialization of an agrarian economy. Dr V. Krishnamurthy, Chairman SAIL from 1985 to 1990, was a young executive working in the planning commission in the mid-fifties. Dr Krishnamurthy wrote about his recollections of those years,

> I was a witness to the successive decisions to set up Rourkela, Durgapur and Bhilai Steel Plants; all such decisions taken within a span of 12 months. To set up and run an integrated steel mill is

> no easy task. It requires a lot of foresight and courage to decide on three such mills, all at the same time. That too at a time when India had no technical expertise and trained managerial and technical personnel to manage it. No country had, till this date, attempted such a thing on such a massive scale. (*SAILNews*, 1997, August)

The three integrated steel plants—each of capacity of a million tonne—were constructed in a record time of four years. The first blast furnaces started their production in February 1959 at Rourkela and Bhilai Steel Plants, while the production of hot metal at Durgapur commenced in December 1959.

The pulsating giants of steel transformed the landscape of the areas they came up at. They employed a large number of engineers, technicians and workers. It is estimated that the total workforce during the peak construction period at Bhilai was around 60,000. The townships of Bhilai, Rourkela, Durgapur and later on Bokaro, became thriving industrial centres with all amenities and facilities for people. Many industrial enterprises—large, medium and small—came up around the steel towns, engaged in cement manufacturing, re-rolling of steel, machine building and chemicals manufacturing.

Mr K. T. Chandy, the Chairman of HSL from 1968 to 1972, wrote in his recollections that the public sector steel industry in India was an exciting story of a large well-knit body of workforce, comprising people at different levels of technical, scientific and managerial responsibilities and others at different lower levels with high technical skills and great operational abilities. It was a story of how the different levels of this composite workforce sought and assimilated successive flows of advancing technology in a complex range of operations, covering, on the one hand, the design, fabrication and establishment of a wide range of production facilities and on the other, the utilization and maintenance of these facilities in the production of an expanding and increasingly sophisticated range of products and services.

Immediately after completion of the one-million-tonne phase at Bhilai, Rourkela and Durgapur, further expansion of the steel plants was taken up. The crude steel capacity of Bhilai Steel Plant (BSP) increased to 2.5 million tonnes in 1967 and further to 4 million tonnes in 1985. The capacity of the Durgapur Steel Plant (DSP) increased to 1.6 million tonnes and that of Rourkela Steel Plant (RSP) to 1.8 million tonnes by 1967.

BSL, which in 1974 had a crude steel capacity of 1.7 million tonnes, also underwent an expansion whereby its capacity increased to 4 million tonnes by 1984. Furthermore, ASP, set up with an initial capacity of 1,00,000 tonnes of ingot steel, was expanded to 260,000 tonnes of liquid steel in 1988.

The performance of the steel plants in the expansion phase however left much to be desired. Mr K. T. Chandy, who visited all the plants after assuming charge, found that as the facilities forming the expansion phase were nearing completion, there were many teething problems in commissioning them and reaching efficient production levels. A heavy load of capital repairs of earlier units had to be carried out simultaneously. Also, certain balancing facilities had to be designed to make expansion projects fully efficient. The technical ability to undertake these tasks not only needed a group to undertake repairs and maintenance but also a group with the ability to plan and design additional facilities, for which the Central Engineering and Design Bureau (CEDB) of HSL needed to be provided with requisite capability.

There were also innumerable disputes with the unions specifically at DSP and to a lesser extent at RSP, regarding manning of new plants and incentive payments. The industrial relations (IR) were turbulent and demanded a great deal of time and effort to manage them.

Further, the economy was characterized by slowing down from the end of the Third Five Year Plan leading to a fall in the domestic demand for steel, which required both undertaking steel exports as well as using rebates and credits as an instrument to resuscitate domestic demand.

Each of the issues needed an innovative approach. CEDB, which had been set up in 1959, played a major role in planning, designing and supervising the construction of balancing equipment for the three integrated steel plants in their expansion phase. It also helped in major repairs and in initiating the work for the construction of BSL. To help CEDB acquire skills of not only making general project reports but also take up detailed project engineering of the designing of facilities of the steel plants, collaborations were entered into with United Engineering and Foundry, Pittsburgh and with Tyazpromexport for the Soviet design institutes, and for the training of Indian personnel in the design institutes. CEDB was spun off in 1973 as an independent company MECON and functioned from 1973 to 1978 as a subsidiary of the holding company SAIL.

To take care of the union issues, a Bipartite Committee was formed for setting the wages for the steel industry through negotiations, instead of through a wage board. The National Joint Consultative Committee for Steel Industry (NJCS) set up in 1969 was a unique experiment in a bipartite relationship and the first bipartite forum of its kind at the national level, consisting of representatives of the trade unions and management. The setting up of the negotiating committee in the steel industry contributed significantly to promoting industrial peace and harmony in the steel sector. The steel industry through NJCS not only established a lead in settling wages in a bipartite forum but also laid the groundwork of a national wage policy.

NJCS over the years has provided the forum to discuss various issues relating to production and productivity with a view to improving the performance of the company. Despite varying ideologies of different trade union organizations being represented in the committee and conflicting situations arising from time to time, the committee has functioned in harmony and contributed significantly to the improved performance of SAIL and the steel industry.

On the marketing challenges faced by HSL, Mr Bhaya who took charge of marketing operations in the late 1960s, made a significant contribution in developing the marketing organization and expansion of markets in India and abroad. The mild recession in the domestic market pushed HSL towards exports, exposing it to highly competitive international markets and prevalent practices.

The 1960s were also a period of evolution of structure and major management systems in the company. Indian standards of steel products were developed along with Indian Standards Institution (now Bureau of Indian Standards). Statistical Quality Control (SQC) and other quality improvement tools were introduced. Materials management as a distinct discipline took root in the company. Procedures for purchase, stores and inventory management were institutionalized. To integrate technical and financial aspects of capital expenditure decisions, a manual laying down a standard procedure for an improved method of appraisal as well as post review was introduced. These processes and systems were emulated by peers both in the public and private sectors.

A large group of graduate engineers, operative trainees, artisan trainees, trainees under the Apprenticeship Act, numbering more than 2,000, were trained under the technical training institutes of the steel plants every year. Engineers were sent for specialized training in foreign countries, viz., USSR, UK, Australia, USA, Japan, Czechoslovakia and West Germany. Advanced courses in different branches of management offered by reputed organizations of the country were also available for training the company's personnel.

Professionalizing various functions was a major step initiated in HSL, under the Chairmanship of K. T. Chandy. He was instrumental in bringing Mr R. P. Billimoria from TISCO to HSL as the Director of Personnel. In finance, qualified and experienced chartered accountants headed the function and academically qualified and experienced HRD experts took over the personnel departments at the plants and the headquarters. Academic excellence in specialized areas became the criterion for the induction of management trainees.

To have a strong and well-equipped R&D Centre within its fold, the Research and Development Centre for Iron and Steel (RDCIS) was formally established in 1972. The primary objective of the R&D Centre was to plan and implement various research and development programmes to achieve continuous improvement in critical performance indices of the steel plants, to increase productivity and lower production cost and improve quality by process optimization or by induction of new technology and develop new grades to cater to the market demand. The R&D complex, as it stands today, became fully functional in 1984–1985 and has been at the forefront of technology improvement of SAIL.

A Center of Engineering and Technology (CET) was set up in 1983 to provide in-house engineering and technology-related consultancy services to SAIL plants, after MECON separated from SAIL in 1978.

In the formative years of HSL, there were some unforeseen outcomes of the situation the company found itself in. One such incident was when heavy riots broke out in the city of Rourkela in 1964 that led to the abandonment of the plant by the workers, officers and the security staff. It created an unprecedented safety situation in the plant as the employees left their post to attend to the security of their homes and families in the township. The situation was somehow managed without any untoward outcome, but the experience led to the setting up of the Central Industrial Security Force (CISF) in the country.

Overmanning has been a historical legacy for PSUs and HSL was no different. The initial numbers came to be high on account of the affected families that gave up their landholdings where the steel plants came up; as other than compensation, employment for persons deprived of land formed a part of the rehabilitation package. Also, in the project execution phase for setting up the steel plants, a number of skilled, semi-skilled and unskilled labour were deployed. After the projects were over, there was a huge pressure on the company to absorb the project labour.

Project management was an area of challenge for HSL and subsequently for SAIL. Frequent change in design, discovering missing components after completion of the project, inappropriate product mix, inordinate delays in ramping up production in the new facilities, were concerns right from the expansion phase taken up in the 1960s.

It was also observed that whenever the projects were awarded on a turnkey basis, the cost became too high while the non-turnkey projects brought an overload of coordination, which the company more often than not, found difficult to manage.

There were two issues, however, which were most relevant for managing HSL. One was to have the professionals within the company rise to its helm and senior positions rather than generalists from outside. The second dealt with the issue of organizational structure and led to the conception of the Steel Authority of India, the holding company.

Steel Authority of India Limited

SAIL was set up on 24 January 1973 following a policy statement in the parliament to evolve a new model of a holding company to manage steel inputs and outputs under one umbrella. It was the concept favoured by the then Steel Minister Mr S. Mohan Kumaramangalam who visualized large holding companies in all the basic industries in the public sector. Chairman designate HSL, Mr Wadud Khan, Principal Secretary to the PM, Mr P. N. Dhar, formed a part of the delegation that went to study the working of such companies in the countries with large public sector enterprises like Italy, France, Sweden and Britain. After implementing the concept, HSL, Bokaro Steel Limited (BSL), Salem Steel Plant (SSP), National Mineral Development Corporation Limited (NMDC), Hindustan Steelworks Construction Limited (HSCL), Bharat Coking Coal Limited (BCCL), MECON and Bharat Refractories Limited (BRL) were brought under the umbrella of SAIL. Additionally, the shares held by the President of India in Bolani Ores Limited, Metals Scrap Trading Corporation (MSTC), Manganese Ore India Limited (MOIL) and Mysore Iron and Steel Limited (MISL) were also transferred to SAIL.

The holding company was to look into the long-term strategic issues, investment planning, securing the input materials, technological upgradation and R&D, developing human resources and marketing, while the companies under it were to perform as operating companies.

The experiment with the holding company however did not last long. 'Russi, the ministry will be the holding company,' was a statement of the then Secretary Steel, to Mr R. P. Billimoria, Chairman of SAIL 1976–1977. In 1978, the government brought the Public Sector Iron and Steel Companies (Restructuring) and Miscellaneous Provisions Act, whereby SAIL became an operating company, retaining the steel-producing assets and linked mines, while the rest of the related business companies were delinked.

SSP incorporated in October 1972, which functioned under the holding company SAIL, merged with the parent company in 1978. It was situated at Salem in Tamil Nadu and had been conceived on the principle of reverse integration. As a part of the first stage of the plant, a stainless steel cold rolling complex came up at SSP in 1981 with a capacity of 32,000 tonnes per year. The capacity of the plant was further augmented to 70,000 tonnes by adding another cold rolling mill in 1991. Subsequently, the plant also acquired a state of art hot rolling mill in 1995.

SAIL, in the late 1970s and 1980s, also acquired three subsidiaries, which later on merged with the parent company.

IISCO was incorporated in 1918. Following a series of mergers in 1952, IISCO became a vertically integrated steel company with its steel-making unit at Burnpur, captive iron ore mines at Gua and Chiria, coal properties at Chasnalla, Jitpur and Ramnagore and a captive foundry and pipe making plant at Kulti. With the ageing of equipment, productivity of the plant started declining in the late 1960s and the plant started incurring losses from the early 1970s. As a result, the Government of India took over the management of the Company in 1972, followed by taking over of IISCO shares in 1976. The shares of the Government of India in IISCO were transferred to SAIL in May 1978, making it a wholly-owned subsidiary.

Maharashtra Elektrosmelt Limited (MEL) was set up in 1974, in Chandrapur, in Maharashtra for production of high carbon ferro-manganese. Due to a variety of reasons including fall in demand for ferro-manganese in the country, high power tariff and process deficiencies, the plant started incurring losses. SAIL took over management of MEL in 1986 for utilizing some of its facilities for R&D work and to maximize production of high carbon ferro-manganese for captive use in its plants.

VISL was established in 1923 in Bhadravati in Karnataka. Known as Mysore Iron and Steel Works, its name was changed to VISL in 1976 as a tribute to its illustrious founder Bharat Ratna Sir M. Visvevaraya. The Government of India, Government of Karnataka and SAIL signed an MoU on 10 August 1989 for taking over majority shareholding of VISL by SAIL. In 1997, SAIL acquired entire shareholdings from the Government of Karnataka making it its wholly-owned subsidiary. VISL merged with SAIL in 1998.

SAIL functioned as a profit-earning company for most of the years after its inception. However, its performance declined in the early 1980s, and it went into loss in the years 1982–1983 and 1983–1984. Dr V. Krishnamurthy was given the charge of Chairman SAIL in 1985 to nurse back the company to health.

Dr Krishnamurthy brought about several changes in the company. He put an end to the practice of additional payment to the workers in lieu of 'overtime'. He gave a thrust to human resource development, specifically training and introducing workshops as a process to collectively brainstorm and arrive at solutions for the problems confronting the company.

The employees felt empowered and there was a general perception that Dr Krishnamurthy restored a sense of pride in the people for the company. A healthy atmosphere of trust was created all around. Interactions with the public and customers were intensified leading to better mutual understanding. In its operating performance, the organization migrated to a higher level of energy and enterprise. There was a complete change of work culture brought about by a disciplined way of working, avoidance of wasteful expenditure and a more transparent way of decision-making. A more harmonious working relationship came about between the workers and executives and there was a focus on quality, concern for customers and improving profits, without resorting to an increase in the price of steel.

The steel industry was amongst the most controlled sectors prior to the economic reforms of 1991. Dr Krishnamurthy discovered to his dismay that SAIL despite being amongst the largest PSE, enjoyed very little freedom to decide on vital matters affecting the operations of the company. 'Market studies were conducted by external agencies on the basis of which the Planning Commission decided on the product mix and additional capacities to be created. It was always the government's decision whether to expand the existing plants or to set up new ones. MECON, outside the control of SAIL, decided on the technologies to be adopted and equipment specifications. The decision to source technology was decided on political considerations and not by SAIL. The Department of Technical Development was the final arbitrator about whether the equipment should be imported or produced in India. Procurement of the machinery was based on credit facilities and not on technical or commercial considerations. The Iron and Steel Controller decided what products should be produced and to whom they should be supplied! The Government regulated the selling price of steel. Another department in the Government dealing with the public enterprises decided the recruitment policies, rates of pay, allowances, perquisites and even the incentive scheme. I wondered what was left for the SAIL Board to manage.'

The Government of India in the 1980s introduced a memorandum of understanding (MoU) system to grant greater functional autonomy to the PSUs. SAIL became one of the earliest PSUs to sign an MoU with the Government of India, its principal shareholder. The MoU was to clearly define the targets to be met and the roles and responsibility for each side towards fulfilment of the targets on an annual basis. Initially perceived as a performance measurement instrument where both the government as well as the public sector enterprises were to lay down the areas of their responsibility and accountability, with the passage of little time it became a one-sided document, which only reflected the targets and the responsibilities for the PSE. The parameters forming a part of the responsibility of the administrative ministry, e.g., in the case of SAIL, say, the availability of railway wagons, domestic supply of coking and thermal coal, etc., were diluted from the obligations and responsibility of the government.

Despite limitations, the performance of SAIL was reasonable for most of the years during the seventies and eighties. It fulfilled to a great extent the purpose for which it had been set up—to be the steelmaker to the nation. It supplied steel for the mega infrastructure projects comprising the thermal and hydel power plants. BSP emerged as the supplier of rails for the Indian railways. SAIL steel was used in the oil sector for the manufacture of large-dia pipes as well as for the manufacture of drums and barrels. It supplied steel for the defence sector—for the manufacture of India's first frigate 'INS Nilgiri', armoured plates for the main battle tanks Vijayanta, Arjun and T-90, as well as the Bofors gun shell. SAIL steel was supplied for the satellite launch vehicles and launch pads, nuclear energy projects and nuclear reactors and its stainless steel used for nuclear fuel complexes.

Its steel touched millions of lives through the supply of construction-grade steel such as TMT bars, structurals and galvanized sheets. SAIL steel was used in the manufacturing of household appliances such as refrigerators, steel furniture and other white goods, as also by the engineering industries, shipbuilders and by the companies engaged in the construction of flyovers, metros, ports and airports. Its steel also found a place in the manufacturing of railway coaches and wagons, commercial vehicles, automobiles, cycles, tractors, etc. The stainless steel manufactured at Salem Steel found its way into everyone's kitchens through utensils and in everyone's pockets through coins!

The company for a few years ran a popular advertisement campaign—'There is a little bit of SAIL in everybody's life.'

The reach of SAIL products was facilitated by its countrywide presence. Over the years, SAIL had developed a network of branch offices and stockyards covering the entire length and breadth of the country. Its diversified product basket helped it penetrate all segments of steel consumption and its wide reach supplied steel at locations far away from its production units. The domestic sales of SAIL were looked after by its marketing wing Central Marketing Organization (CMO), which in 1997 had 42 branches, 37 stockyards and 14 consignment agencies, spread throughout the country.

Erratic supply of industrial power had been a hindrance to the steel plants in managing their operations in the seventies, a constraint pointed out by former Chairmen Mr Wadud Khan and Mr K. C. Khanna. To overcome this drawback, SAIL invested in augmenting the capacity of its captive power assets to reduce its dependence on the grid and also minimize the risk of disruptions caused by the supply of power from the state utilities. By the end of the 1980s, the company insulated itself greatly from the dependence on grid power and has met between 60 to 65 per cent of its total power requirement during the past three decades from its captive sources.

SAIL captive mines form the second biggest mining infrastructure in the country, after Coal India Limited. To provide requisite focus to its mining operations, a Raw Materials Division (RMD) was formed in 1990, to act as the manager of the mines in the eastern region. The captive mines of Bhilai and VISL continued to be looked after by the plants themselves. The erstwhile captive mines of Bokaro, Rourkela, Durgapur and IISCO were brought under the umbrella of RMD. RMD managed the iron ore mines of Kiriburu, Meghataburu, Gua, Bolani, Barsua, Kalta and Chiria; limestone mines at Kuteshwar, Bhavnathpur, ILQ Satna and Purnapani; dolomite mine at Tulsidamar; and collieries at Chasnalla, Jitpur and Ramnagore. The iron ore mines at Dalli and Rajhara continued to be under the control of BSP. The mines took care of supplying the entire requirement of iron ore for the steel plants and met a significant part of its requirement for limestone and dolomite. What, however, is notable is that the iron ore mines of SAIL in the nineties provided it with raw materials input security, rather than being a source of competitive advantage. This was so because iron ore prices spiralled upwards only after 2002 in the international markets, following a surge in the Chinese demand, thereby increasing its significance in steel production. Up to the end of the 1990s, coking coal, for which SAIL was fully dependent on purchased sources, was the main cost driver for steel production through the blast furnace route.

A key contribution of Dr Krishnamurthy during his tenure was to give SAIL a long-term vision. He set up in the company a Corporate

Planning Directorate, which was headed by Mr Arvind Pande as a Director on the Board. Under the Chairmanship of Dr Krishnamurthy, the company came out with its first corporate plan, 'Corporate Plan 2000' which had a 15-year perspective, with five-yearly milestones. The vision of the corporate plan was for SAIL to retain its leadership position in the Indian steel industry, which, however, needed addressing some concerns related to the competitiveness and growth of the integrated steel plants.

Modernization Programme

The oil crisis of the early seventies had brought about a technological transformation in the steel industry worldwide. The open-hearth process of steelmaking had given way to the basic oxygen furnaces (BOF) and the continuous casting process (CC) introduced for improved material yield and product quality, as well as lower energy consumption. There was also a shift towards higher product quality through automation and improved process controls.

The integrated steel of SAIL, however, under the pressure of administered prices had been unable to generate resources for modernization and technological upgradation. To add to the woes, the prices of domestic raw materials had started escalating rapidly, eroding its competitive advantage. In the 1980s, there was a growing realization that the Indian steel sector was becoming uncompetitive due to the backlog of modernization and technological upgradation.

As a result, modernization plans were conceived and approved for three of the integrated plants—the Durgapur Steel Plant (DSP), the Rourkela Steel Plant (RSP) and the Bokaro Steel Plant (BSL). The first plant to be taken up for modernization was DSP followed by RSP and then BSL. Retrospectively, the modernization helped SAIL to compete in the liberalized and competitive market, which unfolded from 1991 onwards. In DSP, the open hearth/twin hearth furnaces were closed, and basic oxygen furnaces were commissioned. A new steel melting shop (SMS) with basic oxygen furnaces was added at

RSP with continuous casting facilities. The continuous casting of steel replaced ingot casting partially at DSP and BSL, while 100 per cent continuous casting of steel was attained at RSP. The combined blowing of LD converters, coil box in hot strip mill and PBCC were some of the new technologies introduced in RSP. Thermax cooling of ribbed bars in the merchant mill of DSP, quick roll changing, walking beam type furnace, hydraulic AGC at the hot strip mill at BSL were other new technologies introduced. The hot strip mills of BSL and RSP, the plate mill of RSP and the merchant mill and wheel and axle plant of DSP were upgraded. Besides improvements in the steelmaking zone and the rolling mills, the modernization strengthened the primary zone of the steel plants in the areas encompassing raw materials handling, sinter production and the blast furnaces complex. The modernization yielded benefits to the company in the form of a higher volume of production, improved efficiency of operations and better quality of products.

Liberalization and the New Economic Policy

The modernization of SAIL plants had just been initiated when the Indian economy faced an unprecedented balance of payment crisis in the aftermath of the Gulf War of 1990. The government on 24 July 1991 announced a bold package of reforms introducing major changes in the trade and industrial policy, which had a major impact on the steel sector, which till then was one of the most regulated sectors in the Indian industry.

To begin with, the iron and steel industry was removed from the list of industries reserved for the public sector and exempted from the provisions of compulsory licensing. Price and distribution regulations were also lifted in January 1992 enabling principal steel producers to fix their own prices. This was followed by the discontinuation of the levy in the form of SDF in 1994 and disbanding the Engineering Goods Exports Assistance Fund in 1996. Further, under the New Economic Policy, the private sector was encouraged to set up steel plants and tariffs on most steel goods; related raw material imports reduced and steel imports were put under the open general licenses.

The decontrol and de-regulation of the steel sector together with the partial divestment of GoI holding exposed SAIL not only to the competition of the market but also to the evaluation of the investing public.

SAIL managed to take up this challenge and could live up to the expectations of its stakeholders in the years up to the mid nineties. Its gross sales, operating profits and net profit improved every year following liberalization up to 1995–1996.

The government introduced the concept of Navratnas in 1997 whereby select public sector companies were to be supported in their drive to become global giants by receiving enhanced autonomy in various areas. SAIL was identified as one of the Navratnas. The autonomy granted by the Navratna status was judiciously used by the company in making suitable investments to improve its performance and in entering into JV for strategic business objectives. In 2010, SAIL was granted the status of a Maharatna company with enhanced delegation.

The liberalization and attaining the status of Navratna significantly changed the decision-making power of the company. SAIL, after the liberalization, was free to set prices for its products and make all decisions relevant to optimizing product-mix and marketing it domestically or abroad. Navratna delegations empowered it to make investment decisions without any limitations and form JVs and strategic alliances, subject to certain limits. The company also received the freedom to effect any organizational changes and create new positions below the Board level.

The year 1996–1997 witnessed a crisis in South-East Asian economies and its effect on the domestic steel scenario. A slowdown in economic activity engulfed almost all the industrial segments, leading to a steep drop in the growth rate of steel consumption. Global steel prices too declined considerably affecting the domestic steel scenario in a liberalized market environment. The rise in the cost of vital inputs brought severe stress on margins. The production had to be regulated due to sluggish demand. This reflected in SAIL's physical as well as financial performance, as its net profit dipped sharply.

The downturn of the economy and subsequent collapse of the steel prices exposed the weaknesses of SAIL as never before. Its high manpower, loss-making subsidiaries, sub-optimal operating efficiency and high capital-related expenses consequent to the modernization investments, hurtled the company to an unknown territory of mega loss.

Corporate Plan Gives Way to a Turnaround Plan

SAIL had given itself a long-term vision—Corporate Plan 2000 in 1987 and followed it with the Corporate Plan 2005 in 1992. Corporate plans, which were aspirational in nature, envisioned a future where the company set goals for itself typically in the form of market share, technological and operational excellence, financial parameters, etc., along with a road map to achieve it, over the medium to long term.

In SAIL, a five-yearly review was the norm for revising the corporate plan of the company and to redesign it afresh in line with the external changes and internal aspirations. The exercise for the new corporate plan had begun in 1997 and the initial interactions were held with the plants and the units, for revising the Corporate Plan 2005.

Around a similar time, an internal working was being done by the managers in the business planning, which formed a part of the Corporate Planning Directorate at the Headquarters, to set up the profit target for the company for next year for the MoU to be signed with the Government of India. The exercise became an eye-opener to the frontline managers when it was revealed that even at 100 per cent capacity utilization the company would not be able to avoid loss! The margins on steel had been severely squeezed due to the falling price line and given the high fixed cost structure of SAIL, a loss was unavoidable.

Clearly, the need of the hour was a Turnaround Plan and not a corporate plan. In an interesting turn of events, the Business Planning managers met their director (Corporate Planning), Mr M. K. Moitra, and informed him that rather than working on Corporate Plan 2007, they would like to work on a Turnaround Plan for the company.

Chairman Pande was quick to grasp the import of having a Turnaround Plan to avoid impending loss. The issue was deliberated in the chief executives meeting which had as its members—all the functional directors and the managing directors of the steel plants. Seven specific areas were allocated to the functional directors/managing directors to draft strategy reports and action plans for bringing improvements; the areas covered comprised Marketing, Technology and Product strategy, Cost Reduction, Raw Materials, Non-core Areas and Non-viable Units, Manpower Planning and Finance.

As a part of the turnaround initiatives, the company immediately embarked on an unprecedented cost reduction drive and a slew of measures for rationalizing inventory and pushing sales was undertaken. As the domestic steel-consuming sectors were impacted by a slowdown, a special thrust was given to exports.

Arvind Pande, Chairman SAIL in February 1998 called the team from Business Planning and told them, 'We will be appointing a consultant of international repute for the Turnaround Plan. Before that I want an internal Plan to be ready. When we do engage the external consultants, I do not want them to recommend anything we haven't already considered. Would you be able to do it?'

The team from Business Planning replied in the affirmative.

CHAPTER 3

Is It the Beginning or the End?

Liquidity Is Usually the First Sign

The environmental changes, which had started impacting the business sentiment in India, were initially perceived as a short-term phenomenon. The collapse in the demand for steel and excess domestic capacity resulted in stockpile of finished and semi-finished steel inventory with SAIL at a time when there was no let-up in the demand for funds for the modernization programmes underway at Bokaro, Durgapur and Rourkela Steel Plants. As a consequence, a significant mismatch between generation and demand for cash started emerging.

Originally estimated at an investment of ₹8,400 crore, the modernization projects at DSP, RSP and BSL faced inordinate delays—sometimes by as much as 5 to 6 years, resulting in the ballooning of project cost. In absence of sufficient generation of own funds, the modernization projects were financed primarily through borrowings. By the time the modernization programmes were over, the time and cost overrun pushed the investments to ₹12,600 crore, higher by 50 per cent compared to the original cost.

Paradoxically, the liquidity constraint had started showing itself from 1995–1996, the year of peak profit for SAIL in the nineties. Although the production increased by about 300,000 tonnes during 1995–1996 compared to the previous year, there was a marginal dip in the overall sales volume, implying that the higher production ended in higher inventories rather than higher sales. As a consequence, the working capital as a proportion to sales rose sharply from 23 per cent to 31 per cent between 1994–1995 and 1995–1996 and further to 42 per cent in 1996–1997 to set the alarm bells ringing!

In absolute terms, around ₹1,500 crore of cash got locked up in the stock of finished and semi-finished steel at SAIL plants and stockyards, in the two years leading to 1996–1997. Managing the funds for the company was becoming increasingly tough. So acute was the demand for cash to finance the capital projects and sustaining high levels of inventory that by 1998, the borrowings for SAIL touched a level of ₹20,000 crore, compared to overall borrowings of ₹12,200 crore in 1994–1995 before the crisis had manifested.

Given the weak balance sheet of the company, it was becoming increasingly difficult to borrow more. Further, other than the quantum of loan, the steep marginal cost of borrowing at 17 per cent and higher, had also started hurting the company. Cash management from being a pure corporate finance function had become a key area to monitor in SAIL Chairman's secretariat.

One of the first indicators of stress in any company's financial performance is when the sources of cash start drying up. The entire business judgement then is in understanding the nature of the phenomenon, something which could be temporary and managed with short-term measures or one which has structural dimensions and requires major surgery. The SAIL team sensed that the market had turned, and relief may not be forthcoming in the foreseeable future.

Maintaining the company's cash flow was one of the most challenging tasks during the crisis years of 1997–2003. The cash flow is akin to the lifeblood of any organization and in those turbulent years, maintaining liquidity was practically a trapeze performance. Finances were hard to come by and if available, the challenge was to reduce the rate of borrowings.

Shri Anil Kumar Chaudhary, who was then Senior Manager (Finance) at Corporate Office and later rose to the rank of Director (Finance) and subsequently assumed the position of Chairman SAIL in 2018 reflected, 'Liquidity management became one of the most critical things for SAIL at that time. I was at the forefront of the liquidity management, continuously interacting with banks and financial institutions and making relentless efforts to reduce the cost of borrowing to keep the lifeblood flowing.'

Liquidity management, which is often perceived as a combination of science and art, required skilfully converting knowledge into execution. Remembering the pioneering role played by Mr V. S. Jain at that time, Mr Chaudhary reckoned, 'I must say that Mr V. S. Jain, who was then the Director (Finance) of SAIL and subsequently became the Chairman of the company played a pivotal role in managing the financial side of the crisis at that time.'

Path to Turnaround and Transformation

Chairman Pande was convinced of the need to initiate a turnaround plan within 6 months of assuming charge of SAIL. Multipronged interventions were initiated in areas covering production, cost reduction, marketing and HR. There was however a need to develop a comprehensive Turnaround and Transformation Plans for the company, as it had started becoming apparent that mere efficiency improvement measures were unlikely to suffice.

At the end of a meeting at Ranchi, which headquartered three units of SAIL—RDCIS, CET and MTI—Arvind Pande asked Executive Director (RDCIS) Dr Sanak Mishra to meet him. Chairman Pande had decided a different role for Dr Mishra—one of the top metallurgists in the country. In his new role, Sanak Mishra was to head the Corporate Planning function at SAIL Corporate Office in New Delhi. Dr Mishra, after some initial reluctance, agreed to a totally different role than he had been associated in his career in SAIL.

Immediately after assuming charge as Executive Director of Corporate Planning, Dr Mishra called his team from Business Planning—the major constituent of Corporate Planning Directorate—for a meeting. Business Planning was a compact team at SAIL Corporate Office, comprising a multidisciplinary group of engineers, economists, marketing and finance professionals. The first job for Dr Mishra as head of Corporate Planning was to prepare a comprehensive Turnaround Plan for the company.

A lot of groundwork for the Turnaround Plan had already been done at SAIL in the 6 months prior to Dr Mishra joining the Corporate Office, through an exercise that engaged a broad cross-section of the company. Wide-ranging discussions and analytical exercises were held to identify the main issues that required attention and the way forward. Seven cross-functional strategy groups were formed under the guidance of SAIL Directors for detailed examination of identified strategic issues and consequent action plans.

Under the leadership of Dr Sanak Mishra, a cross-functional team comprising Sanjay Kumar, Dinesh Likhi and Sumantra Nag from Business Planning, Anirban Dasgupta and Arjun Kumar from CET and J. K. Gupta and C. N. N. Narayanan from Corporate Finance was set up to formulate a 'Turnaround and Transformation Plan' for the company.

The 'Turnaround and Transformation Plan' for SAIL was ready in July 1998. It was an internal document but unsparing in bringing out the pain points for the company and strategies to address the same. The internal plan was adopted by the SAIL Board for implementation. With a Turnaround Plan in its hand, SAIL approached the Ministry of Steel (MOS) to initiate a Cabinet Note on the Financial and Business Restructuring of the company.

At the time when SAIL's restructuring plan was under examination of the Ministry of Steel, SAIL engaged the services of M/s Mckinsey & Co. to validate the critical assumptions for SAIL's Turnaround and Transformation Plan for the short as well as the medium term. The consultants were to assist in the identification of improvements possible in each of SAIL's facilities, formulate recommendations for organizational changes and provide a blueprint for implementation.

Other than benefitting from the vast experience M/s Mckinsey had in the area of corporate restructuring globally, SAIL also knew that its case would gain greater credibility if it was concurred by an independent consultant of global repute. The team from Mckinsey was led by Ashok Alexander, Director of Delhi Office and had Pramath Sinha and Shirish Sankhe as team members. This team was ably assisted by a group of young managers amongst whom Arnab Sen and Divya Sehgal played the lead role. The Mckinsey team worked on the project along with a counterpart team from SAIL which comprised Sanjay Kumar, Dinesh Likhi and C. N. N. Narayanan.

Mckinsey worked on the project along with the SAIL team from November 1998 to March 1999 and came out with a report called the Competitiveness Plan for SAIL. The renaming of the Turnaround and Transformation was based on the logic that the measures of the plan were not only going to lead to a turnaround but were essential for SAIL's long-term competitiveness in a deregulated and competitive business environment.

The Competitiveness Plan

The first thing the competitiveness addressed was the precarious situation of SAIL found itself in. In an 'as is' scenario for SAIL, in case nothing changed, the likely loss figure, estimated in excess of ₹1,000 crore in 1998–1999, was to be followed by further loss, cumulatively adding to more than ₹5,000 crore by 2002–2003. This projection was premised on a weak price line for the steel industry in the backdrop of a persistent medium-term excess capacity, both globally as well as in India.

The poor financial performance was going to be exacerbated by steeply rising depreciation and interest charges consequent to SAIL's modernization programme. The high capital-related charges including interest and principal repayments were likely to result in a cash deficit of nearly ₹3,000 crore a year for the next 3 years, thereby locking SAIL in a vicious debt spiral.

The interest burden was to balloon to over ₹3,000 crore from a level of around ₹1,800 crore for 1998–1999 and SAIL's debt-equity ratio to spiral from 2.3 in 1998–1999 to 7.7 by 2002–2003. Individual plants such as RSP were headed for a financial disaster as the interest burden in their books could grow to over ₹1,500 crore by 2002–2003 compared to an EBITDA of only ₹330 crore.

The above gloomy projection, however, was not attributable only to the external factors. A number of internal factors accentuated the problems triggered by the external business condition.

First, SAIL was burdened with several assets that were either unviable or incompatible with SAIL's core mild steel business. Second, SAIL was unable to match the quality of products of the new entrants in the flat steel segment where its share fell from 61 per cent in 1992 to 33 per cent in 1998. Third, SAIL was yet to start reaping benefits from its modernization programme while incurring substantial expenditure on account of cost and time overrun in the high capital-intensive projects. Fourth, the advantages of captive raw materials in the form of iron ore and flux were more than offset by poor operating efficiency parameters, a large workforce and expenses on social infrastructure. Fifth, the production-dominated incentive structure resulted in high inventories, inefficient supply chain management and high working capital. Finally, there were issues related to organizational structure resulting in a lack of accountability, slow decision-making process and culture of non-performance.

In view of all the aforesaid factors, financial institutions and credit-rating agencies had drastically downgraded SAIL's debt instruments. The deeply pessimistic view of SAIL's future was also mirrored in the decline in market capitalization from around ₹27,000 crore in July 1994 to just over ₹2,000 crore in December 1998.

It was, however, possible for SAIL to reverse its fortunes through a series of interventions, which could potentially boost its bottomline by approximately ₹3,000 crore a year besides conferring a one-time cash generation of around ₹1,000 crore a year. The interventions could broadly be categorized under the following heads:

1. Restore the financial foundation
2. Refocus on the viable and the core
3. Restructure the organization
4. Rejuvenate marketing
5. Reduce operational, social, purchasing and inventory expenses
6. Reprioritise capital expenses

Restore the Financial Foundation

SAIL's restructuring proposal under the consideration of the Government of India, could be seen pertaining to: (a) financial restructuring to improve the company's financial health, in particular its debt serviceability and bankability of future projects and (b) business restructuring to make SAIL a vibrant company, which, on the merit of its own balance sheet and business plan, could raise resources from the market and provide a reasonable return to its shareholders.

Given the fact that SAIL's balance sheet was weak and the company did not have access to the minimum funds required for the business turnaround, the first and foremost task was to restore the financial foundation. A major head in the balance sheet of SAIL in the form of borrowings was on account of the SDF.

SDF was set up in June 1978, through a contribution per tonne of steel sold by SAIL and Tata Steel to provide funds for financing schemes related to projects, modernization, rehabilitation, R&D, renewals and replacement, etc. The contribution to SDF was made only by SAIL and TATA Steel and the fund did not form a part of the consolidated fund of India.

Loans were being extended out of the fund to the contributors for the above activities, which typically had a 12-year maturity with a 4-year moratorium and an average interest of around 7 per cent. The half-yearly interest payments as well as the principal repayments falling due were being rolled back as fresh loans. In effect, the fund was being operated on a non-cash basis.

The pricing and distribution of steel was deregulated in January 1992; however, the SDF contribution was discontinued only in April 1994, after which it became a part of net realization of the main producers. Though the contribution based on steel sold stopped flowing into the fund, inflows in the form of interest and principal repayments rolled over resulted in an increased debt burden on the company. As on 31 March 1998, total SDF dues in the SAIL books on account of loan and accrued interest amounted to ₹6,069 crore.

The financial restructuring proposal for SAIL submitted to the Government of India called for writing off the SDF loans.

Although not providing any cash relief, the proposed financial restructuring was to have a positive impact on the profitability of the company through a reduction in interest and depreciation charges. Also, it was to mitigate financial risk by reducing the debt-equity ratio and improvement in the debt-servicing capability. Furthermore, the lenders/creditors were expected to have a better perception of the company due to the improved financial position.

However, it was recognized that financial restructuring alone would be insufficient for the turnaround of the company. Hence, there was a need for a comprehensive business restructuring for its term survival and competitiveness.

Refocus on the Viable and the Core

The changes in the business environment had exposed the weaknesses with which SAIL had operated for years. Historically, only a few units within SAIL made profits, sustaining the rest of the loss-making units within the company. With the squeeze on the margins, the mounting losses of the non-performing units outstripped whatever profits the performing units could generate.

In SAIL's business portfolio, carbon steel business serviced by the integrated steel plants BSP, DSP, RSP and BSL, had the prospect of becoming internationally competitive due to inherent advantages in raw material sourcing. Even loss-making units such as DSP and RSP had the potential to make profits on the strength of technologies introduced under modernization. Similar potential, however, was not available in the special steels business.

The special steels units, which were neither strong performers nor appeared to have significant potential, posed the toughest business challenge.

ASP: ASP one of the major alloy steels producers in the country, had intrinsic weaknesses and operated in a none-too-favourable environment. Its financial performance had shown a persistent downward trend, culminating in a negative gross margin. Other than functioning in a market where the demand was virtually stagnant for the previous five years, ASP's location in West Bengal made it costlier to serve the major demand segments located in the western and southern regions which accounted for more than 60 per cent of the market for special steels. Operating at a much lower level than its capacity the unit was saddled with a large manpower accounting for 25 per cent of its turnover, compared to 16 per cent for SAIL as a whole. ASP for some time was able to survive by supplying Corten steel slabs to its sister unit at Bokaro. However, after the modernization, the integrated steel plant at Bokaro gained the technical skill to manufacture the slabs supplied by ASP and the interplant transfer was discontinued because of economic considerations.

SSP: The stainless-steel market in India was growing at a moderate rate of around 6 per cent. Broadly categorized as utensil- and non-utensil end segments, SSP was not competitive in the high growth low-nickel market segment aimed at the appliances and utensils market. On the other hand, in the high-nickel category aimed at the industrial end-user segment, SSP was facing tough competition from imports. The erosion of the unit's competitiveness had also caused a loss of export volumes compared to previous years.

The main disadvantage of SSP lay in its high-interest burden on account of the newly commissioned Steckel Mill and lack of steel-making facilities. Originally it had been conceived that SSP would receive the stainless steel slabs for rolling from ASP. However, the high cost of production at ASP and high incidence of freight from ASP to SSP made the option unviable. This resulted in the foreclosure of options for SSP's revival as given the cash crunch, capital expenditure by SAIL for backward integration in slab manufacturing at SSP itself was ruled out.

VISL: The losses of SAIL had increased after VISL became a part of SAIL. Despite being a cash drain, VISL had good assets and locational advantage to serve both the Western as well as the Southern markets. Although BF-BOF technology should have provided VISL with the potential to a cost-effective producer of alloy steels, its performance was yet to match its potential.

MEL: High power tariffs in Maharashtra made ferro-alloys production at MEL un-viable. The only option under the circumstances was to negotiate for a lower tariff with the State Electricity Board, failing which production at MEL had to be truncated to minimize losses.

IISCO: Given its constraints, SAIL was no longer in a position to support IISCO. The only option left for IISCO's revival was through a JV route, where the partner came with the funds for investment. Tyazhpromexport (TPE) of Russia had submitted a proposal for the revival of IISCO with a capital expenditure of around ₹800 crore. The proposal envisaged TPE acquiring 51 per cent of the equity in IISCO. TPE also sought operation on a clean slate basis with accumulated losses and unprovided liabilities being written off, besides other reliefs and concessions. The proposal was awaiting government approval.

Non-Core Assets

Power and Oxygen plants: With a view to long-term competitive positioning, it was important for SAIL to identify non-core assets that could operate better as independent companies.

Power generation and oxygen production were not core activities of the company and could be more efficiently managed by entities, which specialized in these businesses. Also, in the absence of availability of funds, the performance of captive power plants was likely to decline due to the lack of technological upgradation. It was therefore planned to form subsidiary JV companies in power at BSL, DSP and RSP and for Oxygen Plant-II at BSP. This arrangement would have ensured access to these industrial inputs, besides releasing funds that could then be utilized in the core area of steel-making.

Another advantage of this arrangement was perceived in terms of higher power generation from captive sources. Suitable solutions could be worked out for the old power plants to be retired and their duty taken over by new plants with modern technology. However, in the formation of JVs, the jobs of the associated employees were to be protected while ensuring that the net cost of the inputs to the steel plants did not increase.

Rourkela Fertilizer Plant: The fertilizer plant at RSP was a non-performing asset and also non-core to SAIL's business. With the removal of subsidy from the government, it no longer remained a viable proposition. Based on the costly feedstock of naptha, it was intrinsically uncompetitive and had a cost disadvantage vis-à-vis competitors using furnace oil and Low sulphur heavy stock (LSHS). Further, the demand for calcium ammonium nitrate (CAN) produced by the fertilizer plant of RSP had remained low, with farmers switching from CAN to other fertilizers. SAIL, therefore, needed to consider the option of divesting this business.

It was, therefore, decided to focus on the four integrated plants, namely, BSP, DSP, RSP and BSL, while the following actions were recommended for the assets which were either non-viable or non-core to SAIL's business.

Action	*Rationale*
Shutting down ASP and Rourkela Fertilizer Plant	Given the fact that these plants were intrinsically unviable, SAIL was unlikely to get any buyers for these assets. Also, any further investment would have been a waste of precious resources available with SAIL.
Fully divesting IISCO, SSP and VISL	A natural owner was expected to extract a better value out of these assets than SAIL and also afford the required investment. It was possible to find a buyer for IISCO on account of its high-quality iron ore mines, however, a large financial write-off was necessary to clean its balance sheet. SSP and VISL were assessed as intrinsically viable assets which could create more value for SAIL through disinvestment rather than through continued ownership.
Divesting stake in the power plants	Power being a non-core area for SAIL, it should be best managed through a joint venture which ensured SAIL access to cheap and reliable power despite change in ownership.

Restructure the Organization

SAIL over the decades had operated in tight compartments, defined along functional lines. The long-term consequence of this approach was (a) a lack of overall business perspective, (b) conflicting inter-functional objectives, (c) non-commonality of goals and (d) loss of accountability.

As a consequence of SAIL's organizational structure, incentives at various levels had become unconnected with business performance. Also, high levels of manpower and tenure-based promotion policy brought their own pressure in the form of a top-heavy multi-layered organization. In view of the above, it was suggested that SAIL could be reorganized into strategic business units or SBUs.

SAIL's core assets BSL, DSP, RSP and BSL were proposed to be combined into two SBUs, each led by an SBU head, who was to be responsible for the financial performance (Profit & Loss and Return on Capital employed) for the entire SBU. The SBU structure was expected to bring more focus to the overall business and eliminate the inter-plant and production-marketing conflicts that hindered optimal behaviour and performance focus.

BSL and RSP were to form a part of a Flat Products SBU, and BSP and DSP a Long Product SBU. SAIL Board needed to be restructured to include only the following functional directors: SBU (Flat), SBU (Long), Director (Commercial), Director (Finance), Director (HR and Corporate Planning) and Director (Technology). The plant MDs were no longer to be the Board members.

The top management team of each SBU was to comprise two plant MDs, the head of sales and marketing, finance, HR and projects. The sales and marketing functions with the Central Marketing Organization were to split between Flat and Long SBU, while the stockyards were to continue to be a common asset. The Director Commercial was to focus on sourcing centralised items, distribution and exports.

Rightsizing manpower was the other key intervention planned. SAIL's manpower strength of around 1,74,000 was four to five times the global benchmark for the integrated steel plants. Therefore, SAIL needed to reduce its labour force to 100,000 or lower through a combination of natural attrition and VRS.

While around 7,000 employees were to superannuate every year over the next four years, manpower in SAIL would still have been far in excess of the desired level of 100,000 by 2004–2005. Hence, manpower reduction of around 40,000 had to be achieved through the process of voluntary retirement. Simultaneously, all efforts were to be intensified to reduce contract labour.

Incentives systems needed to be modified and aligned to financial performance, productivity, quality, cost and delivery, rather than production. The incentive system for sales performance also needed to be changed. In course of time, sales value and contribution were needed to become the guiding factors in deciding incentives. Redesigned systems and processes for personnel evaluation, reward and promotion were needed to be implemented across all levels of SAIL.

Rejuvenate Marketing

Given the criticality of marketing in the turnaround strategy, several reforms were needed to enhance SAIL's competitiveness in the marketplace. The volatility and intensification of competition called for a refocused product-market strategy, as well as improved marketing processes.

It was estimated that high-end steel consuming segments in the flat product's market such as automobile, white goods and boilers and pressure vessels, were likely to grow about 2 per cent faster than the low and middle-end segments. However, in volume terms, they were projected to constitute only 13 per cent (around 3.5 million tonnes) of the market by 2001, with the low and middle-end segments accounting for the balance 87 per cent (more than 22 million tonnes) of the market. The preferred strategy for SAIL, therefore, was to protect its existing share in the low- and mid-end segments in flats, while selectively moving towards high-end segments. In the long products market, SAIL needed to invest to meet the quality requirements of customers such as the Railways.

With the freeing of imports, the customers of steel had gained access to international quality products. The improved awareness led to high rates of rejection wherever customers encountered quality problems with SAIL products. Poor quality, which occurred at multiple stages, led to large losses on account of high 'arisings', that is, production not conforming to order in the plant, downgrading at the stockyard, customer rejects, lower price realization and loss of sales. This situation was planned to be reversed through improvements in work practices, technological discipline and optimum utilization of the new facilities.

At an organizational level, it was decided to reorganize the Central Marketing Organization under two broad divisions—long products and flats products divisions—which would have led to an improvement in segment specialization and product knowledge of the marketing executives.

An important intervention in marketing was to be in the form of introducing a dealers' network to cater to small, regionally dispersed customers. Traditionally, marketing at SAIL took the form of direct despatch from the plants to the premises of large customers, or supplies from its numerous stockyards, located throughout the length and breadth of the country. A dealers' network had the benefit of reaching out to the small retail customers who typically required products such as galvanized plain and corrugated sheets, bars and rods and light structural, while keeping the marketing cost low.

Introduction of Key Account Management (KAM) was another intervention in the marketing process. It was observed that 2 per cent of SAIL's customers (around 165 in 1999) accounted for more than 50 per cent of the sales. Large customers, who bought multiple products, had to approach separate salespersons in SAIL's marketing set up. Also, salespersons spent far too much time with small customers. The proposed KAM process, which was to involve both CMO as well as plant personnel, was to ensure greater reliability on the quality and delivery of products to the key customers. KAM process was essential for customer retention and improvement both in the share of sales to the customer as well as net sales realization due to better service.

Reduce Operational, Social Purchasing and Inventory Expenses

Given the excess supply that pervaded the global and the domestic market cost-cutting had become a key for the survival of the steel companies. SAIL had already initiated steps in the area with very good results, effecting cost reduction of more than ₹1,600 crore in 1997 and 1998. The cost reduction achieved in the first wave by SAIL was relatively easy to accomplish. A significant opportunity however was available for the company to become one of the lowest-cost producers in the world, by adopting a rigorous methodology.

Four areas were identified which together provided a large potential for cost reduction over the next 3 years:

1. Operational costs in the plants;
2. Purchasing costs;
3. Working capital (supply chain) costs; and
4. Social infrastructure costs.

The prevailing cost of production at each of the four integrated steel plants (ISPs) was higher than the benchmarks for plants with similar technology. The main reason for the inflated cost structure was the low performance on key techno-economic parameters such as energy and yield at each stage of production. It was estimated that SAIL could continue to gain savings of ₹1,000 crore per year by reducing operating costs at its plants/units over the next 2 to 3 years.

Tapping future savings opportunities required a detailed analysis of each plant's technological capability and performance relative to benchmarks, which would then represent parameters or costs achievable without significant investments for upgrading or replacing technology.

SAIL's annual purchase of raw materials and stores and spares items were to the tune of ₹6,400 crore, including ₹3,150 crore on coking coal, ₹1,800 crore on stores and spares and ₹1,400 crore on other raw materials.

In the past, SAIL had selectively focused on some items for cost reduction. It was decided to implement specific strategies, which had a potential for cost reduction of 5–10 per cent on average, such as, focusing on the total cost of ownership (TCO) instead of just the purchase price, developing product-specific and differentiated sourcing strategies instead of the prevalent practice of one strategy for all purchases and coordinated purchases with specific targets for leveraging SAIL's bargaining power and instituting systems that ensured ongoing high performance.

Social infrastructure cost was something that was not visible to the company during the normal business times. SAIL as a leading PSU had been providing employment as well as social benefits to its employees as a part of its motto. The total expenditure on social infrastructure such as township, provision of medical and educational facilities, etc., was over ₹450 crore, which resulted in an additional overhead of nearly ₹500 per tonnes of saleable steel. In a fiercely competitive steel industry, it added another handicap in the company's ability to compete against low-cost players. SAIL, therefore, needed to systematically rationalize its expenses on social infrastructure by gradually reducing the subsidies without affecting the quality of services/social amenities to the employees. Areas such as manpower reduction in schools, hospitals, contract labour and CISF manning, increase in electricity charges, water charges, house rent, medical charges, education and canteen were identified to affect a savings of around ₹100 crore a year.

In addition, spare capacity/opportunity existing in social infrastructure could be utilized to generate additional revenue.

Reprioritize Capital Expenses

The mega-modernization projects of SAIL were fraught with delays and cost overruns, leading to over-capitalization. There was a need in the company to redesign the capital expenditure process keeping in view the changed market scenario and the ongoing cash crunch.

It was decided that the capital expenditure plan should evolve out of rolling corporate and business unit plans, taking into account the market dynamics and with involvement both of plant as well as marketing personnel as a team for idea generation. Furthermore, the returns for individual units needed to be assessed on the entire investment portfolio of the unit and not only on specific projects. Also, the capital budgeting exercise needed to adopt concepts such as a minimum technical solution to avoid extra investments and redundancy.

In the project execution phase, the designated/appointed Project Head was to be fully responsible and accountable for its timely completion and incentives needed to be created right from the start for early completion. There was a great scope within the company for fabricating various engineering items generally required in capital investment projects. Efforts were on to use the in-house facilities and the Growth Division of the company in such endeavours and needed to be better coordinated and streamlined.

Due to difficulties in generation of cash and sluggish market conditions, the capital expenditure programme for the Ninth Plan period had already been reduced from ₹15,000 crore to ₹7,000 crore (inclusive of ₹5,400 crore for continuing schemes and ₹1,600 crore for new schemes). A company like SAIL needed to invest around ₹1,100 crore per year on capital projects towards quality improvements and essential replacements to sustain operations in a competitive market, which translated into a capital outlay to ₹3,300 crore over the next three years.

Realize Shareholder Value

A recommendation of M/s Mckinsey & Co., which was beyond the scope of SAIL was that the government ownership was not consistent with the needs of a company, which operated in a highly competitive industry such as steel. Therefore, once the Competitiveness Plan was implemented over the course of the next 3 years, the government should consider privatizing SAIL. By then, the steel industry would be on an upturn and a competitive SAIL, with its low-cost plants, could be an attractive asset for private investors.

Implementation Plan

Given the organizational needs, it was imperative to move quickly on multiple fronts to implement the Competitiveness Plan.

The implementation of the Competitiveness Plan was a complex and arduous task. Overcoming the implementation challenges, however, was not only significant for SAIL's survival but it was also highly significant given the tremendous social and political repercussions related to a failure. The interlinkages of SAIL with the rest of the economy made thousands of people dependent on SAIL for their livelihood both directly and indirectly, making the social cost of SAIL collapsing unmeasurable.

There was, therefore, a need for full support from the SAIL Board, Ministry of Steel, Ministry of Finance and the Union Cabinet to overcome any barriers to implementation. There were many actions within the control of SAIL while others such as financial restructuring, closures and divestment, Board restructuring and aggressive manpower rightsizing required approvals from the Government of India. It was important for SAIL to implement all actions of the Competitiveness Plan under its own control while pursuing in parallel those actions which required the Government of India's approval.

CHAPTER 4

Impecuniosity Leads to Creativity

The wave of liberalization, initiated in India in 1991, had exposed the Indian steel industry and particularly SAIL to the effects of competition. Major users in India now had access to the quality of the steel they needed from the international market and new entrants in India had the advantage of access to new technologies, which ensured cost-effective production of superior grades. SAIL's modernization programme had been undertaken with the primary object of bridging this gap. Apart from the need to produce to the customer's exact specification, there was the need to produce at low costs, so that, adequate returns could be earned while matching the price of competitors. The stagnation in industrial production in India had aggravated the intensity of competition and piling steel inventories during the fiscal year 1997–1998 signalled a critical situation.

On the demand side, it did not appear that the market was going to provide any respite in foreseeable future. The likely estimate for demand growth was projected at around 2 per cent in the immediate future. In fact, the five-yearly target for the Ninth Five Year Plan (1997 to 2002) for the domestic demand for finished steel appeared overly optimistic and was revised down to 27 million tonnes for the end of the plan period, compared to the earlier estimate of 32 million tonnes.

Under such a situation, the technological capabilities of SAIL inevitably assumed importance, as the quality was to have greater significance than volume. Structures relating to managerial approaches and labour productivity were also expected to become more crucial, as indeed had been the experience of steel plants the world over.

Advancement of technology in steel-consuming applications placed a premium on better grades of steel, viz., those which were more resistant to chemical and physical stresses and at the same time were lighter in weight and cost-effective for the overall application. In many ways, steel as a material and its mode of application had to be re-invented. In the construction industry in the UK, for instance, steel sections had been applied as alternatives to concrete, as a result of sustained development work on designing and building. This was accompanied by a reduction in the cost of production, which made steel more cost-effective than concrete and also by inventing steel with specific properties, such as earthquake-resistant steel structures. In the USA, the transformation in the steel industry had been led by the introduction of thin slab casting and a very high level of automation, coupled with information technology.

The strategy document 'Path to Turnaround and Transformation' was discussed by the SAIL Board in its meeting held on 30 July 1998. Appreciating the efforts and the approach of the Turnaround plan, the Board directed that the implementation of short-term measures contained in the plan should start immediately.

Accordingly, Arvind Pande, Chairman SAIL, wrote to all the managing directors and the functional directors to initiate actions in their respective areas. In fact, in parallel with the formulation of the Turnaround Plan, SAIL had already proactively initiated a series of interventions, which did not require any external clearance. These interventions were inwards-oriented and aimed to improve the efficiency of the business and technical processes.

A Director' Workshop, which was conducted by Mr Arun Maira in Manali from 5 to 7 June 1997, emphasized the need for cost reduction at a pace much faster than had been happening. Improved customer orientation, increase in exports, improved asset utilization and maximization of revenues were the other focus areas for improvement.

Cost Reduction Drive

As the price-line for the finished steel tanked following the Asian Currency Crisis, there was little commensurate relief in the cost of inputs such as coal, petroleum products, power and freight. These inputs that contributed a major component in steel production cost, enjoyed pricing power being state-sector monopolies, irrespective of the market dynamics.

Realizing the criticality of cost competitiveness to stay afloat, a company-wide campaign 'Cost multiplication divides profits' was put up in all the plants and units of SAIL in the form of hoardings and large posters to communicate its importance to the employees, as the company embarked on a major cost-reduction drive.

The cost-reduction plan included innovative ideas and identification of areas where further savings were possible. A detailed comparison of the process cost across the five integrated steel plants was undertaken to have an internal benchmarking for potential cost-saving areas. It was realized that potential existed for further cost reduction through new approaches, such as improvement in techno-economic parameters like energy consumption, yield, etc., identified by the process of benchmarking; improvements by way of substitution of raw materials, technology upgradation through in-house efforts to cut process costs, optimization of cost of imported coal with respect to quality for optimum buying pattern and improvement in captive power generation by 5–10 per cent.

To make the cost-reduction drive a success, teams were formed both at corporate as well as unit levels to identify areas having potential for savings, finalize benchmarks for critical parameters and set targets. The teams were also to coordinate the implementation of cost reduction measures and continuously monitor the implementation for its success. Various levels of authority including the Board of Directors were involved with the exercise of cost reduction. The progress and constraints were periodically reviewed for taking timely action and extending support at the grassroots level.

During 1997–1998, the first year of the cost-reduction drive, the focus was on optimizing material usage and improving operational efficiencies. Thereafter newer approaches to improve savings were adopted. These included reduced diversion to defective and off-grade categories, reduction in purchase prices of various input materials, maximum utilization of in-house manufacturing facilities of spares/refractory materials, increasing direct dispatch of finished steel to customers and optimizing linkages between mines and steel plants, etc. Introduction of new technologies, such as coal-dust injection at the Bhilai and Bokaro steel plants and stabilization of continuous casting units at Durgapur, Rourkela and Bokaro, contributed to substitution of expensive input by cheaper resource and higher yields and quality parameters.

Reminiscing the measures taken up under the cost drive, Mr Suresh Pandey, who held the position as Executive Director (Works) at BSP, Executive Director in-charge at Operations Directorate and later as Managing Director BSL, elaborated, 'Ferro-alloys constituted a major cost item in steel production. SAIL had an in-house facility for the production of ferro-alloys at Chandrapur in Maharashtra. As the unit was underperforming due to a variety of reasons, a small debottlenecking was carried out on priority to maximize the in-house availability and reducing outside purchase, leading to cash savings.'

'Further, to optimize the direct cost of ferro-alloys consumption, a technical balancing was carried out for each plant to estimate the consumption requirement of different alloys, based on the final analysis of the production of different grades of steel. Cumulative normative consumption of ferroalloys so arrived was then compared with the shop supply. A significant gap emerged, attributable both to technical as well as non-technical reasons.

The technical reasons for this were that if a particular grade of steel required a specific physical property which in turn required a certain percentage of alloy additions, there was an opportunity of savings if the alloy addition ensured the presence of the element on the lower rather than the higher end of the desired range.'

Mr Pandey clarified that the optimization of alloys however became a complex exercise during the plant operations, as each plant produced hundreds of grade with multiple physical variations. Each of the physical properties required a different composition, thereby adding complexity to the optimization process.

'The non-technical issues were related to the recovery of elements which depended on local conditions and practices. For the same product-mix, the recovery of elements varied across plants, which required further analysis of factors causing the variance. All this called for a micro-level detailing at the plants to derive the benefits.'

This constituted but one of the numerous cost-reduction initiatives taken up at SAIL. Other than the areas of energy management, yield improvement and reduction in specific consumption of materials and services, a number of opportunities were explored in less prominent areas such as waste management.

For example, a practice followed traditionally was to send the dismantled materials of liquid metal handling system to the waste dumping site. On examination, it was found that it had many usable materials in it. A system was introduced for segregation at the source so that only waste materials were despatched to the dumping site.

Similarly, in the usage of the fire clay bricks at numerous places in the steel plant, an opportunity was seen to substitute some applications with recycled bricks. Further, the purchase of refractory powder of different grades used in the plant could be substituted in some cases by the in-house production by grinding recycled bricks.

Assembly reclamation centre provided another area for cost reduction. When replaced by new assembly sets, the practice followed was to take out the old assemblies and sub-assemblies and dump it in the scrap yard. On inspection of these assemblies, it was found that most of the old sets lying in the scrapyard could be reconditioned for reuse. To accomplish it, a separate reclamation facility was created for mechanical and electrical assemblies and sub-assemblies. A process was put in place whereby it was made mandatory that replaced old assemblies and sub-assemblies would be sent to the newly set up assembly reclamation centres, which would decide repairing the old assemblies for reuse or declare them obsolete. Also, before any purchase indenting, the user department was to take non-availability certificates from these assembly reclamation centres.

Another avenue of cost reduction was substitution of higher cost raw material with waste material. LD slag—a process waste—had very high calcium oxide as well in silicon oxide content. This made it suitable for replacing limestone in the blast furnaces. Charging of LD slag in the blast furnaces was undertaken after solving logistic and sizing issues. It gave added benefit by lowering the coke rate, as there was no requirement of heat for calcification for LD slag, unlike the case of limestone.

Maintenance and repairs imposed significant cost on the production processes. An analysis showed two important facts in the maintenance practice. First, the mean time between two repairs was very low for major equipment. This not only increased the repair cost but also lowered productivity and product quality; thereby resulting in lower sales realization. Second, the cost of maintenance became higher.

To overcome this weakness, good systems of maintenance were reinforced. These included practices such as inspection of equipment, emphasizing preventive and monthly maintenance, which over the passage of time had given way to break down maintenance. Fixing at first sight of leaks had been forgotten. All these interventions needed a cultural change in maintenance practices and its severity varied from plant to plant. To bring about these changes communications exercises were intensified and best inter-plant practices exchanged.

Cost-reduction initiatives at SAIL were encouraging and yielded a savings of ₹732 crore in 1997–1998 and ₹902 crore during 1998–1999.

Ranju Sarkar in his coverage of SAIL in *Business Today* wrote,

> The good news is that SAIL has improved its cost-competitiveness over the years. For example, according to a study by Banque Paribas (October 1998), SAIL has emerged as one of the 5 lowest-cost producers—with a cash cost of $277 per tonne—in the global market. That makes SAIL's steel cheaper than TISCO's ($356) and Nippon Steel's ($441). The bad news: it still has lots more to do to prune costs. (1999, July 22)

Steel Secretary Mr Basu agreed that SAIL needed to focus more on techno-economic parameters so that the cost per tonne came down further. He also explained, 'Adding to SAIL's woes are its social infrastructure costs. The total expenditure on social amenities by SAIL (net of income) rose from ₹271 crore in 1991–1992 to ₹460 crore in 1997–1998, growing, on an average, by 11 per cent every year.'

Going ahead, a process was put in place to optimize the purchase cost of inputs. It was realized that the interests of various stakeholders in the purchasing process differed. For example, the purchasing group's goal was to get the lowest possible price, while the operations group wanted reliability and good quality. It was therefore decided to form specific commodity teams at the plants, comprising people from different streams such as purchasing, finance, operations and maintenance. The overall role of these commodity teams was to focus on reducing the TCO, provide technical problem-solving capability and make optimum cost-quality trade-offs. The new purchase process was overseen by an apex committee of Directors of the SAIL Board. The process was initially put into operation for four commodities—refractories, ferroalloys, rolls and conveyor belts.

Elaborating the initiatives taken up to reduce the cost of refractories Mr Suresh Pandey said, 'Refractory is an important material in steel production process, as liquid metal at low or high temperature can be handled only with the help of this material. With LD converter and continuous casting becoming the dominant technology for steel making, the demand for good quality refractory rose sharply, leading to an increase in its price. To address this issue two-stage actions were undertaken—first, in-house facility utilization and second, the optimization of refractory usage.'

'On examining the in-house facilities, it was observed that since magnesia carbon bricks, which provided higher converter life, had replaced the tar dolo bricks in all the units, facilities provided for tar dolo brick making were idling. Magnesia carbon bricks were being purchased from outside and were very costly. On examination, it was found that with some modification of plant facilities it could be made in-house. At BSP a trial set of magnesia carbon bricks for one convertor was made and put to use. It gave a better life than purchased sets, signifying less consumption of lining brick per tonne of steel. BSP took some more time to make regular production for the full requirement of one unit. With the passage of time quality of homemade bricks improved to the extent that a record life of over 6,000 heats was achieved.'

'Another area of major consumption of refractories was in steel ladles and the concast process. An analysis revealed that certain tapping temperature ranges were giving a better life for the steel ladles. In case of concast, it was found that certain grades and composition range of some elements led to the abortion of casting, leading to higher refractory usage. These were all technical issues controllable by involving workforce and constant monitoring.'

'After monitoring operations, it was discovered that the usage of refractories continued to be much on the higher side despite exercising due controls. This in a way made the quality of supply a suspect. It was, however, difficult to point fingers at any supplier without actual data in hand. Then one plant took a massive exercise of compiling supplier-wise life per ladle of heat cast for the past three years. It was a massive data mining operation and an eye opener. It was discovered that during the last three years the average heat cast per ladle attributable to poor quality refractory, was as low as 1/3rd of the highest heat cast per ladle.'

'Firms supplying suspect quality refractory for ladles were substantial in numbers for every unit. To overcome this issue the purchase system was modified. An average number of heat per ladle was made mandatory, failing which the supplier was made to replace the full set of bricks free of charge. This not only reduced refractory usage but other costs as well. In ladle preparation, other consumables were also used, consumption of which also got reduced. A similar approach was followed for concast refractory, which gave similar benefits. In this case, increased tundish life also increased the yield thereby providing significant gains.'

The cost reduction process got institutionalized in SAIL and continues till date. They were particularly effective in the aftermath of the financial meltdown of 2008, when SAIL emerged as one of the most profitable steel companies globally on the strength of its cost control culture.

Savings in Coal Imports

Coking coal valued at ₹3,142 crore accounted for 58 per cent of total expenses on raw materials consumed for SAIL during 1997–1998 and constituted the single biggest expense item for its integrated steel plants operating on blast furnace route of production. Due to limitations both of quantity as well as quality of the indigenous coking coal, SAIL was dependent on imported coking coal from Australia, New Zealand, the USA and Canada, etc.

SAIL had been importing low ash coking coal of prime quality since 1978–1979 while supplementing it with the indigenously supplied coking coal sourced primarily from BCCL, a subsidiary of Coal India Limited. In addition to importing hard coking coal, SAIL after modernization of its plants started import of soft coking coal beginning 1997–1998 and Coal dust Injection (CDI) coal from 1998–1999. Soft coking coal and CDI coal were relatively cheaper and could be used as a partial substitute for the more expensive imported hard coking coal.

Initially, the process of procurement of imported coal was based on the international competitive bidding procedure of the World Bank.

Under this process, every three to four months, spot tenders were floated to meet the requirement of imported hard coking coal. In 1995, however, SAIL decided to make a change in favour of entering into a long-term contract, which had many advantages over the spot purchase.

These advantages were mainly in the form of security of supply, particularly in the period of shortages, consistent quality, continuity of supply, competitive prices during tight market conditions and tie up with a limited number of good sources of prime quality coking coal.

SAIL entered into long-term agreements (LTA) with four Australian and one New Zealand supplier in 1995 and 1996, for a LTA of three years, which was extendable for another two years depending on SAIL's choice. After extensive negotiations, the price of coal to be imported under the LTA were linked to the Japanese Steel Mill (JSM) prices. This was a big achievement as the JSMs purchased around 40 million tonnes of hard coking coal compared to the annual purchase of around 6 million tonnes by SAIL. In September 1997, SAIL opted for an extension of the LTA for two years, that is, for the deliveries up to 1999–2000.

However, there was a fall in the international prices of coking coal in 1998. Given the sensitivity of the price of imported coal in the cost structure of steel manufacturing, SAIL resorted to renegotiation of JSM linked LTA for imported coking coal. After a protracted negotiation, the procurement price was brought down to US $43/tonne against the earlier contracted price of US $51/tonne, giving a savings of approximately US $50 million per annum. In addition, fresh LTAs were signed for a period of 3 years, which were extendable by another 2 years at the purchaser's option, with annual price negotiations to be held between the buyer and the supplier.

In 1999, SAIL laid down a sound policy for coal imports, which was an optimal combination of procurement under long-term contracts vis-à-vis spot purchases. While the hard coking coal was to be purchased under LTA, the soft coking coal and CDI coal was to be purchased under spot tender as their requirement was relatively small.

There was also an option to tie up hard coking coal through spot tendering whenever an opportunity of competitive price became available. In the same year, that is, 1999, SAIL negotiated a long-term supply price for hard coking coal for US$ 36–37 per tonne, which was lower than the JSM price by around US$ 5 per tonne, thereby evolving an Indian steel mill pricing.

The system of coal procurement devised in mid-nineties has been of great significance to SAIL. Increasing hot metal production and dwindling domestic supply of metallurgical grade coal has increased the dependence on imported coal significantly over the years. SAIL continues to procure coal through a mix of LTA and short-term contracts with some modifications since the system was put in place.

Marketing Initiatives

Steel prices in India post liberalization moved synchronously with the international price trends. The initial years, immediately after liberalization, presented the existing integrated steel producers with an opportunity. Unshackled by the administered prices, companies such as SAIL and Tata Steel were able to mop the premium available between the administered and the market price, thereby boosting their revenue earnings and profits. Also, relatively stable international prices and depreciation of the Indian rupee provided adequate cushion consequent to disbanding of quantitative restrictions on imports and slashing down of customs duty.

However, the period of easy earnings for steel players was relatively short. Initially, the problem manifested in terms of sluggish domestic demand, which immediately afterwards got exacerbated by a sharp decline in the price line following the East Asian Currency Crisis. To overcome it, SAIL started several initiatives to keep the company afloat in the face of an unprecedented dull market.

The focus of these marketing measures was a vigorous thrust on exports and sales to projects and construction segments by exploiting SAIL's inherent advantages of a wide product range.

Signing annual MOUs with the key customers was taken up as an instrument for nurturing long-term relationships with customers. Participation in tenders was emphasized to improve the order book position. To improve sales-force effectiveness, higher delegation of power was accorded to the force on the field.

One of the most innovative steps taken by SAIL Marketing was the 'total package deal'. The Scheme, extended mainly to projects, was conceived keeping in mind the wide range of SAIL products. SAIL undertook supply of full requirement of a particular project through (a) conversion route, where semi-finished steel supplied by SAIL was converted to finished steel by suitable arrangement with rolling mills in the private sector and (b) buy-and-sell schemes in order to supplement its own product range. These schemes were quite successful and helped in bagging many project orders.

During 1997–1998 the company was able to reverse the decline in sales, which had taken place during two successive years—1995–1996 and 1996–1997. Besides, it earned higher sales realization despite adverse conditions both in domestic as well as international steel markets.

SAIL's marketing transformations were noticed by its rivals, as the media reported Lloyds Steel's Mr Gupta saying, 'Earlier, SAIL produced first and then sold. Now, it sells first and then produces.' That's why, despite the production drop, SAIL managed to improve its sales volumes by 7.60 per cent to 8.70 million tonnes in 1998–1999 even as the domestic steel market grew by just 1.5 per cent to 23.20 million tonnes.

Revenue Maximization Team (RMT)

Conflict between production and marketing is an oft-observed phenomenon in manufacturing enterprises. To minimize these conflicts and for optimizing the supply chain, SAIL instituted a new forum in the company.

A top management team was constituted to give direction to the marketing force as well as to formulate policies related to pricing and product mix. It was a new concept in SAIL as the pricing earlier was looked after entirely by Director (Commercial). After setting up of RMT, pricing and product mix became the responsibility of the Director (Commercial), Managing Director of all the SAIL Plants and Director (Finance). The Constitution of RMT helped in bridging the gap between marketing and production units and made the production units more aware of the market dynamics. Enabling an early adjustment of production in line with fluctuations in market demand, this practice set up in 1997 continues to date in the company.

RMT became an effective mechanism for reorientation of product mix towards production of higher value-added products and management of dispatches to the market providing higher net sales realization (NSR). It also resulted in a renewed thrust on direct dispatches thereby economizing on the storage and handling cost incurred at the stockyards.

Closer coordination between the marketing and production units led to a renewed support to the marketing by the production units. New facilities such as continuous casting, secondary refining of steel and renovation of mills helped in improved product quality.

Maximizing production from the modernized facilities helped in meeting the requirement of specific industry segments in terms of size, tolerance, quality, packing and delivery. The long products mills maintained shorter campaigns of profile/size for long products in line with market requirements. There was close cooperation between R&D Centre and the production units to develop new grades and process routes to capture new markets. This led to augmented production of special quality steel such as boiler quality, high tensile, API, high carbon, TMT and EQ wire rods.

Thrust on Exports

SAIL led the thrust on exports as the international markets started showing signs of firming up at a time when intense competition prevailed in the domestic market. Its exports hit a record growth of 120 per cent in 1997–1998, crossing the level of one million tonne mark for steel and pig iron for the first time since inception. Encouraged by export earnings of more than ₹1070 crore, an export target for 1998–1999 were set at 1.5 million tonnes.

Amongst SAIL's export products, Bhilai's plates were well accepted in the markets in the USA and Canada and contributed a major component of SAIL exports because of their quality. Strict adherence to shipment schedules helped SAIL in earning a good reputation in the international market.

Middle-East was identified as a zone for the high demand for construction-grade steel by SAIL. Dubai, being the hub for commercial activities, was considered an ideal location for serving customers of the region. To ensure ready availability of materials at a stockyard from where the customers could buy their requirements, SAIL entered into a strategic alliance with an LLC Bhatia Brothers in Dubai. Different types of materials such as TMT bars, structurals, plates, wire rods, etc., were shipped to the LLC at Dubai, to be kept in their stockyard.

Increasing export volumes, however, became a challenging task given depressed demand from South-East Asia. The European and the American Markets were flooded with cheap steel from South-East Asian countries, which before the crisis were net importers; thereby constraining exports from India.

Marketing Channel Optimization

SAIL had a nationwide marketing network spread all across the country comprising more than 40 branch sales offices and more than 50 stockyards.

Over the years SAIL had been servicing its customers by supplying materials from its stockyards as well as directly from its plants to the premises of customers, called direct despatch, for large order quantities. A competitive market forced it to look at its marketing cost, which was higher compared to its competitors. An analysis revealed that the net earnings for the company were higher for direct despatch than from stockyard sales. Hence, the volume of direct selling by the integrated plants was planned to be increased, by prioritizing supplies to the customers who received direct dispatches. Direct dispatches were also planned to be increased by supplementing it with the road dispatches which hitherto had played an insignificant part in SAIL's transportation channel.

In 1997–1998, the quantum of direct dispatch almost doubled compared to the previous year. Road dispatches from the plants and nodal stockyards were also augmented to provide doorstep delivery to the customers. The direct dispatches led to better prices to the customers on account of non-applicability of Excise on freight and distribution charges, which were applicable to stockyard delivery. In addition, it also led to the timely delivery of materials to the customers and avoided multiple handling.

Rationalization of the stockyard was another intervention to streamline and improve the marketing supply chain. The concept of nodal stockyard was introduced for the stockyards at Hyderabad, Chennai, Bhilai and Kanpur. Nodal Stockyards were introduced to ensure supplies to locations where material could not reach due to constraints of limited availability of piecemeal wagons from Railways and route restrictions/movement suspension imposed by Railways from time to time.

With increased direct dispatches to customers and the operation of 'mother stockyards', it became possible to close un-remunerative stockyards. Some stockyards whose presence was beneficial were given over to consignment stockists operating on behalf of SAIL. Since satellite locations had limited demand, the concept of nodal stockyard was also helpful in avoiding movement of such materials which had a disposal problem and either got stuck or required backward movement for sales. With the focus increasing on direct dispatch, the viability of operating certain stockyards was reviewed and most cost-effective alternate arrangements were undertaken.

Another area in marketing that needed attending related to developing cost-effective channels in distant areas/small towns, as well as to service dispersed demand of small volumes in major consuming centres. A dealers' network could contribute to sales both by improving access to customers and also by reducing 'cost to serve'.

The dealers and distributors were to provide better market accessibility, particularly in rural and hinterland areas. Better access to materials was a key buying factor for retail customers. Dealers in small towns (where no SAIL branch/stockyard existed) could sell retail products like TMT/TOR, light structural and GP/GC. Also, restricting the dealers to retail products ensured that they did not compete with SAIL for the existing large non-retail customers. Non-retail products like HR coils bought by larger customers were to be sold by SAIL maintaining direct contact.

In line with the above approach, it was decided that the stockyard to direct sales mix of 42:58 would be changed to accommodate 10 per cent of sales through the dealers' network.

Initiatives to Enhance Sales Force Effectiveness

SAIL marketing professionals were highly experienced in the marketing of steel. Unfortunately, a greater part of their experience pertained to marketing steel in the time of shortages. An excess supply market called for a very different approach.

The changing market dynamics demanded a transformation in the mindset of SAIL's Market Divisions, Central Marketing Organization (CMO) and International Trade Division (ITD) from mere selling to actual marketing. There was a need for institutionalization of structured customer contact as well as the development of an integrated customer database management system for better customer orientation. Bringing in new systems and processes was important as it was realized that the existing marketing condition was not going to be wished away for a long time.

To combat severe competition, CMO introduced many customer service measures. These included flexible and market-driven pricing mechanism, strengthening the Application Engineering Group for technical support to customers and appointment of service agents.

Concentrated customer contact and close monitoring of orders led to reduced lead time and kept the customers informed about the progress of their orders. Prompt settlement of customer grievances and a focus on project construction schemes where the door delivery was undertaken for the entire package of requirement in a time-bound manner were the other measures introduced in the marketing practices.

In order to ascertain the effectiveness of initiatives undertaken and identify areas of improvement, a composite performance index for measuring satisfaction level for customer retention was developed.

Special attention was given to improve the effectiveness and efficiency of the salesforce. It was observed that CMO personnel needed to spend more time on customer contact and less on paperwork. There was also a need for upgrading the critical selling skills of sales executives by a thorough knowledge of customers and products. The existing incentive system for the sales force was modified to aid high performance by basing it ultimately on contribution, NSR and volume (and not volume alone).

Besides the above, a number of other changes were introduced, viz., transfer of suitable executives from the plants and CMO headquarters to the branches and transfer of CMO salespersons to plants and vice-versa; training non-executives to perform low-skill activities such as paperwork and follow-up with plants and introducing an IT-enabled environment for faster information flow. Increasing face-to-face time with customers/prospects, assigning the best sales people to key accounts were some other measures introduced. The marketing of chemical and by-products was left to the purview of individual plants. Further, training programs were undertaken to improve communication, negotiation and planning skills of the sales force.

Finally, the criteria for performance excellence in marketing were restructured to bring in attributes such as cash collection, NSR and reduction in marketing cost.

Production Planning and Supply Chain Optimization

With cost and sales realization both under pressure, it was evident that the utilization of SAIL's assets would have to be optimized in order to maintain profitability. Some of the imperatives that needed to be examined and implemented included preservation or discontinuation of product lines, sizeable reductions in cost and excess manpower and a product mix, which could be continually tuned to the needs of the market.

SAIL plants belonged to a period when the maximization of production was seen as primary objective in a near monopoly situation. The products of the steel plants were a natural input for large public projects and industries, manufacturers of capital goods, or tonnage industries of the kind represented by tube makers and producers of drums and barrels. The rise of alternative sources of supply, both indigenous and international, with sophisticated product ranges and a rapid increase in customer expectations for better grades, forced a reassessment for SAIL's business practices.

The action plan for Turnaround and Transformation was formulated with the realization that any attempt at assuring SAIL's profitability will require deliberate steps aimed at turning the company around from a path of decline. These steps entailed a transformation in the business structure of the company and its mode of operation. The entire analysis was carried out both at an organizational level as well as at a unit level by assuming that each one of the units should be independently profitable.

To bring about a transformation it was imperative that each plant under SAIL operated at 100 per cent of its capability. The word capability denoted that in select circumstances capability could exceed capacity. Also, there was realization that the qualitative parameters of importance needed to be maintained and improved. A key area of focus was to achieve quality parameters without an uneconomical generation of arisings, along with excellence in operational efficiency parameters which governed productivity and cost optimization, viz., energy consumption, coke rate, coal-to-hot metal ratio, linking of imported coal supply to specific cost-effective ports, etc.

Improving supply chain management was critical to reducing both working capital and lead times at SAIL. Systemic changes were required in both marketing as well as production-related processes to minimize inventory levels and also ensure minimum lead-time for delivery to customers. Lack of supply chain was evident in the built-up of a total inventory of more than 166 days of sales - a ratio unaffordable by any steel company.

A revised target was set to reduce the inventory level from 166 days during 1997–1998 to around 70 days of sales turnover progressively. This reduction was to be effected with an aim to target 40 days of sales for finished goods and semis and two weeks each for raw materials and stores and spares.

To bring about production discipline SAIL needed to stop the 'production maximization' philosophy and shift to maximizing contribution, taking into consideration costs on account of inventory carrying, obsolescence, etc. Further, it was pointed out that whenever inventory built up it invariably led to further discounts, thereby depressing prices artificially. The strategy, therefore, was to maintain a constant level of inventory and produce only what could be sold, instead of producing in anticipation.

In line with the above, production was to be tailored strictly to avoid the generation of material, which could not be sold early against an assured demand and to reduce and maintain inventory at a level healthy enough to preserve the quality of stock, avoid psychological pressures for downward revision of prices and, above all, to reduce the interest cost of inventory. To implement the above at the shop floor, production not covered by order (NCO), was to be taken out of the purview of production reporting. Given the incentive structure operating at the SAIL plants, there was a monetary gain for the employees if the production of the shop went up. However, in a depressed market scenario excess production resulted in soaking up of liquidity and a net loss when the products were eventually sold at discount. The necessary steps for production planning, therefore, entailed (a) adopting a product mix which improved overall net sales realization and increased the proportion of value-added products with higher realizations, in total production, (b) reducing the levels of arisings and the products which had to be downgraded and (c) improving market share by improved quality and implementing successful strategies.

SAIL had often faced the problem of receiving fewer orders than anticipated, leading to unwarranted production and inventory pile-up. There was hence a need to institutionalize systems to forecast the stockyard demands better, based on genuine information (e.g., customer orders) and sophisticated market intelligence. On the production front, it was imperative to decrease the levels of downgrades and diversions.

Accountability needed to be fixed on concerned marketing and production personnel for managing inventory levels. Failure to sell committed volumes needed to reflect in the performance incentives of marketing personnel and unplanned over-production by the plants their performance incentives. Overall, CMO was to be accountable for inventory levels, particularly at the stockyards, while the plant MDs were also to be made accountable for inventory levels in the plants.

A specific policy was to be developed for the production, costing, pricing and marketing of HR coils/plates/CR coils/sheets and export of HR coils and plates. These were the products most vulnerable to the threats of competition from fresh capacity and imports and were the top candidates for inventory build-up.

Unit specific strategies were developed to optimize operations at each of the integrated steel plants of SAIL.

The modernization projects in Durgapur, Bokaro and Rourkela needed to be stabilized to the full, in order to derive the full competitive benefits up to the hot rolling stage which were covered under the modernization undertaken. For DSP, the priority was to reach the modernized capacity and attain production of one million tonne through the continuously cast route, which provided benefit both on account of improved quality and yield as well as lower cost compared to ingot casting. JVs/Conversion Agents were to be identified for a long-term arrangement, where DSP's surplus semi-finished steel could be converted to finished products.

The fertilizer plant of RSP was to be closed down. If RSP as a whole was unable to improve productivity and profitability through improved performance despite modernized assets and facilities, its divestment from SAIL was to be taken up as the last option.

Sale of Idle Assets

Other than efficiency improvement, it became important for the company to explore avenues for cash generation to provide immediate relief. SAIL had a non-moving store and spares inventory level of more than ₹300 crore. There were various reasons for this—items turning obsolete, purchases lying unclaimed which had become unusable over time, 'non-moving' inventory of parts not needing replacement for more than three years, maintenance of 'insurance' inventory, etc. There was a need to reduce the stores and spares inventory by at least 50 per cent, by fixing a maximum 'insurance' level. Any excess that emerged based on this criterion was to be declared as 'obsolete' inventory for disposal.

Also, after the introduction of new facilities under the modernization, many facilities such as those related to ingot casting and rolling of ingots in blooming and slabbing mill, etc., had become redundant and disposing of them would have provided much-needed cash for the company.

SAIL a Navratna PSE

An important public sector enterprise (PSE) reform introduced by Janata Dal United Front Government during 1997–1998 was the concept of Navratna PSEs. As a part of its common minimum programme, the new Government planned to give enhanced delegation to the Boards of select PSUs to manage their affairs. SAIL was one of the nine PSEs along with BHEL, BPCL, HPCL, IOC, IPCL, NTPC, ONGC and VSNL identified under the concept.

Navratana concept required the Board of the PSE to be restructured to induct eminent professionals and experts as non-official part-time directors. The restructured Board was to enjoy enhanced delegation encompassing areas pertaining to investments (without any monetary ceiling), formation of JVs and strategic alliance, organizational restructuring, including the creation of profit centres, creation and winding up of all posts below the Board level, implementation of schemes related to HR, training and VRS, etc.

The SAIL Board in 1998–1999 was restructured to induct Dr D. Basu, former Chairman SBI, Dr Y. R. K. Reddy, HR Expert, Prof. Atul Sharma, Prof. ISI, as independent Directors.

The number of independent Directors was further increased in 2000-2001 to comply with the SEBI Corporate Governance requirement that mandated 50 per cent of the Board to comprise independent Directors for the publicly listed companies. Some prominent independent Directors inducted in the SAIL Board were Shri R. V. Gupta, former Dy Governor RBI and Dr Isher Judge Ahluwalia, Economist and the then Director of ICRIER, amongst others.

The empowered Board could take decisions particularly in the area of human resource restructuring, investments and JVs, which were useful in restructuring SAIL.

The transformation initiatives brought in 1997 and 1998 were enduring. Set in motion two decades back, cost reduction drive has become an integral part of SAIL's annual exercise. Similarly, import of coking and CDI grade coals continue to serve the company through a mix of LTA and spot purchases.

The Fateful Flight

The year 1998 was a year a tragic incident in SAIL's history. Six senior executives of the company lost their lives when the aircraft in which they were travelling crashed due to a freak storm over Chiklakasa on 2 February 1998, about 28 km from Dongargarh in erstwhile Madhya Pradesh. Travelling in the fateful flight were Dr S. M. Aeron, Director (Operations); Mr T. K. Ghosh, Executive Director (Operations); Commodore Varghese; Mr K. S. Chandra, Additional Director (Computerization, Communication & Control); Mr U. K. Sharma, GM (Projects), Bhilai Steel Plant; and Mr K. Padmanabh, Senior Manager (Finance), Chairman's Secretariat. In a communication to the organization Chairman Pande recalled the contribution of the officers and their commitment to SAIL and dedicated the SAIL's Silver Jubilee to their memory.

CHAPTER 5

The Balance Sheet Matters

At the time SAIL was working on its internal strategies for effecting a turnaround and transformation, changes were taking place in the industrial policy domain which had specific relevance to the public sector enterprises.

The genesis of these changes could be traced to the policy of liberalization ushered in by the Union budget and the new industrial policy announced on 24 July 1991. Under the new policy, the focus of the public sector was to be on strategic, high technology and infrastructure sectors and the sectors reserved for the public sector drastically pruned down from 18 to 8. Industrially sick PSEs were to be referred to BIFR for the rehabilitation/revival scheme; and in order to raise resources and encourage wider public participation, disinvestment of government's shareholding in the public sector enterprises was to be carried out with offerings to mutual funds, financial institutions, general public and workers.

A committee headed by Dr Rangarajan was set up to recommend the policy for disinvestment of equity in Central Public Sector Enterprises (CPSEs). The committee submitted its report in April 1993 and recommended that the percentage of equity to be disinvested should be generally under 49 per cent in industries reserved for the public sector and over 74 per cent in other industries. The target ownership for CPSEs ranged from 0 per cent where there was little justification of Government presence, to 26 per cent for exercising limited control and 51 per cent or higher for effective control.

The disinvestment of the government's equity in CPSEs had started in 1991–1992, when minority shareholding of the central government in 30 individual CPSEs was sold to selected financial institutions (LIC, GIC, UTI) in bundles. Subsequently, shares of individual CPSEs were sold and the category of eligible buyers expanded to include individuals, NRIs and registered Foreign Institutional Investors (FIIs). SAIL was in the initial list of CPSEs identified for disinvestment. Following a series of disinvestment undertaken in 1991–1992, 1992–1993, 1994–1995, 1995–1996 the Government of India's holding of SAIL's equity came down to around 86 per cent by March 1996. The total realization to the government from the sale of SAIL's equity (not accounting for 1991–1992 when the sale was in bundles) was around ₹736 crore.

A new United Front government came into power in 1996. In the budget speech delivered on 27 July 1996, the then Finance Minister P. Chidambaram announced, 'Government has approved the proposal to establish a Disinvestment Commission. Any decision to disinvest will be taken and implemented in a transparent manner. Revenues generated from such disinvestment will be utilized for allocations for education and health and for creating a fund to strengthen public sector enterprises.'

Following the budget announcement, a Public Sector Disinvestment Commission was established on 23 August 1996, as an independent, non-statutory, advisory body with Shri G. V. Ramakrishna as its full-time Chairman. The task of the Disinvestment Commission was to prepare an overall long-term disinvestment program for the Public Sector Undertakings referred to it, determine the extent of disinvestment, manage and supervise the process of disinvestment and advise the government on capital restructuring to ensure maximum realization through disinvestment. Initially, 40 CPSEs were referred to the Commission and more CPSEs were added later.

The Disinvestment Commission covered SAIL as a potential company for disinvestment in its 7th Report submitted in March 1998.

Seventh Report of the Disinvestment Commission

The Commission analysed the business of SAIL and noted the decline in its market share, particularly in the flat products segment where it dominated in the early 1990s. SAIL's market share in this segment came down to 43 per cent by 1996–1997 from a level of 71 per cent in 1993–1994, primarily on account of increased competition from domestic sources as well as imports. The loss of market share was steeper in high-value segment of CR coils where although accounting for 60 per cent of domestic capacity, SAIL's market share was only 43 per cent in 1994–1995, which further slipped to 32 per cent in 1996–1997. With more capacities due for commissioning, further intensification of competition was imminent in the flat products segment.

A major area of concern for SAIL was its manpower strength of around 180,000 out of which 125,000 were located at its manufacturing units. The large workforce and the nature of technology affected SAIL's labour productivity adversely at around 94 tonnes of crude steel/man-year compared to international standards of 350 to 400 tonnes of crude steel/man-year. As the labour cost accounted for anything from 15 to 18 per cent of the cost of sales, manpower rationalization was a critical component for long-term competitiveness of the company, especially as new steel companies were entering the field with state-of-the-art technology and limited workforce.

Gross sales for SAIL in 1996–1997 had dipped by 4 per cent compared to 1995–1996, the first instance of a decline in more than a decade. Attributable both to a lower sales volume as well as realization,

SAIL's operating margins were under great pressure given the subdued market and increasing cost of materials, stores, employees and energy. In addition, SAIL's massive modernization program required raising external resources, which increased the company's debt-equity ratio from a level of 1.8:1 in 1992–1993 to 2.2 by March 1997.

A typical challenge faced by SAIL came in the form of the loss-making subsidiaries it was nurturing, amongst which IISCO dominated. In fact, the criticality and complexity of IISCO were such that it lent itself to an independent evaluation by the Commission.

The Indian Iron and Steel Company Limited

IISCO was a private sector steel company, the management of which was taken over by the government in 1972 due to mismanagement. Subsequently, the Government of India acquired the shares of IISCO through a nationalization act in 1976 and transferred it to SAIL in 1978, thereby making it a 100 per cent subsidiary of SAIL.

IISCO had an integrated steel plant operating at Burnpur, a foundry and a casting unit at Kulti, three captive collieries and two captive iron ore mines. IISCO as a company was in losses due to the ageing of its equipment and very high manpower—numbering around 29,000 in 1997–1998.

Several attempts to modernize IISCO in the past could not materialize because of the want of funds. The Public Investment Board (PIB) of the Government of India in 1991 suggested MOS explore the possibility of private participation in IISCO modernization. However, a bill introduced in the parliament to enable the transfer of shares to private party encountered all-round opposition and was shelved. In the meantime, with amendment in the Sick Industrial Companies Act (SICA Act), IISCO became referable to the Board of Industrial and Financial Reconstruction (BIFR). IISCO was referred to BIFR in June 1994 and was declared a sick industrial company in August 1994.

In 1997, the Government of India was considering a revival plan for IISCO involving capital expenditure of ₹2107 crore which was to be infused by SAIL with the simultaneous conversion of an equivalent amount of SDF loan in the books of SAIL to the capital reserve without any tax liability. In addition, accumulated losses of IISCO were to be written off by corresponding writing off from SDF loans to SAIL.

It was apparent that pending modernization the losses of IISCO would continue. SAIL had been providing financial support to IISCO in the form of minimum capital expenditure to keep the operations going. This, however, was becoming increasingly difficult as SAIL's own finances came under acute stress.

SAIL's Financial Performance

Disinvestment Commission observed that SAIL's funding options were gradually growing narrower, while the company was seized with significant investment needs, existing debt repayments, high leverage and rising interest burden.

While SAIL needed to raise resources to finance its ongoing modernization and investments envisaged in the Ninth Plan period, it was in no position to raise resources from the equity market because of low share price. Also, raising debt was becoming difficult due to high debt–equity ratio and the downgrading of SAIL's credit rating.

The structural problems faced by SAIL, such as high fund requirement for technological up-gradation, loss-making subsidiaries, high manpower cost, etc., made it difficult to gain an advantage of any upturn in the industry, should it happen in the future. Further, the uncertainty of IISCO's revival and potential cash outflow from SAIL on account of SDF loans made SAIL's share unattractive. It was therefore difficult both for the company as well as the Government to raise funds by selling SAIL's equity in the market. The Commission, therefore, recommended that the Government should not disinvest its holding in SAIL and instead initiate actions to address the issue of IISCO and SDF immediately.

Steel Development Fund

SDF had an interesting history.

There were only a handful of Financial Institutions during the seventies which could finance the modernization and expansion of the integrated steel plants, as given the capital-intensive nature of the projects, the requirement of funds was very high.

The Indian steel industry at that time had only three steel producers—SAIL, IISCO and TISCO, which were acknowledged steel producers with integrated facilities. Unless main steel producers modernized their plants, kept pace with the global steel producers and expanded their capacity, they were under threat of becoming non-productive and eventually sick, IISCO, Burnpur, being the case in point.

Realizing the concern, the Government of India decided to create a Fund for addressing the investment need of the integrated steel producers. SAIL, TISCO and IISCO were to put a small element of the price of their iron and steel products into a fund which could, later on, be utilized for financing modernization of the main steel plants and research and development activities, etc.

For a number of years after setting up of the SDF, SAIL, TISCO and IISCO who were member steel plants and contributors to the SDF, as well as members of the Joint Plant Committee (JPC) set up in 1964 for guiding the production, allocation, pricing and distribution of iron and steel materials in the country, were also the authorized users of the SDF. Later, IISCO was exempted by the government, through the JPC mechanism from contributing to the SDF account.

Nature of the Fund

Steel was classified as an essential commodity under the Essential Commodities Act 1955. The central government framed and issued the Iron and Steel (Control) Order in 1956, under the Essential

Commodities Act, for the purpose of regulating the price of steel and steel products. Several notifications were issued from time to time under the Iron and Steel (Control) Order, referred to as the 'Control Order' in ensuing sections.

SDF was created by a notification dated 27 December 1978 under the Control Order, whereby the main plants named in the notification were made members of the JPC. Only the member steel plants (or the main steel plants in this case) were required to add an element of their ex-works price and remit the same to the SDF.

In common parlance, the contribution to SDF was expressed by JPC and the MOS as 'JPC Levy' though no such expression was used or expressed in the notification issued for the creation of SDF. The Fund was created for the purpose of modernizing the steel plant as well as for research and development, with the object of ensuring the production of iron and steel in desired categories and grades by member steel plants.

The member steel plants named in the notification were BSP, BSL, DSP, RSP of SAIL, Indian Iron Steel Company Limited (IISCO) (under the control of SAIL) and TISCO. After a passage of time, the steel plants of SAIL and TISCO only remained as the member steel plants for SDF. Secondary Steel producers were not members of the SDF and did not contribute to the Fund.

The SDF was managed by a high-level committee constituted by the central government under the chairmanship of secretary (steel) along with secretary (expenditure) MOF and a representative of the Planning Commission, amongst others. SAIL and TISCO used to participate in the meeting of the SDF managing committee as invitees when needed to assist the committee with their suggestions.

The secretariat of JPC used to maintain the loan accounts of SDF. As per the practice adopted, separate SDF accounts were maintained for SAIL and TISCO—something akin (not exactly) to the practice adopted by the Provident Fund Trusts for its members.

Elaborating on the nature of the fund, Mr A. K. Shahi, Former Executive Director and Head of Law SAIL, said, 'There were differing views on the nature of this Fund among the Ministries under the Government of India. While Finance Ministry and the Law Ministry treated the collection and contribution to SDF by member steel plant as an element of ex-works price, thereby becoming eligible to attract Excise Duty, the Steel Ministry and JPC perceived that such a collection was in the nature of JPC Cess.'

Mr Shahi said, 'The correct legal position was that though SDF was formed under the Iron and Steel Control Order, it did not have any statutory backing. SDF was created under the administrative orders of the Government. Both Law Ministry and the Supreme Court on deeper examination later confirmed this position in law. However, many in JPC and Steel Ministry perceived it differently.'

Post-economic liberalization, the central government withdrew the administered pricing of steel under the Control Order, vide its notification dated 16 January 1992. Thereafter, by a notification dated 21 April 1994 contributions by the member steel plants towards SDF were discontinued, however, the Fund continued to exist.

Over the years, the size of the fund swelled to a significant level—more than ₹8,000 crore, the bulk of which was availed as SDF loan by SAIL and TISCO. The fund benefitted SAIL and TISCO immensely and helped them in managing investments for modernization of their steel plants and R&D activities. Both SAIL and TISCO right from the beginning paid interest on the loans undertaken at the specified rates and reflected the SDF loan and interest payable thereon in their balance sheets and P&L accounts.

The SDF loan formed a substantial part of borrowings in the books of SAIL. Total borrowings and accrued interest on account of SDF in SAIL's balance sheet as in March 1997, aggregated to around ₹5755 crore. At a time when SAIL's financial performance had become precarious SDF appeared to provide a window of opportunity for restoring the financial health of the company.

Recommendation of Disinvestment Commission

The Disinvestment Commission recommended that for improving the attractiveness of IISCO as an investment prospect, the government should write off its accumulated losses against loans provided by GoI (routed through SAIL) and SAIL's loan to IISCO. Further, to safeguard SAIL from the impact of waiver of loans to IISCO; a matching waiver of equivalent SDF loans should be provided to SAIL. After cleaning the balance sheet, the government should allow SAIL to disinvest its stake to a strategic buyer, through a transparent competitive bidding process.

The Commission was of the view that although SDF was a debt in the books of SAIL it was more in nature of quasi-equity, as the money was contributed out of sales realization of the integrated steel producers—SAIL and Tata Steel. However, appearing as debt, SDF loans had an adverse impact on the debt-equity structure of SAIL. Given the adjustment of SDF loans against cleaning of IISCO's accumulated losses, out of a total amount of ₹5,755 crore in the books of SAIL as of 31 March 1997, only ₹1,022 crore would have been adjusted, leaving a balance of ₹4,733 crore.

The Commission, therefore, recommended that SAIL's SDF loans together with its accrued interest (after adjustment against IISCO loss write off), should be converted into equity capital at a fair price.

The Commission's recommendations were expected to bring many benefits.

Cleaning up the balance sheet of IISCO would have made it attractive for private investors, thereby leading to the protection of jobs for 29,000 employees. The drag on SAIL to fund the losses of SAIL would end. Equity investment by SAIL in IISCO would be recovered and the debt-equity ratio lowered from 2.2 to 1.

Furthermore, the reduced interest burden would improve the net margin of SAIL leading to improved shareholder value. Also, it would have saved SAIL management's time on IISCO. For the Government of India, it meant avoiding the large funding required for IISCO's revival. Also, in place of unrealizable SDF loans Government would have a larger number of shares of SAIL, which would have provided better value in future disinvestment.

The recommendations of the Disinvestment Commission were an interesting way to kill multiple birds with one stone. However, as was seen a few months later it was possible to improve the suggested financial restructuring of SAIL.

The plan to convert SDF loans into equity got wide coverage in the business dailies. Singdha Sengupta of *Business Standard* wrote on 15 May 1998,

> The Steel Authority of India Ltd (SAIL) plans to expand its equity base in the current financial year by converting a ₹5000-crore Steel Development Fund (SDF) loan into equity... The principal objective of this proposal is to pump in much needed funds into modernizing its ailing subsidiary, Indian Iron & Steel Company. It could not, however, be ascertained what the size of the equity would be if the proposal for converting the loan was approved. The Disinvestment Commission is believed to have made certain recommendations for conversion of the SDF loan into equity at a fair price and these are presently under the consideration of the Union government... The financial restructuring is of crucial importance to SAIL as the Disinvestment Commission has set this as a pre-requisite to further disinvestment in the company by the government.

The *Business Standard* article also noted the tight cash situation of the company. In 1997–1998, SAIL had raised ₹767 crore through the issue of bonds on a private placement basis and another ₹1000 crore from financial institutions and banks as term loans. Despite tight money market conditions, the steel major also raised a syndicate loan of $85 million from overseas debt markets. Furthermore, SAIL's net deposits under the Public Deposit Scheme in March 1998, increased 32 per cent to ₹2,520 crore as against ₹1,908 crore in March 1997.

The above developments took place even as SAIL was giving final shape to its internally developed Turnaround and Transformation Plan. To explore the available options, SAIL decided to engage services of the Industrial Development Bank of India (IDBI) as a consultant to examine its financial restructuring plan.

IDBI Report on Financial Restructuring of SAIL

The IDBI team which worked on a financial restructuring plan for SAIL comprised a set of young professionals, full of energy, led by their Executive Director Mr V. P. Singh. They took a period of three to four months to finalize the report. In the process, they also developed a detailed financial model to assess the impact of each of their recommendation on SAIL's financials.

IDBI submitted its report on the financial restructuring of SAIL in August 1998. It concurred with the Disinvestment Commission to the extent of writing off loans and advances to IISCO against the SDF loans in SAIL books. However, it differed with the Commission's recommendation of conversion of the remaining balance in SDF to equity. This was based on the reasoning that the equity return parameters (dividend, earnings per share, return on net worth) of SAIL were already very low and the shares were quoted below par. Any further increase in equity was likely to impair the chances of improvement in the perception of the capital market and adversely affect the future equity raising capability of SAIL.

IDBI in their recommendation brought in a new dimension, viz., correcting the value of capital expenditure (CAPEX) in the books of SAIL. There were cost overrun in the modernization projects of SAIL by nearly 50 per cent, accounted mainly by interest capitalization and expenditure during construction. There was thus an inflated value associated with the fixed assets without any corresponding increase in income generation capacity. The interest capitalized, forming a part of the project cost due to delayed implementation over the previous 5 years, amounted to ₹2618 crore. IDBI recommended that the value of fixed assets be written down to the extent of ₹2618 crore.

Also featuring in the books of SAIL were loans and advances to IISCO aggregating to ₹1685 crore (including accrued interest) for which no provisions had been made. IDBI recommended that as the probability of recovery of these loans was doubtful, the loans and advances to IISCO should be written off.

SAIL had SDF dues of ₹6069 crore as of 31 March 1998 (inclusive of accrued interest of ₹1112 crore). IDBI recommended that the SDF dues of SAIL be used for correcting the inflated value of capital projects, extinguishing loans and advances to IISCO, writing back past waivers granted by SAIL to IISCO and the remaining balance transferred to capital reserve as shown in the following table:

Financial Restructuring Recommendation of IDBI

Recommendation (₹ in crore)	Assets	Set Off Against		Comment
		SDF	GoI Loan	
• Write down of fixed assets	2,618	2,618		
• Write-off of loans to IISCO	1,685		362	GoI loan routed through SAIL
		1,323		
• Interest written back on loans to IISCO	506	506		
Subtotal	4,809	4,447	362	
• SDF balance to be transferred to capital reserve		1,622		
Total SDF dues incl. interest for SAIL		6,069		

The proposal suggested by IDBI had the following advantages for SAIL. First, reducing the liabilities of SAIL by ₹6431 crore (₹6069 crore of SDF loan and ₹362 crore GoI loan routed to IISCO through SAIL) and at the same time increase the reserves by ₹2128 crore

(₹1622 crore conversion of balance SDF loan to capital reserve and write back of ₹506 crore interest earlier waived). Second, on the assets side, the fixed assets would have reduced by ₹2618 crore and current assets by ₹1685 crore. Third, cleaning up the balance sheet of IISCO by writing off the accumulated losses and its dues to SAIL would make IISCO attractive for prospective investors.

The financial restructuring would thus lead to enhanced profitability, improve the debt–equity ratio, thereby mitigating the financial risk, provide access to debt for funding the modernization project and enhance the shareholder value.

Lastly, the Government of India while giving up its right on SDF to the extent of ₹6431 crores would be compensated as a shareholder by way of accretion to reserves and improved market capitalization.

IDBI recommendations were an improvement over the Disinvestment Commission as in addition to cleaning up the balance sheet of IISCO and correcting DER (Debt-equity ratio) for SAIL, it also corrected the inflated value of capital projects. Further, it would not have hampered SAIL in providing an enhanced shareholder value in the future.

Optics Matter, but Cash Is the King

IDBI recommended that till business restructuring measures for SAIL came into force, SAIL would have to look beyond capital restructuring to bridge its cash flow needs for funding the capex programme.

Given the negative perceptions associated with the sector, raising fresh equity from the market was not an option. Moreover, as the government was 'in principle' inclined to divest its shareholding in non-strategic sector to 26 per cent, it could have happened only after SAIL's share price improved. As an interesting alternative, the government's equity equivalent to ₹1,000 crore could be converted to non-cumulative preference share, which would have improved the earnings per share by 30 per cent and reduced the GoI's shareholding to 61 per cent. After an improvement in market valuation and depending on GoI's disinvestment program, SAIL may then be able to raise fresh equity.

IDBI recommended that SAIL should adhere to DER of 1:1 for additional funding, to mitigate financial risk.

To synchronize debt outflows with additional revenue generation from capital expenditure undertaken, IDBI proposed that SAIL should go for a debt arrangement, which was long term and back-ended. However, IDBI realized that the restructured financial ratios for SAIL alone would be insufficient to attract back-ended long-term loans from the lenders. It, therefore, proposed a government guarantee for additional loans for credit enhancement.

Another interesting dimension brought forth by IDBI related to the state Government schemes, which allowed for sales tax deferrals and exemptions for industrial units set up in their states. The sales tax and other concessions by the state Government to new units were not made available to the PSEs in the past on the plea that they operated in a protected and controlled environment. However, post-liberalization, SAIL had to compete with newer units, which did not have to spend on social infrastructure and also enjoyed the added benefits in the form of sales tax deferrals enabling them greater flexibility in pricing.

SAIL plants contributed considerably to the economy of their respective states in the form of social infrastructure and employment opportunities. SAIL had also invested huge sums in the capital projects for revamping and capacity additions. IDBI, therefore, recommended that SAIL should seek sales tax deferrals similar to that available for new units in the private sector from the State Governments of Madhya Pradesh, Orissa, Bihar, Tamil Nadu and West Bengal (Bokaro Steel Plant was in Bihar and Bhilai Steel Plant in Madhya Pradesh prior to the formation of the states of Jharkhand and Chhattisgarh in 2000). This could enhance the cash flow available to SAIL over the medium term to the tune of ₹160 crore per annum.

On the expenditure side, IDBI advised SAIL to defer capital expenditure, which was not already committed or essential, beyond the 9th FYP. This potentially could release ₹2900 crore over a period of five years. It was, however, inevitable that SAIL in the future would have to incur additional expenditure for expansion as well as in the new product lines for product quality and market share. IDBI recommended that additional capital expenditure should be justified by independent assessment by a term lending institution, accompanied by a more vigorous project monitoring mechanism.

So far the financing of subsidiaries was concerned, IDBI suggested that given its own problems SAIL should re-examine its role in rehabilitating IISCO and VISL.

IDBI also pointed out the scope of freeing up cash and reducing financing charges on bank borrowings by rationalizing finished goods inventory which by FY 1998 had touched a level of ₹5,300 crore, accounting for around five months of sales. This was clearly non-sustainable given its impact on liquidity, carrying cost, interest cost and value deterioration. Given the finished steel, inventory SAIL was carrying, even a reduction in inventory by two months would have resulted in interest savings of around ₹300 crore. Further, given the extra expenditure on every tonne of material dispatched to the stockyard in form of excise duty and transportation cost, it was important to plan production and dispatches strictly as per market requirements.

The last area of liquidity management was in the form of rupee and foreign currency loans. Foreign currency-denominated loans of around ₹3,052 crore exposed SAIL to exchange risk, as forex interest and principal payments were not fully covered by export earnings. In addition, SAIL had rupee borrowings of around ₹1,400 crore from FIs and banks on a floating interest basis. IDBI recommended that SAIL should minimize the interest and exchange rate risk through an appropriate hedging mechanism.

In conclusion, IDBI stated that financial restructuring would result in an improvement in leverage enabling access to funds to maintain operations. However, the larger issue of improving operations and competitiveness would still need to be addressed. This could be only achieved through business restructuring.

SAIL wrote to the MOS in September 1998 for implementation of the Financial Restructuring Plan, as recommended by IDBI. Also communicated to the MOS was the comprehensive turnaround and transformation Plan of SAIL of which financial restructuring formed a part. Approval was sought from the Government of India for recasting the SDF loan as recommended by IDBI, hiving off the non-core assets and divestment of special steels plants of SAIL. MOS, in turn, started consultation with other Ministries of the Government of India, viz., Finance, Law, etc., as well as the Planning Commission on the merit of SAIL's restructuring plan.

CHAPTER 6

Courts Pave the Way

The inevitable happened. 'SAIL sinks into net loss of ₹1,573 crore' read the headline of the news item covering SAIL's financial results for the year 1998–1999 in *The Telegraph*. Published on 28 May 1999, the news item said, 'Steel Authority of India Ltd (SAIL) today reported a mind-boggling net loss of ₹1,573.66 crore in 1998–1999 on a higher turnover of ₹15,484 crore. In 1997–1998, the company recorded a profit of ₹132 crore on a turnover of ₹15,127 crore.'

The newspaper quoted SAIL Chairman Arvind Pande, saying: 'We have drawn up a strategy for turning around the company on the basis of two reports prepared by IDBI and McKinsey. We are clear in our minds on how to get out of this.'

Mckinsey and Co., the consultants engaged by SAIL, had endorsed the financial restructuring plan prepared by IDBI. They also prepared a report after reviewing the internal plan prepared by SAIL and after holding a series of discussions and workshops at SAIL's Corporate Office, plants and CMO. In the process, they also interacted with SAIL's customers and received inputs from some of the union leaders on the key recommendations. The insight of the consultants was captured in a document called the 'Competitiveness Plan' and was considered by the SAIL Board in its meeting in April 1999.

Recollecting those times Mr R. K. Garg who was then the Company Secretary of SAIL, said, 'SAIL suffered a massive loss of over ₹1500 crores in 1998–1999 for the first time in 15 years. During this period, detailed deliberations took place in the Board meetings where the Independent Directors supported the management for the proposed restructuring despite reservations from the nominee directors of Government of India. Discussions in these Board meetings used to be very professional with the objective to bring SAIL back to its glory.'

SAIL Board, while agreeing with the broad approach of the Competitiveness Plan, asked McKinsey to work out pros and cons for specific areas of asset restructuring (related to closure and divestment) which required approval from the Government of India. Accordingly, the consultants detailed their recommendations considering different options and presented a supplementary report to the SAIL Board in May 1999 specifying the best option for SAIL and a fallback option in case the best option could not be implemented in the immediate future.

Outside of SAIL, extended discussions were held with a broad section of senior Government functionaries and with officials in the Ministry of Steel, Ministry of Finance and Planning Commission, to build consensus on the recommendations on SAIL's restructuring plan.

The Government of India in the meantime had circulated a draft Cabinet Note on SAIL's Financial and Business Restructuring proposal to the Ministry of Heavy Industries and Public Enterprises, the Ministry of Law, Justice and Company Affairs, the Planning Commission and the Ministry of Finance for their comments. SAIL also made a detailed presentation to Secretary Expenditure, Ministry of Finance in September 1999, pressing its case for Financial and Business Restructuring. However, the Government of India was taking its time in understanding the implications of the write-off of the SDF loans sought by SAIL. Also, as the general elections were to be held in September–October 1999, it was unlikely that SAIL's restructuring proposal would have been cleared in a hurry.

SAIL's financial restructuring proposal was examined by Mr P. P. S. Brar, the Joint Controller General of Accounts, Department of Expenditure, Ministry of Finance, who while agreeing to the provision of funds from the National Renewal Fund (NRF) of ₹1,500 crore for supporting VRS and Government guarantee for an additional ₹1,500 crore for raising loans, did not favour write-off sought by SAIL on the SDF loans.

Mr Brar gave several reasons for not favouring the write-off of the SDF loan. In a voluminous report prepared by him on the issue, he mentioned that write-off of the SDF loans through book adjustments would reduce the operating cost by less than 10 per cent of total potential and that rest of the savings were expected to come by asset and business restructuring measures. He pointed out that the SDF loans in the past had been written off only for the revival of the sick company and that all steel producers needed to benefit from SDF corpus, which was similar to the Oil Industry Development Fund (OIDF).

In response, SAIL pointed out that while SDF loans write-off did signify only 10 per cent of the potential savings, it was a necessary first step to ensure SAIL's financial viability. Write-off of the SDF loan would lead to improved investor confidence and restoration of a degree of financial health in SAIL's balance sheet, which was essential for meeting the required cash deficit over the next 3 years. SAIL pointed out that even after implementing the business restructuring programmes—the benefits of which would accrue with a lag, SAIL needed to mobilize around ₹5,000 crore over the next two years, absent which there was a likelihood of the company turning sick. It would indeed be unfortunate if the support from SDF was to take place only after the occurrence of that event.

Further, SAIL indicated that the parallel between SDF and OIDF was improper. Although a large number of small producers operated in the steel industry, SDF was only applicable to the main steel producers. OIDF on the other hand was applicable to all producers.

In the meantime, SDF had attracted the attention of a number of entities who started eyeing the funds to their advantage. The list of such entities included the private steel companies starved of cash as well as organizations such as the Federation of Engineering Industries of India (FEII) who wrote to the Prime Minister for using the SDF funds for setting up a steel plant in Northern India.

Recounting the legal challenge faced by SAIL in seeking relief on SDF loans, Mr A. K. Shahi, who headed SAIL's Corporate Law division as an Executive Director and Principal Law Officer, recalled, 'Forewarned of the critical position of SAIL, Mr Arvind Pande, the Chairman of the Company, had already put in place a strategy team comprising members from Business Planning, Finance and other related functions to identify and work out suitable strategies to overcome the turbulent terrain ahead. The strategy group comprising economists, business planning managers, engineers and accountants, benefitted from the guidance of the then Director of Finance of SAIL, Mr V. S. Jain, particularly on the issue of SDF.'

Initially, there was a suggestion of seeking the government's help to merge a sizeable portion of the SDF in SAIL's account into Government Equity in SAIL, to save the company from becoming sick and getting referred to BIFR. The proposal was discussed with the MOS and on getting their informal nod, was approved by the SAIL Board.

SAIL's endeavour for financial restructuring also benefited significantly from the support extended by Mr Ashok Basu, Secretary, Ministry of Steel. The media quoted Mr Basu on the SDF write-off, saying, 'The final proposal will be a combination of part-waiver, part-conversion of debt into equity.' The financial restructuring proposal approved by the SAIL Board was endorsed by the Steel Ministry and sent for the concurrence of the Ministry of Law and Justice before being placed for approval of the Union Cabinet.

While the financial restructuring proposal was under examination of the Government of India, there were two different views pertaining to the restructuring of the fund. The MOS was of the view to convert the SDF loans into a part waiver and part equity. Within SAIL there was a view that conversion of part SDF loans into equity will further enlarge SAIL's already large equity base, impairing its ability to mobilize equity funds in future. A solution to this dilemma came in a most unexpected manner.

Recounting the developments at Law Ministry, Mr A. K. Shahi, then SAIL's head of law stated, 'Mr Ram Jethmalani, a veteran amongst the eminent senior lawyers of the country, at that time was the Minister of Law and Justice. The financial restructuring proposal put up to the Government of India, was for the conversion of SDF loan to Government's equity in SAIL to enhance the equity base for SAIL. Mr Jethmalani queried if Government was the owner of the Fund? Until it owned the SDF, Government of India could not put a portion of the Fund into SAIL's equity!'

This led to a further re-examination of the nature of the fund by the Ministry of Law and Justice which concluded that the central government through its functionaries was only managing the fund. As SDF was not part of Consolidated Fund of India or Public Account Fund and was not owned by the government, conversion of SDF or a portion thereof into equity by the central government was not legally tenable.

The Law Ministry, however, advised that under the circumstances, MOS in consultation of Ministry of Finance, may decide to waive any portion of the SDF loan taken by SAIL inter-alia to support and sustain the operation of IISCO which was brought under its control and for time and cost overrun of SAIL's modernization projects at Durgapur and Rourkela which had been impacted by the disintegration of USSR and other factors, thereby affecting financial strength of SAIL.

While efforts for financial restructuring in SAIL were on, new players who had entered the steel industry after its delicensing in 1991 were in the need of more capital to finance their projects involving thousands of crore. They represented to the MOS to be allowed access to the SDF and to be provided loan from the fund in a manner similar to that enjoyed by SAIL and TISCO. Their contention was that the contribution to SDF by SAIL and TISCO was in a real sense paid by the buyers and consumers of steel and therefore was public money. Hence, they could not be denied access to money available in the SDF. Some of them went to the extent of proposing that part of the loan given to SAIL and TISCO be taken back from them and given to the major new entrants.

The Legal Battle

The concept of the new claimants to the SDF did not find much favour in the Steel Ministry though some functionaries at lower level perceived it with greater accommodation. While their representations were pending in the Steel Ministry, one such new player moved Calcutta High Court by way of a Writ Petition during mid-1999, claiming their rights over the SDF, which according to them comprised of public money and therefore could not be converted into equity for SAIL.

SAIL was apprehending such judicial intervention and promptly defended its position in the High Court. Resultantly, the Writ Petition was dismissed by the single judge at the threshold. Aggrieved by such an order, the Petitioner preferred to appeal before Division Bench of the Calcutta High Court, where despite its presentation it failed to succeed.

The Division Bench of the High Court pronounced a well-reasoned judgement on 3 February 2000, justifying the right of SAIL and the Central Government over the SDF. This in effect cleared the deck for Financial and Business restructuring proposal of SAIL, which was pending for long and shuttling between the Steel and Finance ministries.

Backed by the Calcutta High Court Judgement, SAIL and MOS acted promptly and took immediate steps to move the Cabinet Note for approval of SAIL's comprehensive proposal for Financial and Business Restructuring, which included the waiver of SDF loan to SAIL and other financial reliefs. The proposal of SAIL as recommended by the Steel Ministry was thereafter accepted and approved by the Union Cabinet.

Approval of the Central Government was communicated to SAIL by the Government of India, MOS by letter dated 18 February 2000. Financial Restructuring approved by the Government included the waiver of a loan of ₹5073 crore from SDF and ₹381 crore from the Government of India and further reliefs by way of Government guarantees for raising a loan of ₹3000 crore including ₹1500 crore to be raised by SAIL from the market to finance VRS and ₹1500 crore to be raised to meet repayment obligation on the past loans. The government also granted 50 per cent interest subsidy for loan and interest thereon for VRS. After the waiver, an amount of around ₹1200–1500 crore remained in the SDF in SAIL's account.

In the meanwhile aggrieved by the judgement of Calcutta High Court, the Writ Petitioner filed Special Leave Petition before the Supreme Court, which was dismissed on 28 February 2000.

Supreme Court Has the Final Say

Explaining the judgement, Mr A. K. Shahi, said, 'The Supreme Court, in a well-reasoned judgement dated 31 March 2000, put a final seal mandating SAIL and TISCO's exclusive right to use the money in their respective accounts in SDF. The Apex Court improved upon the judgement of Calcutta High Court and further clarified the matter in controversy to give it finality. In its judgement, the Supreme Court affirmed the exclusive right of SAIL and TISCO to use the SDF. While Calcutta High Court had not placed SAIL and TISCO on equal footing for use of the Fund, the Supreme Court judgement treated the two equally for use of the Fund from and out of their respective accounts in SDF.'

Recalling the proceedings in the Supreme Court, Mr Shahi said, 'The case was very well presented and forcefully argued by eminent Senior Counsel Mr Harish N. Salve for SAIL in the Supreme Court.' Earlier, Mr C. S. Vaidyanathan, eminent Senior Counsel and the first ASG had led the team of lawyers for SAIL in Calcutta High Court.

Mr Shahi cited the following conclusive findings of the Supreme Court on the nature of SDF, which formed a part of the judgement:

> While there was price control under the control order during the period 1978–1994 when the remittance to SDF was made by main steel producers, the petitioner was nowhere in the picture

> and was not subjected to any price control like the main steel producers. The petitioner and the other steel producers were free to produce and sell the iron and steel products in the market on the prevailing prices. It has been pointed out that price fixed by the petitioner of its products was higher than the control price which included elements of SDF. While the collection and remittance to SDF have been discontinued with effect from April 1994, the petitioner made its claim for the first time in 1999 which appears to be rather incongruous. It is submitted that the claim made by the petitioner is not bona fide and writ petition has been filed with ulterior motives, which are not difficult to fathom. SAIL had stressed immediate need for restructuring and modernizing all the main steel plants. Due to recession, SAIL has been passing through severe financial position and has to suffer a loss of ₹1,574 crores in 1998–1999. It has further to suffer the burden of interest to the tune of ₹2,017 crores per annum for modernization. In the aforesaid circumstances, the petitioner does not have any right to claim any relief in the writ petition pertaining to utilization of SDF. It is quite apparent from the very nature of the creation of SDF, the manner of remittance to SDF and purpose of its utilization, it is a fund created ultimately for utilization by the member steel producers only.

Mr Shahi recounted, 'There would not have better clarity on the nature and right to use the Fund than the one given by the Apex Court'.

It is worth mentioning that prior to pronouncements of the judgement of Calcutta High Court and the Supreme Court; there were multiple queries from the Finance Ministry repeatedly on the proposed waiver of SDF loans for SAIL, which delayed the concurrence to Steel Ministry's proposal on SAIL's Financial Restructuring. The possibility of lobbying by the new entrants in the corridors of power to present their case could not have been ruled out. The Calcutta High Court and Supreme Court judgements and views of the Law Ministry cleared the cloud over ownership and use of SAIL and TISCO's account in SDF maintained by JPC. Thereafter, it became easy for the Central Government to clear the proposal of SAIL and waive a substantial amount of loan taken out of SAIL's account in SDF.

With the passage clear for SAIL's Financial Restructuring from a legal perspective, it became easy for the Government to clear the comprehensive Business and Financial restructuring proposal of SAIL. Being backed by the Supreme Court Judgement, Tata Steel (the current name for TISCO) later pressed for disbanding SDF and giving back the amount lying in their account—after adjusting the loan amount disbursed to them, as the contributions to SDF had stopped long ago.

Sizeable Funds Attract Attention

Mr A. K. Shahi, former head of law, SAIL recounted an interesting anecdote, 'After a few years, sometime around 2005–2006 JPC functionaries considered diverting the SDF into Public Account Fund of India through an act of Parliament, possibly through the Finance Act and also obtained the views of Law Ministry in this regard. However, the move was shelved on further examination by the SDF Managing Committee when I attended the meeting along with Mr V. S. Jain, the then Chairman, SAIL and assisted the Committee in providing clarifications on the contentious matter. SAIL and Tata Steel have all through adopted a conciliatory approach with Steel Ministry, while at the same time consistently making the legal position clear.'

Nod to SAIL's Restructuring

In February 2000, the Government of India accorded approval to the Financial and Business restructuring proposal sought by SAIL in its letter dated 16 September 1998 to the Ministry of Steel. Several clarifications and discussions had taken place during the interregnum; the clinching point, however, was the adjudication of the court case on SDF in favour of SAIL. The GoI noted that it was one of the largest restructuring proposal considered by it and involved an amount of over ₹8,000 crore.

The restructuring proposal of SAIL approved by the Government of India was under two broad categories of financial and business restructuring.

Financial Restructuring of SAIL

- Waiver of loans and advances from the SDF to SAIL up to a value of ₹5073 crore and ₹381 crore from the GoI provided to IISCO by routing it through SAIL
- Provision of government guarantee with 50 per cent interest subsidy for loans and interest thereon amounting to ₹1,500 crore; to be raised by SAIL from the market to finance manpower reduction through VRS
- Provision of government guarantee for loans and interest thereon of ₹1,500 crore, to be raised from the market for meeting repayment obligations on past loans

Business Restructuring

- To initiate the process of divestment of the following non-core assets while protecting the jobs of existing employees:
    - Power plants at Bokaro, Durgapur and Rourkela (Subsequently power plant at Bhilai was also included in the list)
    - Oxygen Plant 2 of Bhilai Steel Plant
    - Salem Steel Plant, Salem
    - Alloy Steels Plant, Durgapur
    - VISL, Bhadravati
    - Fertiliser Plant, Rourkela
- Conversion of IISCO into a JV with SAIL holding minority shareholding

For implementing the Business Restructuring proposal MOS and SAIL entered into an MoU on 13 March 2000, with detailed milestones. It was decided that a Committee of Secretaries would examine and review the progress on business restructuring plan against detailed milestones and submit a report every six months to the Cabinet Committee on Economic Affairs (CCEA).

Based on the MoU signed with the Ministry of Steel, responsibilities were assigned in SAIL to senior executives for carrying out the implementation and accomplishing the milestones within an agreed timeframe. An Office of Restructuring was set up at the SAIL Corporate Office, headed by Dr Sanak Mishra, Executive Director (Corporate Planning) to continuously plan, monitor and maintain the status of restructuring in SAIL and assist the Chairman in the implementation of restructuring initiatives.

Mr Garg, then Company Secretary, narrated an interesting anecdote on the process regarding the implementation of SAIL's restructuring approved by the GOI. 'The approved restructuring package for SAIL, other than a waiver of outstanding loan of around ₹5,400 crores, included divestment of certain non-core and loss-making assets/units. Before taking further action on divestment, approval of shareholders in the general meeting was required as per the Indian Companies Act. Being a listed company having more than two lakhs shareholders, an extraordinary general meeting was called in May 2000 for getting the requisite resolution(s) passed from the shareholders. The permission was sought from the shareholders to sell, lease or otherwise dispose of by divesting either by JV or otherwise some of the identified units of the company while protecting the jobs of the existing employees.'

As 85.82 per cent of the equity share capital was owned by the Government of India, technically passing of a resolution in the shareholders meeting should not have had any concern since the GOI had already approved the restructuring plan. However, in view of the perception of 'selling the family jewels' created amongst employees, public and media, getting the shareholders' approval amicably was a priority. It also became important in the backdrop of certain questions/concerns raised in the parliament by the opposition party members against the divestment approved by the government. Some employee union leaders (motivated by political agenda) in SAIL plants were also objecting to the proposed divestment.

Mr Garg recalled, 'A detailed planning was done to ensure smooth conduct of the shareholders meeting without any untoward incident. Some of the union leaders along with around 500 employee shareholders from SAIL plants had planned to visit Delhi to attend shareholders meeting with the objective to object to the resolution and disturb the proceedings. However, all the activities of the shareholders meeting had been planned meticulously and the proceedings were conducted in a timely manner to ensure all statutory compliances. Shareholders resolution was therefore passed with requisite majority.' It also helped that the outside participants who wanted to object to the resolution initially went to Talkatora stadium where SAIL's Annual General Meetings were held traditionally. The Extraordinary General Meeting, however, was held in Airforce Auditorium at Subroto Park. By the time the employee shareholders realized their mistake and reached the right venue, the proceedings were more or less over.

Thereafter, certain employee unions filed the writ petition in Delhi High Court questioning the conduct of shareholders meeting and requesting to quash the resolutions passed by shareholders. They were represented in the court by eminent lawyer Mr Prashant Bhushan. The court case was forcefully argued by SAIL management based on merits and the writ petition was rejected by the Court, paving the path for initiating activities related to divestment.

Waiver of SDF loan of ₹5073 crore helped in improving SAIL's balance sheet, profitability and creditworthiness. However, the waiver of a portion of SDF did not bring any cash to SAIL which was most needed at that time. It is worthwhile to note that despite severe financial constraints SAIL never made a single default in servicing its loan obligations, thereby maintaining the confidence level amongst its lenders. Also, SAIL never delayed payment of wages and salary to its employees who reciprocated in equal measure and co-operated fully in its endeavour to come out of the woods.

CHAPTER 7

Dynamics of Power Asset Transfer

Divestment of captive power plants of SAIL was one of the tasks identified for early completion in the area of asset restructuring. While Financial Restructuring was a difficult task due to reasons explained earlier, asset restructuring tasks came with their own unique challenges.

The Power Group of SAIL in its approach paper on the restructuring of power generating facilities in May 1998 had concluded that the company could focus on its core business of production of quality steel at a competitive cost and allow some of the vitally important support function like the power to be handled by specialized groups under independent management. Underlying logic to this was the recognition that steel making and power generation were two distinct businesses in terms of technology, operating skills, statutory rules and regulations and financing. Also, as the Government policy was favourable to the power sector for raising resources, it made sense for SAIL to float an independent power company.

Covering SAIL restructuring strategy in July 1999 in *Business Today*, Ranju Sarkar wrote,

> Such divestments have, suddenly, become de rigueur for steel companies limping from the effects of a crushing recession. Essar

> Steel has struck a ₹720-crore deal to sell its 500 MW power unit to Marathon Power while TISCO has done the same with its 1.73-million tonnes per annum (tpa) cement unit, selling it to the French major, Lafarge. And SAIL has already got offers for its power plant from Enron Corporation and BSES.

The article, however, cautioned on the problem related to such a move quoting Mr Rajesh Gupta, CEO, Lloyds Steel, 'When you sell your power plants, the cash inflow will be neutralized in the long run. For, the power cost is likely to increase once you buy power from outside at the market rate.' Elaborating the above point, the article mentioned that in 1997–1998, SAIL paid ₹2.93 per unit for power that was outsourced while the cost of its captive power generated through steam turbines was a mere ₹1.52 per unit.

In response to the above, the article mentioned Chairman Pande saying that the long-term power purchase agreements would be negotiated with the new JVs in a manner that the cost of power to SAIL remained largely unchanged. What, however, was crucial for him was how soon the power assets could be hived off. Sarkar noted that the entire process could take five years or longer as each of the decisions was likely to be debated, tossed and turned between the Steel, Finance and Industry ministries as well as SAIL's trade unions.

Captive Power Plants for Divestment

SAIL's captive power plants traditionally were classified under two categories PP-I and PP-II. Power plants I (PP-I) built in the initial years of construction of the steel plants were used for supplying air to the blast furnaces, meeting the process steam requirement and generating emergency power for the safety of the steel plants. Power plants II (PP-II) came up in the late 1970s and early 1980s to supplement the power supply from different public utilities, against the backdrop of acute power shortage in the states of Orissa, West Bengal and Bihar at that time. The list of power assets identified for divestment comprised all PP-II of the steel plants other than Bokaro Steel Plant where Both PP-I and PP-II were offered for divestment, as segregating PP-I and PP-II was not possible because of technical reasons.

The locations of power plants slated for divestment were Bokaro (PP-I & PP-II), Durgapur (PP-II) and Rourkela (PP-II). Initially, the 74 MW power plant at Bhilai (PP-II) did not feature in the list of power assets for divestment in the approval granted by the Government of India in February 2000. A separate approval, however, was obtained on 29 March 2001 for divestment of PP-II of Bhilai Steel Plant (BSP). The reason for non-inclusion of PP-II of BSP in the initial divestment proposal lay in SAIL promoting a 574 MW power company in Bhilai in a JV with L&T and PGEG Global, USA. The JVC named Bhilai Power Supply Company (BPSCL) was incorporated in 1995 and a JV agreement signed in 1997. However, SAIL withdrew from the project in May 2000, as the financial closure for the project could not be accomplished for want of escrow commitment from the Government of Madhya Pradesh, despite five years elapsing from the date of the project approval.

The Psychology of Resistance

Divestment of power assets into a JV company was not an easy task. There was strong opposition to such a move within the company due to a variety of reasons. It was in a way very different from the classical divestment of a company, as the captive power plants formed a unit of the integrated steel plants. In fact, it amounted to the divestment of a part of the plant and not the entire plant; also it was not disinvestment of SAIL the company.

Resistance to divestment emanated from a threat perception amongst the employees regarding the impending change. Employees in each of the steel plants—Bhilai, Bokaro, Rourkela and Durgapur, had lived together for many years. Their lives had been interwoven in the social fabric as they enjoyed commonly shared social facilities in education, health and other civic amenities. As the social facilities under SAIL Townships were much better compared to the rest of the state, there was reluctance in the employees to live under a different banner in a society they had become a part of. Also, being a part of SAIL—a faltering and yet very respectable company, they were unprepared to move to a new company with an uncertain future. They were in a way being coerced to become an employee of a company with an unknown management and therefore felt belittled and were unwilling to accept a secondary status.

Furthermore, there was no certainty that they would not be removed or retrenched under the new management before attaining the age of superannuation prevalent in SAIL. There was also no clarity about their service conditions in the new company and little was known of any incentive or severance package available in the proposed new entity.

The stance of the employees of SAIL's captive power plants under divestment received support from their fellow workers in the other departments, as they perceived a similar threat in future. Within a short span of time, the matter became a subject of conversation in every family living in the steel township. Unlike the Financial Restructuring, these issues created IR problems across the steel plants in the years 2000 and 2001.

Assuaging the apprehension of the employees called for an intense dialogue with the unions and an effective communication exercise with the affected employees. This challenge was taken up by SAIL's HR department headed by Mr Mihir Moitra, who at that time was the Company's Director Restructuring and Corporate Planning.

It soon emerged in the internal discussions that prior to initiating any discussion with the affected employees and the unions, the company's IR managers themselves needed clarity and a common understanding of the issues they were expected to deal with.

Preparation for Divestment

Although the business restructuring proposal was approved by the Government of India in February 2000, the preparation for divestment of captive power plants by SAIL had started as early as February 1998 and the Merchant Bankers—M/s SBI Caps & M/s Dresdner Kleinwort Benson (DKB) appointed in September 1998 for divestment of the power assets.

On the buyers' side, there were only a handful of players with good experience in the business of power generation, interested in taking over captive power plants of SAIL along with its employees. In the beginning, five parties expressed their interest in the proposed divestment, namely, M/s National Power International Ltd, M/s ENRON, M/s BSES, M/s Consolidated Power Asia Ltd and M/s PSEG. Subsequently, three parties, National Power International Ltd., Consolidated Power Asia Ltd and M/s PSEG withdrew from the bidding process. The remaining two parties, M/s ENRON and M/s BSES, completed the data room visits in February 1999 but were unable to undertake plant visits due to stiff opposition from the trade unions of Bokaro, Rourkela and Durgapur.

After GoI's approval of the business and financial restructuring of SAIL, letters were written to both BSES and ENRON to reconfirm their interest in the proposed divestment of captive power plants. BSES, a power distribution company in Mumbai, was headed by Mr R. V. Shahi, Ex-SAIL man and former director of NTPC. Against a background of serious opposition to the planned divestment, no response was received from M/s BSES and M/s ENRON in their reply informed that they would not like to pursue the opportunity any further.

Public–Public Partnership

With the players in the private sector backing out, it became imperative to focus on the public sector companies. NTPC the largest power generating company in the public sector had many positives associated with them. Initially, NTPC was not enthused with SAIL's proposal and did not show much interest. It needs mentioning that SAIL had identified NTPC as a potential partner at the outset, however, it did not find NTPC' s proposal for complete sell-off of its power assets acceptable, as under such a condition power plants of SAIL would have lost their captive status. Subsequently for a variety of reasons NTPC agreed to participate in the divestment process and became the preferred choice for SAIL.

From the SAIL side, Mr Pande entrusted Mr A. K. Shahi, Executive Director Law and PLO with the task of building bridges between the two organizations for a successful outcome. After a series of meetings and discussions between the management of SAIL and NTPC, the ice was broken enabling the two large companies to work together under a JV for running, operating and managing SAIL's Captive Power Plants approved for divestment. SAIL had put in place a strong cross-functional team to work on the power assets divestment. The members of this team comprised Mr V. Shyamsundar, Tejveer Singh, Neeraj Sharma from the Power Group, Umesh Kumar from Corporate Law, K. Krishnakumar from Business Planning and Devinder Kumar from Finance Directorate. In addition, heads of power units of the integrated steel plants formed a counterpart team from the plants.

Back-Channel Efforts

Mr Shahi, head Corporate Law, SAIL, had a number of sessions with Mr B. N. Ojha, Director (Operations) NTPC, during July and August 2000 and ultimately succeeded in convincing him that SAIL's proposal was a desirable and beneficial arrangement for both the organizations.

It could be seen by experts of both the companies that the proposed venture would benefit from NTPC's well established O&M practices, as and when SAIL's captive power plants came under the watch of the JV. Another area of synergy was that a number of engineers and managers in NTPC were ex-SAIL men, thereby ensuring compatibility between the two large organizations.

Mr Shahi narrated that after Mr Ojha was convinced of the positive synergy of the venture, he did all the in-house work for getting a favourable decision at NTPC. Although the formation of JV was in the functional domain of the Director (Technical) at NTPC, Mr Ojha took all the initiatives to take the process forward. He won the confidence of Chairman NTPC Mr C. P. Jain on the proposed venture and was successful in selling the idea within NTPC.

Another favourable event that helped in finalizing the partnership was that Mr Ashok Basu, Secretary Steel at the time of SAIL's restructuring plan was approved by the GoI, had moved to the Power Ministry as Secretary Power and helped NTPC in getting the nod of the Power Ministry, wherever required.

SAIL NTPC JV Conceived

After the groundwork was done and an informal consensus reached, Mr Arvind Pande with his team of functional Directors of SAIL went to NTPC with a formal proposal and was received by Mr C. P. Jain, Chairman NTPC, along with his directors. A formal channel was thereby established and no one opposed the move.

With the groundwork having been done, the task became less arduous with only a few points for the two Chairmen to decide. Thereafter, in only two or three meetings of the high-level teams of the two organizations, almost all issues were frozen and agreed upon. An MoU was signed between SAIL and NTPC capturing the basic understanding of the proposed formation of the JV.

The JV was to have a 50:50 JV structure, with an equal number of directors on the Board from SAIL and NTPC. Day to day management, executive and O&M functions were to be exercised by NTPC. SAIL on the other hand retained certain affirmative rights, including those to protect the interests of the employees to be transferred to the JV Company.

Devinder Kumar, a member of the cross-functional team, working on the power asset divestment reminisced an interesting anecdote on the valuation of power assets, which were to come under the proposed JV with NTPC. M/s MECON was the consultant for the valuation of power plants under the above divestment scheme and he was the lone official from finance handling the case. A day before the Board meeting where the proposal was to be placed for approval, he requested two-three times to the then company secretary of SAIL to show him the contents of the Board note. However, as the Board note was a confidential matter, he was refused every time.

'It was past 8 PM in the evening and the company secretary had already left the office when there was a sudden power outage. Finding no one around, Devinder Kumar took a candle to the photocopying room where he read the main contents of the Board note. The note stated that at the valuation amount determined by MECON the identified power plants together with all connected movable and immovable assets, stores, spares and consumables would stand transferred to the Subsidiary/JV Company. Recounting the incident Devinder Kumar exclaimed, 'I was totally taken aback as MECON had determined the value only of the power generating units. The value of the inventory of movable assets, viz., stores, spares and consumables were not included in the valuation report.' The next morning, he checked with his colleagues from Power Group and came to know that value of stores, spares and consumables, not considered by MECON in their valuation report, was to the tune of almost ₹35 crore. Just before the Board meeting, he brought these facts to the notice of the then Director (Finance) Mr V. S. Jain and requested him to get the additional amount, equivalent to the value of the inventory of stores, spares and consumables under transfer communicated to NTPC, which was to make a payment equivalent to valuation determined by MECON. In the evening, after the Board Meeting, a meeting was arranged between Chairman SAIL and Chairman NTPC, where it was decided that in addition to the value determined by MECON, NTPC would make an additional payment of around ₹35 crore to SAIL, towards the transfer of inventory of stores, spares and consumables pertaining to the units under transfer'.

A distinctive condition in the MoU between SAIL and NTPC was that the service conditions of the personnel transferred to the JV Company from SAIL, would not in any manner be inferior to what they had in the parent company. Also, to enable smooth operations of the JV Company with no undue dependence on NTPC or SAIL, a mechanism was to be put in place whereby payment of the monthly power tariff was to be made within the first week of the succeeding month.

The IR personnel at the SAIL plants till then had been unsuccessful in addressing the concerns raised by the local trade unions and officers association. The matter, in fact, had become so grave that the Corporate Office functionaries, who had gone on a visit to one of the plants, were asked by the local IR Department not to visit the Power Plant site office when they offered to meet the workmen there.

Armed with the MOU, which adequately protected the interest of the employees of the Captive Power Plants of SAIL; IR functionaries from SAIL's Corporate Office reached out to the IR personnel working in the Steel Plants.

Winning the Confidence of Employees

A communication plan was developed to address the concerns of the impacted employees. As a first, a meeting was held with the entire cross-section of power plant employees at Bokaro Steel Plant. It was a well-attended meeting where the employees listened patiently, though with some apprehension, the presentation on measures undertaken to address their concerns and protect their interest. Following a series of such meetings and presentations, things started looking up.

However, in one of the plants where a team comprising senior officers from NTPC had gone for a visit of the Captive Power Plant, the workers got so agitated that the NTPC team was pulled out of the train and not allowed to carry out the inspection. It was a big embarrassment for SAIL Management and the NTPC engineers reported the incident to their management. The visit however was re-organized after a lapse of a few days.

The strong resentment affecting SAIL power plant employees was in fact more noticeable at the executive levels, where many officers had had a long tenure in power plant operations and maintenance. Their plea was that NTPC engineers were not more capable or competent than the SAIL counterparts working in the power stations of SAIL. The opposition led by the executives was firmly backed by the workforce that brought with them the strength of the numbers.

It took time and patience to overcome the resistance of the affected employees. Likely benefits resulting from the proposed JV was shared across a large cross-section of employees. It was explained to them that under the SAIL umbrella utilities such as Power Plants, Oxygen Plants etc. do not get the focus and priority given to the main metallurgical process units. Due to fund constraints, even the preventive maintenance and capital repairs at power plants sometimes tend to get delayed. Hence, it was not a question of individual competence or capability but the process of improved synergy by bringing in a partner for whom power was a core business that would lead to an improvement in the performance of the power plants.

Unlike SAIL, where the main focus was on augmenting the production of steel, SAIL NTPC JV would concentrate on timely maintenance and capital repairs of the power plants. Not constrained for funds, the improved operating and maintenance practices would result in better health of the plants and improve their efficiency. Also, under the new arrangement, it would be easier and more convenient to arrange capital for expansion of the plants wherever required. Thus, following a continuous process of engagement, the power plant employees were brought to the table and their resistance pared.

The resistance to change in a way was natural. It was anticipated that any change in the status of employees working in Power units of SAIL plants, without their consent, was likely to create a hindrance. Being conscious of the fact, the Government of India also while according approval to the divestment of assets, directed that the jobs of the employees be protected.

After signing the MoU with NTPC, the National Trade Unions was requested to help. Most of the trade unions did not oppose the move of power plant divestment after they were informed through a detailed presentation, the substance of the MOU between SAIL and NTPC. The meetings held with the cross-section of workers helped them in realizing that they stood to gain in the years to come and that none of their benefits was going to be curtailed. There was, in fact, a real possibility that they could enjoy more benefits than they had under SAIL.

The transfer of any generating station by SAIL to another entity—the proposed JV of SAIL and NTPC—required statutory permission from the Electricity Regulatory Body. SAIL was able to obtain such permission for Durgapur, Rourkela and Bhilai from the respective regulatory authorities. However, when similar permission was sought from DVC for Captive Power Plants of Bokaro Steel Plant, Chairman DVC Mr Jaitley proposed to become a JV partner with SAIL for the power plants of Bokaro on the same terms and conditions as agreed between SAIL and NTPC. It became difficult for SAIL to reject the offer of Chairman, DVC. Permission was thereafter granted and an MOU signed in a similar manner with almost identical terms and conditions, as agreed for SAIL–NTPC JV Company. Bokaro Power Plant thus came under a JV of SAIL and DVC.

The time taken for completion of the divestment process for the power plant was impacted by the large size of manpower which at different locations were represented by different trade unions and needed to be separately convinced. In the case of a rigid attitude of executives in some steel plants, options were given to them to opt-out and remain in SAIL.

The support received from the National Trade Union leaders like Shri Gopeshwar, Shri Passey and Shri Arya of INTUC, Shri Samant Roy of HMS, Shri Gaya Singh of AITUC, Shri M. K. Pandhe of CITU and others, for the power plant divestment was invaluable. Some of them were Members of Parliament and viewed the entire issue in a larger perspective. Being mature they understood very well the future interests of the employees working in power plants. Mr Arvind Pande and Mr Mihir Moitra talked to them in person and succeeded in conveying the rationale behind a move which ultimately was to benefit the workers in the long run.

'Launch of SAIL–NTPC Joint Venture for Power' read the maroon gold banner at a gathering of top executives of SAIL and NTPC, senior bureaucrats and media persons on 16 March 2001, assembled at Hotel Le Meridien, New Delhi, to witness the signing of share-holders' agreement between the country's largest steel producer and the country's largest power producer. Historic was how Arvind Pande,

Chairman SAIL, described the event in his address on the occasion. Thanking NTPC, which had been given management control in the JV, Mr Pande said that the JV Company will initially maintain two power plants located at Rourkela and Durgapur. All employees of power plants at RSP and DSP would be deputed to the JVC for a period of six months, during which they could decide to remain there or return to the SAIL fold, he added and assured that interest of SAIL employees would be fully protected. In his address, Mr C. P. Jain, Chairman NTPC, agreed with Mr Pande that an alliance between two big giants was indeed momentous and hoped that with liberalization of the economy, the JVC would definitely come away in a big way. The formalities were over within an hour with Mr M. K. Moitra, Director (Restructuring & Corporate Planning) SAIL, Mr V. S. Jain, Director (Finance) SAIL and Mr A. Palit Director (Technical), NTPC affixing their signature on the document on behalf of SAIL, SPSCL and NTPC respectively.

The JV Power Companies

Initially, two JV companies, one with NTPC for captive power plants at Rourkela and Durgapur and the second JV with DVC for captive plants at Bokaro, were formed. The designated power plants were then transferred to the JV companies. Subsequently, a third JV Company for a 74 MW captive plant at Bhilai was added. The power companies so formed were:

- NTPC SAIL Power Supply Company Limited (NSPCL) for Rourkela and Durgapur Power Plants: 220 MW.
- Bhilai Power Supply Company Limited (BPSCL): 74 MW plus 150 t/hr steam generation capacity
- Bokaro Power Supply Company Limited: 302 MW plus 660 t/hr steam generation capacity

The transfer of assets to the new power companies took place under a well-designed mechanism. Firstly, three wholly-owned subsidiary companies of SAIL for Rourkela-Durgapur, Bokaro and Bhilai Power Plants were formed and assets belonging to the designated power pants transferred to the respective subsidiary companies. This helped in nullifying stamp duty implications amounting to more than ₹100 crore. Thereafter, JV agreements were executed and 50 per cent equity of the subsidiary companies was transferred to NTPC and DVC in the respective companies.

Valuation of power plant assets was done by a mutually appointed valuer. SAIL received a sale consideration of around ₹1060 crore by the way of asset sales of its power plants, resulting in a net cash inflow of more than ₹900 crore and a capital gain in excess of ₹770 crore. A few years later in the year 2005–2006, Bhilai Power Supply Company was merged with NTPC SAIL Power Supply Company.

The valuation of power assets of the JV with DVC had its own element of drama recalled Devinder Kumar. In this case also, M/s MECON was the technical consultant for determining the value of power plants under transfer to DVC. He had gone with Mr Shyamsundar, then GM, Power Group, to MECON Office, Ranchi to meet the MECON Officials. 'I requested DGM, MECON, who was assigned the task of carrying out the valuation of power units, to show me the workings for arriving at a valuation', narrated Kumar. The MECON official, however, declined to share details of the valuation which was about ₹119 crore on the plea of confidentiality.

Recounting the event Devinder Kumar said, 'The discussions continued with the MECON official in the hall till late evening when he left his seat for a few moments. As he left his seat leaving behind his desktop computer, I hurriedly went through the financial model which showed that based on the discounted cash flow; the valuation of power plants was about ₹119 crore. I noticed that some of the assumptions considered by MECON were apparently incorrect and depressed the cash generation. In the meantime, the MECON official returned and got annoyed with me. I apologized and politely brought the shortcomings in the model to his notice. He did not commit anything at that time. After discussing the matter perhaps with his seniors, he modified and corrected the financial model, which resulted in the enhancement of value to about ₹180 crore.'

The power JV companies were Board managed with a CEO who was not a Board member. The Boards of all the three JV Power Companies were constituted with an equal number of Directors from SAIL and its JV partners—NTPC and DVC. Ex-officio Chairmen were the nominees of NTPC and DVC. Being small and compact, decision-making in the JV Companies was quick and effective, issues were better identified and corrective measures were taken without delay.

Mr B. N. Ojha Director (Operations) NTPC, was nominated as the first Ex-officio Chairman of NTPC SAIL JV (NSPCL) and Mr A. K. Basu, Secretary DVC, was made first Ex-officio Chairman of SAIL-DVC JV (BPSCL) at Bokaro. Executive Director (Works) of the respective SAIL Plant was made Director on the Board of the respective JV Company so as to represent the Plants. Contrary to the apprehension among certain quarters, the Power JV Boards worked with good harmony and were able to provide the requisite focus for improving the performance of the divested captive power plants. Mr A. K. Shahi, ED SAIL and PLO, being involved at every step of the JV formation since SAIL's initial attempt to form a JV with NTPC, was made part-time nominee director in all the JV companies in 2001, a position he held up to his superannuation in SAIL in 2006.

It was interesting to note that the NTPC and DVC work culture was visibly different. NTPC-SAIL JVs, within a short time, became sensitive to the burning issues faced by the power plants under their control. Prompt in identifying the issues affecting the plant's performance, they took corrective actions without any loss of time or delay. The JVs worked with complete harmony amongst SAIL and NTPC nominee directors, with commonality both in their thinking as well as in their approach towards decision-making.

Unconstrained by any lack of resource or expertise, the performance of NTPC SAIL JVs Power Plants at Rourkela, Durgapur and Bhilai started improving significantly within a short period of time. The Bhilai Power Supply Company performed so well that within three years of its formation it planned a mega expansion for adding 500 MW and become a 574 MW plant. Order was placed on BHEL for 2 × 250 MW Turbo Generators in 2005–2006. The expansion plan was implemented in record time.

With the expansion at Bhilai, SAIL–NTPC JV, which had a capacity of 294 MW at the time of its formation, became a 794 MW captive power generating company by 2008–2009. NSPCL (NTPC SAIL Power Supply Company Private Limited) helped the Bhilai Steel Plant significantly in meeting its enhanced power requirement through captive supply and reduce overall power cost.

The power plant at Bhilai under the JV was later adjudged as one of the best power generating stations in the country. NSPCL has since embarked upon the expansion of a captive power plant at Rourkela as well (250 MW), which is now under advanced stage of completion.

Divestment of Oxygen Plant-2 of Bhilai Steel Plant

Oxygen Plant-2 was the other non-core asset identified for divestment under SAIL's restructuring plan. Attempts were made by SAIL to divest the Oxygen Plant-2 (OP-II) of Bhilai, beginning April 2000. The rationale for divestment was that the induction of a JV partner would bring benefits of technological expertise and operating experience and also release significant cash proceeds for SAIL, estimated at ₹400 crore against a book value of ₹205 crore.

Four parties who fulfilled the eligibility criteria of a proven track record of 10 years with generation capacities of at least 2000 TPD of industrial gases and net worth around ₹200 crore, expressed interest in participating in the divestment process. These interested parties were:

- M/s Messer GmBH (through Goyal MG Gases Ltd)
- M/s Inox Air Products Limited
- M/s Praxair Inc. through PraxAir India Ltd.
- M/s BOC India Limited

All the four parties were shortlisted for the divestment process. Subsequently Praxair and BOC India Limited withdrew from the race as they did not find the proposal viable.

After the due diligence process, offers were received from the remaining two parties, which however were conditional in nature. Negotiations were taken up with the higher bidder; however, despite protracted discussions, no meeting point could be reached. The two issues which remained unresolved related to (a) return on equity and (b) the method of computation of depreciation. What was significant was that other than a deviation from the tender bid, the above two factors proposed by the H-1 bidder resulted in a higher price of oxygen for BSP.

Consequently, the bidding process of divestment of OP-II at BSP was terminated and a fresh Expression of Interest invited on relaxed eligibility criteria. However, the response was limited to the two parties with whom the negotiations had earlier failed and no improvement came about despite extension of the deadline for bid submission.

Later on, the oxygen producers came with offers to build a new oxygen plant at Bhilai on BOO (Build Operate and Own) basis and not under a JV arrangement. This looked logical and a policy decision was thereafter taken to have new oxygen plants at the steel plants built on a BOO basis and not under a JV as envisaged earlier. Consequently, the new oxygen plant at Bhilai Steel Plant set up in 2012 to meet the enhanced requirement of oxygen came up on BOO basis. Other Steel Plants also followed the suit and their enhanced requirement for oxygen has been met by oxygen plants built and operated on a BOO basis.

CHAPTER 8

Challenges in Divesting Loss-Making Units

Despite divestment of loss-making units featuring high on the agenda of the then Vajpayee government; it was not easy for a democratic government to sell businesses that engaged a large number of employees and formed a part of a mammoth public sector enterprise.

The divestment of various assets of SAIL was to take place against the background of the progressive economic reforms undertaken by the Government of India whereby a separate ministry for disinvestment was created with Mr Arun Shourie as the Minister at the helm. Although determined measures were taken up by the government for the privatization of identified public sector enterprises, there was resistance from employees in each case.

There was also uncertainty about the number of buyers interested to take over businesses engaging a large number of employees on its rolls. A few who were prepared to bid for such government-owned businesses, albeit at a highly discounted value, provided no assurance or guarantee for the continuance of the jobs of the employees. The apprehension regarding job security was so deep in the minds of public sector employees that they were unwilling to listen to anything favourable related to divestment.

Furthermore, it was easy for the public sector employees to gain access to political power centres in their respective states and thwart the disinvestment process. The case of SAIL business units approved for divestments was no different; in fact, it was even tougher as the unions operating in SAIL wielded substantial political clout.

That the opposition to privatization would be swift was predictable. *The Hindu* reported in February 2000, the state committee of CPI (M) of Tamil Nadu condemning the Centre's decision to hive-off SSP. The committee said that the move was like adding salt to the injury in the context of the long-pending demand for converting the plant into an integrated steel plant. The newspaper also reported the PMK founder, Dr S. Ramadoss saying that the move to privatize Salem Steel Plant was very unfair and the decision had created strong resentment among the people of Tamil Nadu. Mr Vazhappadi K. Ramamurthy, former Union Minister and president of the Tamizhaga Rajiv Congress, urged the Prime Minister to reconsider the decision to privatize Salem Steel and in a telegram sent to the Prime Minister said that the NDA partners in the State under the leadership of the Chief Minister, Mr M. Karunanidhi, were opposed to the proposal.

The opposition to divestment was voiced even more strongly by the AIADMK general secretary, Ms Jayalalitha, who asked the Chief Minister, Mr M. Karunanidhi, to 'call a halt' to the move to privatize the Salem Steel Plant. 'If, in spite of opposition from the entire populace of Tamil Nadu, the Central Government sells the Salem Steel Plant to private hands, I have to state that there will be a time in the future when we will restore the plant to the public sector,' she said in a statement.

In a move that cut across the party lines, the Tamil Nadu Assembly on 8 March 2000, in a unanimous resolution, appealed to the Centre to take steps to ensure the continuance of the Salem Steel Plant in the public sector. The resolution moved by the Chief Minister, Mr M. Karunanidhi, wanted the Centre to prevent the privatization of the plant.

Against a determined opposition to privatizing the loss-making units, Chairman Pande in an internal communication to the employees of the company in February 2002, highlighted the obstacles which thwarted efforts to divest ASP and SSP. He said that while efforts were on to minimize the losses of ASP before a solution could be found for its survival or otherwise, the situation at SSP was worrisome. Continuous opposition to the divestment plan would only result in the plant being pushed further into the red, he reasoned, and added that a capable JV partner could invest much-needed funds into SSP for its long-term viability.

The rationale for divesting special steels business was very clear for the decision-makers in SAIL. While the special steels business accounted for only a small part of the turnover, it was a significant contributor to the losses incurred. Moreover, future projections for the special steels plants did not provide any comfort in terms of any reversal in fortunes. It was therefore prudent to concentrate on carbon steel as the core business and divest the speciality steels business.

Alloy Steels Plant, West Bengal

Alloy Steels Plant (ASP) was set up at Durgapur in West Bengal in the vicinity of the integrated steel plant. The plant was built to produce different grades of alloy steels required for defence, automobile, engineering and other related sectors.

ASP at one time was considered a centre of excellence where the leading metallurgists in SAIL were deployed to produce the best quality alloy steels needed by the country. The excellence in the high-end metallurgical operations was planned to be achieved in collaboration with SAIL's R&D Centre at Ranchi, with the production facility located at Durgapur. Late M. N. Dastur, who used to be a doyen amongst the engineering consultants for the metallurgical industry, once narrated how the location for ASP was finalized. 'I was on my honeymoon at Pahalgam, when I got a message that

Pandit Nehru wanted my presence at Delhi,' narrated Mr Dastur. When he reached Delhi to meet the Prime Minister, he found that Chief Ministers of the then States of Madras (now Tamil Nadu), Maharashtra, West Bengal etc., were also present in the meeting. A new special steels plant was to come up in the country and each of the Chief Ministers wanted it in their state. The Prime Minister, however, left the decision to a specialist—M. N. Dastur. Mr Dastur asked for some time to firm up his views. He was on a visit to Durgapur when it struck him as the ideal location for the proposed new special steels plant.

ASP over the years produced eminent metallurgists, which included Dr P. L. Agarwal, Former Chairman SAIL, Mr D. Mukherjee, Mr DeTarafdar, Dr S. K. Bhattacharyya and Mr U. P. Singh, all of who later on rose to became MDs of SAIL's integrated steel plants and members of the SAIL Board.

Set up with Electric Arc Furnaces for steel making, ASP used steel scrap as input, which was sourced primarily from its sister units—the integrated steel plants of SAIL. However, with the passage of time, it started facing stiff competition from the larger integrated steel plants that were able to improve their product quality by introducing continuous casting and secondary refining facilities.

The special steels plants of SAIL, ASP and VISL, operated in a market where the domestic demand for alloy and special steel during the late nineties had stagnated at around 1.5 MT. The capacity utilization for the industry was less than 50 per cent and the market highly fragmented among various small and regional players.

To enhance the cost competitiveness of the unit, the options of transfer of hot metal and/or molten liquid steel from the Durgapur Steel Plant located adjacent to it were explored. However, on account of some technical reasons such as the absence of torpedo ladles, the transfer of liquid steel of Durgapur Steel Plant could not take place. Also, the limited quantity of hot metal sourced from DSP did not result in any significant reduction in cost economics. The locational dis-advantage of being away from the large markets of Western and Southern regions and a large workforce of more than 5,000 employees were some key factors that kept the bottom line of ASP in the red. As the operations of the unit had become unviable a decision was taken to disinvest the unit.

The divestment process for ASP was initiated with the issue of a global advertisement on 26 June 2001 inviting Expression of Interest from potential partners in the JV process. Efforts were made to contact potential bidders and persuade them to participate in ASP's divestment process. The preliminary Information Memorandum was issued to four private alloy and steel manufacturers in India. However, it elicited no response from them.

As ASP supplied about 20 per cent of its production to Defence and had the potential to increase supplies further, attempts were made to persuade the Ministry of Defence to take over ASP. Despite repeated efforts, the Ministry of Defence informed the MOS that it will not be possible for them to take over ASP. Due to the aforesaid reasons, it became imminent that the divestment of ASP was not feasible and it was decided to shelve the divestment.

VISL Karnataka

Set up in 1918 as a wood distillation plant with the name 'Mysore Wood Distillation & Iron Works', the VISL Plant at Bhadravati in Karnataka was one of the oldest steel plants in the country. Going through successive phases of evolution it emerged as 'Mysore Iron and Steel Ltd' (MISL) under the then Government of Mysore in 1962.

Its name was changed to Visvesvaraya Iron and Steel Limited in 1976 as a tribute to its founder—the great engineer and Bharat Ratna Sir M. Vivesavaraya. VISL was a symbol of pride for the people of Karnataka. The plant had a large area of land close to Shimoga and some associated iron ore and flux mines in the nearby mineral zones of Karnataka. VISL became a subsidiary of SAIL in 1989 and merged with it to become a unit of SAIL in 1998.

Burdened with very high manpower, VISL produced alloy and special steels through electric pig iron-LD route and electric arc furnace routes of production. It also produced ferrosilicon and some small quantities of manganese-based ferro alloys. Acute shortage of power in the state of Karnataka during the 1970s with attendant high tariff resulted in sub-optimal plant operations and concomitant loss of financial viability of the steel plant.

SAIL acquired a majority stake in VISL during Dr V. Krishnamurthy's tenure as Chairman, SAIL. After taking over, the ferrosilicon production at VISL was discontinued and investments made by adding one small size blast furnace of 530 cubic metre capacity. It was anticipated that the new blast furnace in the plant would help reduce dependence on the purchasing power, enabling it to migrate to a relatively cheaper production process.

However, the problems of old technology and high manpower (5656 numbers as in March 1997) continued to burden VISL's financials, providing the unit little respite. After the mid-1990s pressure was being put on SAIL by the state government of Karnataka to take over the plant fully by transfer its shares it held in VISL to SAIL. By then Shri Deve Gawda had become the Prime Minister and a decision was taken to merge VISL with SAIL.

An advertisement was placed in March 2001 inviting Expression of Interest (EOI) from parties interested in taking over VISL in a JV. The Preliminary Information Memorandum (PIM) was circulated widely and the opportunity to participate in the divestment process was communicated to many national and international steel companies, investment banks in Indian and abroad, as well as to the trade attaches of Indian consulates abroad and foreign missions in India. After extending the last date for submission of EOI, two EOIs were received from M/s Sunflag Iron and Steel Company Limited and M/s Indian

Seamless and Metal Tubes Ltd. (ISMT), both of whom fulfilled the eligibility criteria.

A Confidential Information Memorandum was circulated to the two parties and the due diligence including site visits organized when ISMT expressed its inability to proceed with the transaction citing certain developments within the group and in the external environment.

Sunflag completed the due diligence and site visit in February 2002 and was provided with the Confidential Information Memorandum Part II containing the offer procedures, terms and conditions of the offer and the draft contractual documents. Despite an extension of the last date for submission of bid on more than one occasion, Sunflag requested additional time and further information related to cost, contribution, sales realization and customer-wise analysis. In view of the above, the Merchant Banker for the divestment process, M/s IDBI, advised that the bidding process for VISL be treated as closed.

It needs to be stated that there was a lot of resistance by the unions and the officers' association with the proposed divestment of VISL. Mr R. K. Nagabhushana, who at that time was the technical assistant to the CEO of VISL, Mr R. Kumar, recalled, 'Employees of VISL had stalled the due diligence process. So an arrangement was made for the Sunflag team to access the documents pertaining to VISL in the Bangalore branch office. Also, there was a big protest at the factory gates when the Sunflag team arrived for the plant visit. The team was taken inside the plant through a back entrance and given the situation, it was not possible to have a prolonged tour of all the shops. So, the visit was curtailed to about an hour or so.'

To conclude, both Alloy Steel Plant at Durgapur and VISL Plant at Bhadrawati did not attract genuine buyers. No expression of interest was received against the Preliminary Information Memorandum (PIM) issued for ASP. VISL attracted one response, where the party apparently was more interested in accessing sensitive commercial information than the acquisition of the plant. The efforts of divestment for ASP and VISL were dropped once the United Progressive Alliance (UPA) Government assumed power in 2004.

Salem Steel Plant (SSP), Tamil Nadu

Commissioned in 1981, Salem Steel Plant had a cold rolling mill (Z mill) for stainless steel coils and sheets production. An additional cold rolling Z mill of similar capacity was added in 1991, taking the overall production capacity of SSP to around 70,000 MT of cold-rolled stainless steel coils and sheets per annum. The plant also set up a blanking line with a capacity to produce 3,000 MT of coin blanks per annum.

Set up initially only with cold rolling lines, Salem Steel Plant produced stainless steel coils and sheets with a very good finish. It used to import hot rolled stainless steel coils from abroad and roll them in its Z mills for supplying the finished stainless steel products in the domestic and international markets. Prior to decontrol of the sector, an option of supplying hot rolled stainless steel for SSP's Z mills was to take the stainless steel slabs from ASP to Finland (Outokumpu), roll them to SS HR coils and bring them back to India for cold rolling at SSP!

Till around mid-1990 there was no other stainless steel producer in India whose products met international standards. Jindals, who had installed a stainless-steel production facility at Hisar in Haryana, were in the process of expanding their base.

SSP had a limited presence in the stainless steel market, the size of which at that time (later half of the 1990s) was around 6 lakh MT, with moderate growth of about 4 per cent per annum. The market comprised industrial end-use segment which required high nickel categories of stainless steel and non-industrial segment which had under its fold mainly the utensils manufacturing that required low nickel varieties of stainless steel. SSP produced stainless steel of high nickel variety for industrial applications, concentrating mainly on 300 and 400 series where its market share was around 40 per cent.

Salem Steel Plant had been exporting a significant part of its stainless steel production in those times. It exported nearly 25,000 MT or around 40 per cent of its total sales during the years 1996–1997 and 1997–1998. However, in 1998–1999, its exports dipped by almost 50 per cent; the depressed international market being the main culprit, which dented the unit's sales realization and made its exports unviable.

As a part of backward integration, a Steckle Mill with a capacity of rolling 1,86,000 MT of hot rolled coils had been set up at SSP in the year 1995 at a cost of ₹623 crore. It had been envisaged that after commissioning of the Steckel mill the requirement of SSP of purchased inputs would reduce as the desired input stainless steel slabs could be sourced from the sister unit, ASP. The option, however, did not fructify because of the high cost of production at ASP and the high transport cost for transferring SS slabs from ASP to SSP. So acute was the issue of feed materials for SSP that not even 50 per cent of its new Steckel mill capacity was utilized. The only difference after installing the Steckel mill was that SSP became dependent on purchased stainless slabs instead of purchased stainless steel HR coils.

Salem Steel Plant had many strengths. Foremost amongst them was the brand equity it enjoyed as a producer of high-quality stainless steel. Salem's rolling mills were the finest and steel sheets rolled by these mills sold at a premium in the South Asian market. The plant also had an excellent work culture. SSP's operational performance was quite good and its mills operated at high operating efficiency levels comparable to the European producers. The plant had an additional parcel of 1,500 acres of developed land, adjacent to the existing plant for further expansion.

It was conceived that divestment of SSP to a strategic partner would help in tiding over the constraints faced by the plant. The strategic partner could fund the backward integration into steel making at SSP and also reduced the capital cost for the project to less than ₹200 crore by sourcing second-hand equipment from overseas. Also, the strategic partner could potentially be a stable source of supply of stainless steel slabs, till the backward integration was achieved. Furthermore, the JV partner could open up new export markets for Salem product and improve the working capital management

Initially, an advertisement inviting EOI was issued for setting up stainless steel melting facilities in a JV. However, as no response was received, an alternative option was given for setting up a JV company through equity participation in SSP, with SAIL holding minority shareholding.

The move to hive-off SSP, however, was strongly resisted by employees who formed a 'Save Salem Committee'. *The Hindu* reported on 28 May 2000 that 'Save Salem Steel Committee', comprising at least eight trade unions, voiced its apprehension over the 'stealthy move to privatize the Salem Steel Plant'. In a statement signed by all the affiliated trade union leaders, the committee noted that it had registered its strong protest against the privatization of the Salem Steel Plant on many occasions and that their stand had been endorsed by the State Assembly through a resolution.

Expressions of Interest against SAIL's advertisement were submitted by Avesta Sheffield, TISCO/Usinor, Jindal Strips (with MOU signed with NTK Japan and INC) and Shah Alloys. Avesta Sheffield and TISCO-Usinor were shortlisted while clarifications were sought from JSL regarding their consortium partner. After receiving additional information from JSL, the consortium was cleared for participating in the divestment process. M/s Avesta Sheffield later withdrew from the process leaving only two parties in the field. Subsequently, a request was received from JSL that they qualified the specified criteria on their own and would like to be considered on a standalone basis. Since the deviation in the case of JSL was minor they were allowed as a qualified bidder to continue participation.

However, Salem workers and executives were opposed to divestment en masse and wanted to remain in SAIL. They approached the High Court of Madras against the divestment process and the qualification of M/s JSL for participating in the divestment process.

Their resolve was so deep and opposition so grave that they did not allow entry of the senior management team of TISCO-Usinor inside the plant. Employee's resistance was also supported by the local MPs and by the State Government.

The TISCO-Usinor team arrived at SSP in November 2001 but was prevented from conducting the due diligence. The incident was narrated by Mr K. K. Khanna, who was heading the team which had been set up for divestment of SSP. Mr Khanna at that time was GM (Projects) at Project Directorate, SAIL Corporate office and later on, held the position of Director (Technical) in the company. He had spent a number of years at Salem when the plant was in its construction phase and was familiar with the plant. He was also was well known to the employees of Salem Steel Plant.

Mr Khanna arrived at Salem a day earlier than the scheduled date of plant visit by the Tata Steel team. Mr M. K. Moitra, Director (Restructuring and Corporate Planning) had also gone for the planned interaction with the Tata team, which was led by Mr R. P. Singh. The next day, as Mr Khanna accompanied the Tata team for the plant visit, their progress to the plant entry gate was blocked by an irate crowd of around 200–300 SSP employees.

'I came out of the vehicle to plead with the crowd,' narrated Mr Khanna. 'I tried to convince them that it was a win-win situation for both SSP and Tata-Usinor combine. I reasoned with the crowd that SSP would be able to gain by a partnership with Tata–Usinor JV, particularly when Usinor was one of the leading manufacturers of stainless steel in the world. But they were unwilling to listen and shouted that the due diligence would not be allowed to take place,' recollected Mr Khanna. Eventually, the Tata team had to go back to the guest house, where meetings were organized with them for discussion. When the impasse continued the next day also, the visiting team from Tata had to go back without the plant visit.

The press in May 2002, reported that the Union Minister of State for Steel Braja Kishore Tripathy had written to the Chief

Minister Ms Jayalalitha, seeking the cooperation of the Tamil Nadu government for converting the Salem Steel Plant into a JV company. When asked about the status of the Assembly resolution, Mr Tripathy told *The Hindu*, that plant was the centre's property and, therefore, it had the prerogative to decide the future course of action. But since the Assembly resolution reflected the aspirations of the people of the State, it would be given due regard and respect. Mr Tripathy argued that the Steel Authority of India Ltd. would not be able to sustain the operations of the Salem plant for long without a JV partner. The newspaper reported that SAIL had invited expressions of interest from probable JV partners for divestment of SAIL's equity of the Salem plant. Two parties had been identified (Tata Steel and Jindal), but they could not carry out the 'due diligence', owing to resistance by employees.

In August 2002, TISCO-Usinor combine withdrew their interest from the JV participation in Salem.

As Jindals were eying for Salem Steel Plant for some time and probably had all the required information about its facilities, they did not press for inspection. Resultantly, only Jindal Stainless remained in the field. They completed the data room visit organized at SAIL Corporate Office during August-September, 2002. Additional information sought by them was provided and the RFP and the other contractual documents were issued. The price bid of JSL was expected in January 2003. However, owing to consistent opposition by the employees and the State Government, the divestment could not be pushed and was shelved.

Divestment of Rourkela Fertilizer Plant (RFP)

The Rourkela Fertilizer Plan was set up in the year 1962 adjacent to the Rourkela Steel Plant to profitably utilize its by-products, such as hydrogen from coke oven gas, waste nitrogen of oxygen plant and the limestone fines, for fertilizer production. Naphtha Refining Plant I & II were installed in the year 1970–1971 for an achievable production capacity of 3,60,000 MT of Calcium Ammonium Nitrate (CAN).

The financial performance of RFP was greatly dependent on the retention price mechanism administered by the GOI which was discontinued with effect from June 1994, while its substitute fertilizer-urea continued under the subsidy scheme. Although the quality of Rourkela fertilizer in the brand name of 'Sona' was well accepted in the market; its obsolete technology, high cost of production and removal of price subsidy made the operations unviable. RFP had a low market share of 19 per cent in the CAN market and its capacity utilization was only 26 per cent. Its high number of employees and the route of production deployed resulted in a high-cost structure, making the unit fundamentally uncompetitive.

The reasons for RFP's non-competitiveness were many. RFP's feedstock naphtha was costlier than furnace oil and LSHS oil used by its competitors, Gujarat National Fertilizer Company (GNFC) and National Fertilizer Company (NFL). This resulted in a cost disadvantage of around 40 per cent for RFP vis-à-vis competitors. So far as the substitute urea was concerned, most urea-based fertilizer plants were switching from naphtha to natural gas, thereby attaining higher cost efficiency.

RFP's main product CAN, accounted for only 1 per cent of the market for fertilizers in India. The demand growth for CAN had become stagnant during the nineties, but the market had continued to be competitive with an aggregate capacity utilization of 56 per cent. On the demand side, farmers had started switching from nitrogen-based fertilizers, such as CAN to NPK Complex Fertilizers. Also, the competitors to RFP had integrated fertilizer plants capable of producing other fertilizers such as urea, and unlike RFP, were not solely dependent on CAN.

Given the above context and the lower cost structure of its competitors backed by the advantage of cheaper feedstock, it was foreseeable that the net sales realization of CAN supplied by RFP would not increase. Thus, divesting the fertilizer plant or closing it down were the only options left to plug the annual cash loss incurred by RFP.

Efforts for Divesting RFP

As Rourkela Steel Plant was dependent on RFP for the supply of synthesis gas for use in its cold rolling mills, it was imperative that synthetic gas generation facilities be set up in RSP before divestment of RFP. Hence, the divestment process for RFP was taken up only after the synthetic gas generation facilities were set up in the Rourkela Steel Plant.

An advertisement inviting EOI was issued on 16 March and the last date for submission of EOI extended twice. The EOI was submitted only by two parties, Deepak Fertilizer Petro-Chemicals Corporation Ltd (DFPCL) and Rashtriya Chemicals and Fertilizers (RCF). The parties undertook due diligence visits to RFP in November and December 2001. Confidential Information Memorandum and draft contractual documents were issued to them for submission of the bids.

M/s DFPCL insisted that they will like to inspect the running plant before submission of their bid. As RFP was not operational with effect from September 2001 up to March 2002 due to the non-availability of some critical spares, DFPCL undertook another due diligence visit during May 2002 when the plant had become operational. Deepak Fertilizer submitted their bid in 2002 while M/s RCF sent their regret letter declining further participation in the JV.

The Hindu, in its coverage of the divestment of the Rourkela Fertiliser Plant, wrote on 9 September 2002, 'The Steel Authority of India expects to wrap up the divestment of the fertilizer unit in Rourkela Steel Plant (RSP) in the next two to three months. According to sources, the company is now negotiating with the only bidder for the plant, Deepak Fertilizers. The latter had already carried out a due diligence exercise of the plant and was subjected to submit its financial bid following the negotiation.' The newspaper cited Dr S. Mishra the then Managing Director of RSP telling that the fertilizer unit was incurring a loss of ₹5 crores a month and that it would be a great relief to the ailing RSP if it was divested in the proposed JV.

M/s Deepak Fertilizer had put certain conditions in their price bid. After receiving a response from SAIL on the issues raised by them, they re-submitted their final bid in November 2002. However, the bid amount from DFPCL was lower than the reserve price and also had a set of conditions attached.

The valuation of the reserve price for RFP by independent consultants was based on the realizable scrap value of the fertilizer plant and a small value attached to the building and the structural and civil works. Negotiations were held with the party to explore the possibility of improving the price bid to match the reserve price. However, the final bid submitted by M/s Deepak Fertilizer continued to be lower than the valuation done for RFP by the independent consultants.

Deepak Fertilizer had also indicated that they would absorb no more than 175 employees of RFP thereby implying that the remaining manpower of about 600 would continue to be with SAIL. As the negotiations with the party were not leading to resolution, it was decided to close the divestment process, suspend the operations of RFP and reduce the manpower by giving VRS to all the employees. The assets of RFP after that could then be taken up for disposal.

Divestment of Indian Iron and Steel Company (IISCO)

IISCO was a chronically sick plant with old assets and outdated technology. It was referred to BIFR in June 1994 and declared a sick company under SICA Act. As a part of the restructuring plan of SAIL, GOI had approved the conversion of IISCO into a JV with SAIL holding minority shareholding.

A number of attempts earlier had been made to modernize IISCO. M. Vinayak in an article 'The Corrosion within SAIL' published on 15 June 2000, in *The Hindu* wrote on the previous attempts to modernize. In the eighties when modernization and rationalization became the key for survival and growth of steel plants, differences between the then SAIL Chairman, Mr V. Krishnamurthy and Dr M. N. Dastur of Dastur and Co., who had become the steel consultant to the Union Steel Ministry, surfaced at a seminar though both agreed on the urgency of modernization to save the Burnpur plant, wrote M. Vinayak. For IISCO's modernization, several plans had been chalked out, some commissioned by the centre. The British consultants had done a study but it was the Japanese consultants of Nippon Steel who had prepared a ₹6,000 crore plan that stirred a needless controversy and virtually stalled the modernization.'

The article pointed out that Dr Dastur favoured optimum use of indigenous capability in designing the equipment, which could have led to delayed deliveries; while the SAIL Chairman preferred a time-bound programme with a judiciously balanced participation of indigenous equipment manufacturers and overseas suppliers.

M. Vinayak wrote that had the Union Steel Ministry not stalled the Japanese plan for modernization of IISCO, the steel scene at the Burnpur and Kulti works would have dramatically changed. The Japanese Government had paid for the consultancy and a consortium was to implement the modernization scheme on a turnkey basis but the scheme was stalled by a vacillating centre. Within SAIL, however, the perception was that the Modernization of IISCO took a back seat when the Congress government under Rajiv Gandhi was replaced by a new government in 1989 under Prime Minister V. P. Singh.

The Hindu article cited earlier attempts to privatize IISCO when apart from the London-based Mr Swaraj Paul, the chairman of Mukand Iron and Steel Works, Mr Viren Shah, made a bid to acquire the Burnpur works. However, none of these proposals materialised as IISCO was trapped in the political quagmire of West Bengal politics.

The SAIL restructuring proposal approved in February 2000, which proposed privatization of IISCO was based on the fact that SAIL did not possess the financial wherewithal to modernize IISCO.

It was expected that IISCO would attract private entrepreneurs as it had some of the best iron ore and coking coal mines and huge real estate assets.

EOI were invited from prospective partners in April 2000 for divestment of IISCO. EOI were received from five parties out of which three parties were shortlisted for further process. The shortlisted parties were BHP Minerals Marketing, Australia, Mitsui & Co., Japan and Tyazhpromexport (TPE) Russia. BHP and Mitsui later decided to operate jointly for IISCO's disinvestment.

Due diligence was conducted by TPE in March 2001 and jointly by BHP and Mitsui in March and April 2001.

BHP and Mitsui combine informed in May 2001 that they were unable to take equity interest for the rehabilitation of IISCO Steel Works and were assessing a proposal for the development of IISCO's iron ore assets only. Finally, on 16 November 2001, BHP and Mitsui combine sent a proposal for the development of Chiria Iron Ore Mines only, which was not accepted.

M/s TPE the only party left, submitted a proposal in November 2001 for JV participation in IISCO with TPE's equity holding in the JVC at 51 per cent. The proposal envisaged increasing the production of steel to 5.45 lakh MT at an investment of ₹820 crore to be funded from Rupee-Ruble Escrow Account.

A high-level Indian team from MOS and SAIL discussed the proposal and its funding in Russia in March 2002. During the visit, TPE indicated that their experts would visit Burnpur for on-the-spot assessment of facilities, especially the BF and that they would engage mining experts for evaluating prospects in mines. The TPE indicated around three months to come up with a viable proposal for IISCO's revival. However, no response received from them thereafter despite follow up.

Financial Express while covering divestment of SAIL units reported on 2 December 2003, 'For the sale of Indian Iron and Steel

Company (IISCO), a wholly-owned subsidiary of SAIL, three overseas firms had shown interest—BHP of Australia, Mitsui Company Ltd of Japan and Tyazhpromexport (TPE) of Russia. They also carried out the due diligence exercise. BHP and Mitsui, however, lost interest. In the middle of last year, it appeared that TPE may take over IISCO. In fact, in his November 2001 visit to Moscow, Prime Minister Atal Bihari Vajpayee had discussed the acquisition of IISCO by TPE with Russian President Vladimir Putin. But the acquisition never took place.'

Given the uncertainty regarding the JV, SAIL had submitted a proposal for the revival of IISCO to the MOS in August 2001. The proposal envisaged total fund amounting to ₹1,081 crore comprising ₹540 crore as grant for funding VRS, ₹341 crore towards investment at Burnpur Works and mines and collieries against a soft loan and ₹200 crore for meeting anticipated cash loss during the period of construction.

SAIL's proposal was based on a grant of funds from GOI and certain concessions from the Government of West Bengal. It was decided in a chief executives meeting of SAIL in November 2002, that the divestment process for IISCO may be suspended for the time being and the rehabilitation plan pursued for implementation; and that at an appropriate time, depending upon market conditions, the disinvestment may be re-examined by fresh effort either by SAIL or through Ministry of Divestment.

In line with the rehabilitation plan for IISCO, operations at Kulti works were closed down. A fund amounting to ₹186 crore had been approved by the Government of India for providing VRS to employees at Kulti Works. The downsizing of the work-force was taken up at Kulti and Burnpur Works to improve the viability of IISCO.

In the meantime, the steel market started improving by the second half of 2002–2003. In 2005–2006, IISCO was merged in SAIL and became a unit and the fifth integrated steel plant of SAIL.

Conclusion

One can only speculate on the impact of the condition put by the Government of India in its letter approving business restructuring that the jobs of the employees were to be protected, had on the disinvestment process of loss-making SAIL units. In all fairness, such conditions were kept by the central government in all cases of dis-investments or divestments and were not specific to SAIL. This condition could have been a disincentive for probable buyers of ASP, VISL, IISCO and Rourkela Fertilizer Plant. At the same time, it was difficult to dilute this condition due to the reasons explained above.

CHAPTER 9

The Human Dimension

SAIL had a rich legacy of human resource or HR engagement since its inception. Its HR practices gained maturity at the time Dr V. Krishnamurthy became the Chairman of the company. Krishnamurthy made the company realize that the people were its most important resource. He took pains to point out that while resources such as money, machines and physical assets had limitations, there was no limit to human ingenuity and creativity, a renewable resource with unlimited possibilities.

Creating a committed workforce has been the focus for HR management and development in SAIL over the years. This approach enabled adaptability to change, whenever necessitated, by leveraging the strength of cooperation and involvement of the SAIL collective. The decision of restructuring the company's businesses, which inter-alia called for manpower rightsizing and divestment of the non-core and unviable production facilities, was a big challenge that confronted SAIL in the turbulent nineties.

Arvind Pande, Chairman SAIL had realized right at inception, that employees were central to the turnaround endeavour. Despite rightsizing manpower being one of the key interventions in the turnaround strategy; rather than seeing employees in an adversarial role, Pande made all efforts to co-opt them in the turnaround initiative. He believed that accomplishing the turnaround needed the involvement of a wide cross-section, across different functions and locations in SAIL. Furthermore, he knew that success critically hinged on implementing actions that required topmost priority by all concerned. He was confident that by working collectively the period of adversity could be overcome. Accordingly, the communication channels were kept in a hyperactive mode and the unions, officers, associations and other interest groups kept in confidence at each stage.

When SAIL's restructuring package was cleared by the Government of India on 15 February 2000, Pande lost no time in reaching out to the employees. In his communication to the SAIL collective, he said, 'I am confident that we can restore past glory and ensure long-term viability of our company. By clearing one of the largest restructuring proposals ever considered, the Government has reposed great confidence in the entire SAIL collective. The time has come for us to discharge our responsibilities by emerging winners once again. We owe this to ourselves as well as the Government and the public at large.'

Manpower Rightsizing

As a public sector enterprise SAIL historically had a huge workforce—a legacy of the post-Independence policies under which the industrial organizations in the public sector had the onus of providing employment in large numbers. Ranked amongst the biggest employers in the country, SAIL was burdened with a huge man-power cost accounting for around 21 per cent of its turnover. This placed the company at a disadvantage vis-à-vis the competitors, especially the new steel companies that emerged following delicensing of the sector and operated with much lower manpower costs ranging around 6 to 7 per cent of their turnover.

From 1991–1992 to 1995–1996 labour cost at SAIL had gone up at an average of 18 per cent per annum compared to 11 per cent for the other cost component. This steep rise in manpower cost happened despite a net reduction of 6,200 in the workforce. The cost structure for manpower at SAIL was such that for each 1 per cent increase in the basic pay of employees, the company had to bear an additional burden of ₹13 crore. It was an important element while taking into account normal increments on promotion which on average constituted 10-11 per cent of the wage bill. Trapped in an intensely competitive market, SAIL was no longer in a position to support the large workforce and its attendant cost, which nullified the benefits of the latest facilities at its production units installed under modernization.

Modern steel-making technology had sharply reduced the manpower-intensity in the production process. This was an outcome of superior automated production techniques which made the requirement of the large workforce redundant. Internationally, leading steel procedures employed only around 1,000 persons in the works area to produce one million tonne of steel. With the passage of time, the steel companies outsourced the industrial services which traditionally constituted a part of integrated steel plant operations. With over 1.83 lakh employees on its rolls in 1997, SAIL had a huge handicap in its efforts to become globally competitive.

Overmanning in SAIL was also a result of political intervention and pressure over the years. Many officials held that a time had come to overcome these pressures, as many employees did not have sufficient work on hand to justify their continuance and yet the political pressure kept them going. They were of the view that it was time for the top management to take a tough stand, and that one did not require consultants to tell that many stockyards and branch offices were redundant.

The company strategists were aware that all the interventions identified in the turnaround plan would come to nought unless SAIL rationalized its manpower. With overmanning an acknowledged element of high fixed costs in SAIL, a concerted plan to reduce manpower to less than 1,00,000 within the next 5 years was initiated. In fact, much before the turnaround plan was approved by the Government of India, SAIL had already initiated actions to downsize the organization.

Manpower Planning

SAIL followed a well laid-out process for manpower planning exercise every year. Starting around six months in advance of the ensuing fiscal, the manpower planning exercise was synchronised with the annual budget exercise. Various steps forming a part of manpower planning included preparation of a detailed designation-wise inventory of retirements and likely separations due to various reasons; categorization of jobs where separations were to take place and the basis of replacement needs—full, partial or none—for the year under consideration; calculation of phase-wise manpower requirements for sustenance investment programmes (called AMR: Additions, Modifications and Replacements) and modernization schedules; identification of work practices needing improvement and the savings in manpower on that account; accounting number of people who could be redeployed from existing areas to new positions; and finally, calculating the gap to be met through external recruitment.

Manpower planning in management literature is normally associated with placing people in the right numbers at the right place at the right time. In application, however, manpower planning also engages with qualitative aspects such as age-mix, skill-mix, redeployment and retraining of the workforce, etc. As a part of the restructuring initiative, SAIL undertook an extensive manpower planning and design exercise to have a fair assessment of optimal manpower for the present as well as future needs. It took into account progressive improvement in work practices for arriving at optimal manpower and improving manpower productivity. An assessment was also done of the changes in the skills required due to the adoption of new technologies. This exercise enabled identifying surpluses, assessment of manpower potential and their retraining and redeployment, in the context of future needs. It also led to carefully controlling recruitment to avoid year-to-year fluctuations in the intake.

The implementation of the HR plan on the other hand entailed constant monitoring and analysis of manpower trends to keep the management informed about deviations and the need for taking pre-emptive action for correcting distortions if any.

Voluntary Retirement Schemes

VRSs in SAIL were introduced in the late 1980s for the first time. These schemes were operated up to 1992–1993 and were availed by more than 17,000 employees during the period. However, liberalization and competitive pressures made the introduction of VRS a necessity in the late nineties, with much larger numbers as the target group.

SAIL launched a newly formulated VRS for its employees on 1 March 1998. It was a generous package keeping in mind the length of service of the employees and providing them with a comfortable post-retirement life. To have a focused strategy for manpower downsizing, specific sets of criteria for granting of VR were evolved.

The eligibility criteria for applicants for VR was kept at a minimum of 20 years of service in SAIL or 50 years of age. The target set of employees for VR was to come from those working in departments to be phased out or likely to be phased out or facing technical obsolescence. Departments that were economically unviable and non-Works areas constituted yet another target segment for granting VR. At an individual level, VR targeted employees having actual attendance of fewer than 240 days in a year or those who had been underperforming due to physical loss and injury or illness, or employees with qualification below graduation, or surplus and non-deployment of employees.

Initially introduced for six months, the VRS was to be reviewed based on the need and response. It was however conveyed to the employees that VR was not a matter of right and would be discouraged for high performers as well as for departments recently modernized.

Under VRS, an employee was to be given a monthly benefit ranging from 80 per cent to 100 per cent of the Basic Pay and DA, depending on age group category, for a maximum period of 10 years or till the date of superannuation, whichever was earlier. The payment of Provident Fund and Gratuity under the rules was payable in lump sum. In addition, the recipient employee was also to be given leave encashment for the un-availed Earned Leave and Half Pay Leave within the ceiling limit. This payment was to be made in equal instalment along with monthly benefit. Also, the retiring employee was eligible to receive the benefit of Mediclaim facilities for self and spouse at the plant/unit hospital in line with the general benefits available on superannuation.

The VRS of SAIL was a brilliant innovation. It allowed the company to run a VR scheme despite the crunch in financial resources. The payments towards VR—spread over a period of up to 10 years—enabled SAIL to meet the cash flow required to finance the scheme. At the same time, it resulted in an average savings of around 30 per cent in the cost borne by the company for the employee opting for VR. The employee on the other hand was assured of 70 per cent of his current income and could supplement it with other income opportunities after leaving SAIL. It was, hence, a win-win outcome for both the company as well as the employee.

The VRS of SAIL found a good response and around 6000 employees opted for the scheme across SAIL plants and units. SAIL launched a slightly modified VR scheme in June 1999. The benefits under the scheme were further improved to a range from 85 per cent to 105 per cent of the basic pay plus DA. The eligibility criteria were also relaxed from 20 years of service in VRS 1998 and minimum of 50 years of age to 15 years of service and minimum age of 40 years in VRS 1999. VRS 1999 was a success and 13,600 employees opted for it. Thus, SAIL through its innovative VR scheme was able to reduce its manpower strength by nearly 20,000 within a span of two years.

The deferred payment VRS operated in 1998 and 1999, were designed to take care of SAIL's finances which were then under acute stress. After the approval of the SAIL restructuring plan by the Government of India, it became possible to mobilize funds for VRS based on government guarantee and also benefit from the interest subvention on the loans. SAIL, therefore, launched a VR scheme on a lump-sum payment based on the DPE pattern in 2001. All three VR schemes overshot their targets. A total number of 26,102 employees availed VR between 1998 and 2001.

The hugely successful VRS operated by SAIL in 1998–1999, 1999–2000 and 2001 provided the right impetus to the manpower rightsizing exercise. Selective recruitments also helped restrict numbers to the targeted levels. An analysis of the three VR schemes indicated some interesting facts. To begin with, VRS was availed by more numbers than targeted. Secondly, VR was more in the 55+ age-group and low in the below-52 age-group. Third, it was higher in non-works areas. Fourth, as a percentage of manpower VR was higher in the loss-making plants. Fifth, the Executive category had a marginally higher response for VR. Lastly, VR was availed by less professionally qualified employees and consistently high performing executives

The VRS scheme was relaunched in three phases during 2002–2003 and was availed by 7,099 additional employees. Thus, the total number of separations in the company from 1997–1998 to 2002–2003 through VR schemes aggregated to 33,201 numbers or around 20 per cent of the workforce in 1997.

SAIL followed a policy to neither have any recruitment against VR nor engage contract labour in areas where VR separations had taken place. Taking the company's interest into account while granting VR to employees, the management retained the right to reject applications from employees working in key functions/categories such as telecommunications, instrumentation, computers—especially software, professionally qualified finance personnel, specialist medical personnel, critical categories for the plant/unit, and also executives having ACP above 40 in their previous 10 appraisals. A thrust was laid on targeting higher responses in the age group of 40–55 years, which constituted the bulge so that VR was optimally spread across all age-groups.

Sabbatical Leave Scheme

The Sabbatical Leave Scheme was another interesting innovation for the company. Introduced in March 1999 as a means of manpower rationalization, the sabbatical leave scheme encouraged the employees to avail leave for self-renewal with minimal risk. It provided the employees with the opportunity to voluntarily seek employment elsewhere or take up self-employment to utilize their professional and technical expertise.

The scheme provided an alternate option to the employee and at the same time helped SAIL in its manpower rationalization drive. It was open to all regular employees who had completed 10 years of service in the company. Under the scheme, leave of absence was granted to the employee for a period of one to three years, in lieu of earned leave and half pay leaves in his or her credit. The remaining period after the adjustment for earned and half-pay leaves was to be treated as extraordinary leave. In case the employee took employment with another organization during sabbatical leave, then the person had to avail extraordinary leave for the entire duration. The employee continued to receive benefits related to medical facilities, housing and education in accordance with his entitlement. The Sabbatical Leave scheme provided the freedom to the employees to explore opportunities outside SAIL with minimal risk and the company a means of manpower rightsizing.

SAIL Manpower Trend

Manpower in SAIL was steadily decreasing over the years. Separations during the early 1990s were in the range of 8,500 numbers per year, due to a high number of superannuation. However, this period was also characterised by high recruitments. In the latter half of the decade, the number of separations fell mainly because for two years up to

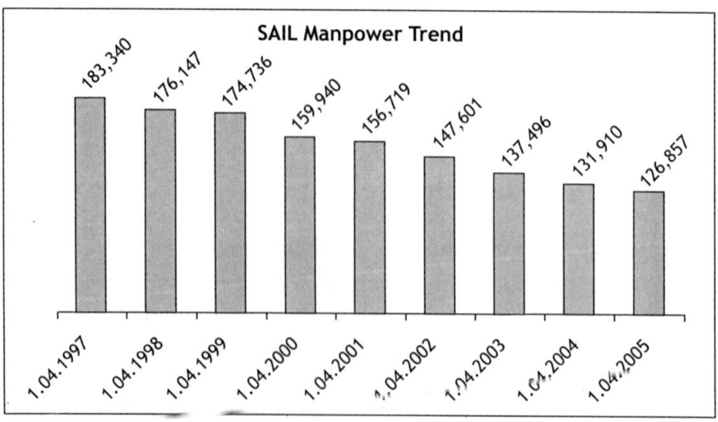

May 2000, there were no natural separations due to the raising of the retirement age to 60.

The graph captures the trend in SAIL manpower from the years 1996–1997 to 2004–2005 for which a target of 100,000 had been set.

Manpower rightsizing implementation at SAIL was very effective. While the total number of employees on the company's rolls came down by more than 50,000 between 1997 and 2004, there was an equally impressive reduction in contract manpower reduction.

Contract Labour Management

Another avenue for manpower rationalization pertained to the reduction in contract labour in operations. The company had around 29,500 contract labour in 1998 handling incidental jobs in its plants, mines and stockyards, including those in its subsidiary units.

To reduce dependence on contract labour, SAIL had previously adopted measures like VR, mechanization of mines etc. to reduce labour dependent jobs. The effort to rationalize contract labour was strengthened further by the adoption of stringent guidelines for contract labour management, of which awarding jobs only to bona fide recognized contractors was the most significant measure.

While measures to regulate contract labour managements were being taken up in SAIL there was a mega change in the policy regime related to contract workers. The Honourable Supreme Court pronounced a judgement in December 1996, in the Air India Statutory Corporation case, making a legal declaration that all contract workers engaged in jobs for which prohibitory notification under section 10 of the Contract Labour (Regulation and Abolition) Act, 1970, prohibited employment of contract labour; by the effect of law, became regular employees of that establishment from the very date the notification under section 10 was issued.

The Supreme Court ruling affected PSUs in two distinct ways. The immediate impact was that lakhs of contract workers had to be absorbed which could lead to industrial sickness in many cases. The long-term impact was in terms of the emergence of a discriminatory situation between PSEs and private companies, whereby the PSEs were going to lose competitiveness.

This created an alarm across the industry, particularly for big companies like SAIL, which engaged contract labour in large numbers. With the change in law, there were beelines before the Contract Labour Advisory Boards, both central or state, by contract labour unions justifying their case for the issue of prohibitory notifications for contract workers who had been working for long.

Several notifications were issued for different establishments of SAIL and more were on their way. Similar was the case with many other organizations. The Personnel Directorate of SAIL was the first to realize the grave implication of this judgement. Without losing time, Mr Arvind Pande Chairman, SAIL and Mr Mihir Moitra, Director (Personnel and Corporate Planning), assisted by Mr A. K. Shahi and his legal team, held a detailed conference with Mr Soli Sorabjee, the then-Attorney General for India for his guidance in seeking a review of the Air India judgement.

Mr Shahi, who headed SAIL's legal team worked hard and with the involvement of the top leading lawyers of the country, got the judgement referred to the Constitution Bench which finally overruled the Air India judgement, in August 2001. The prompt and timely action by SAIL averted the absorption of several thousands of contract workers in SAIL at a time when it was implementing its manpower reduction plan through the VR Scheme. The constitution Bench Judgement widely known as SAIL judgement of 2001 helped many organizations in the public and private sector to streamline their contract labour management. This initiative is remembered as SAIL's gift to Indian industries. This judgement holds to date and is relied upon in the cases pertaining to contract labour by the Supreme Court and various High Courts.

At the operational level, a number of initiatives were undertaken at SAIL for the reduction in contract manpower. For example, a reduction in contract labour was a key consideration while signing new contracts. It was kept as one of the main action points to follow for all plants and units and monitored at the highest level. Registration of contractors, proper documentation and computerization was ensured for close monitoring and control of the number of contracts and contract labours. A number of voluntary separation schemes were introduced at Raw Materials Division Mines and Bhilai Steel Plant Mines for a reduction in contract labour strength. Also, a massive communication exercise was conducted to point out the importance of reduction in contract labour, particularly in view of the Supreme Court judgement in the case of Air India and subsequent judgement in the case of the National Waterfront Union.

Reduction of the Central Industrial Security Force (CISF) was another area of focus for expenditure rationalization. Over the years, expenditure on CISF personnel engaged at many SAIL plants/units for providing security cover to vital installations had increased significantly. This was particularly true after implementation of the recommendations of the Fifth Pay Commission, after which their wage bill had gone up sharply. Several measures were taken up to reduce expenditure on account of deployment of CISF, in consultation with concerned ministries.

Rationalization of CISF strength was complemented with the implementation of various advanced security and surveillance measures such as joint surveys conducted with CISF at plants/units to reassess the requirements, closure of some of the stockyards, replacement of the CISF with DGR sponsored security agencies, introduction of Dog Squad, use of Wireless/Walkie-Talkie/VHF Sets by CISF for better coordination and security, use of Electronic Surveillance Systems, modern gadgets like CCTV, intrusion alarm system and Electronic Sensors and reduction in the number of followers (Drivers, Cobblers, Washermen, Barbers, Cooks etc.). By making use of the above initiatives it became possible to reduce the CISF strength to the tune of 25 per cent with 1999 as the reference year.

All the above measures were taken to restrict expenditure on contract labour in addition to those for rightsizing regular manpower

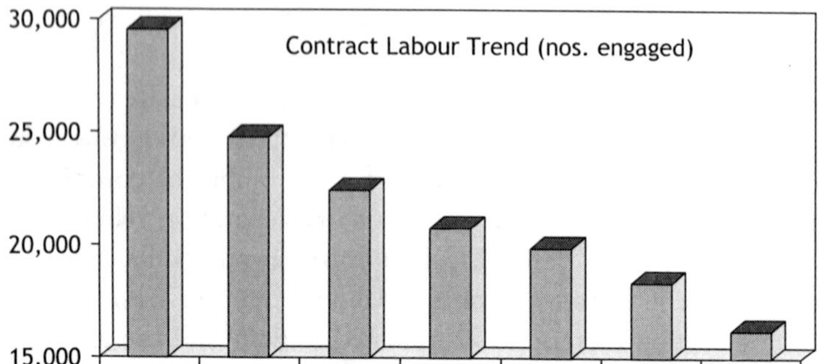

	1998	1999	2000	2001	2002	2003	2004
■Cont. Lab.	29,565	24,812	22,494	20,789	19,901	18,385	16,270

provided a great relief in reducing the fixed recurring expenditure for the company.

The MoU signed with the Government of India for financial and business restructuring in the organization module also had milestones other than manpower rightsizing. Timelines were set in the MoU for redesigning and implementing key corporate processes, viz., incentive structure, promotion policy, change from a functional to a business unit structure etc.

HR Policy Initiatives

It was evident that in order to harmonise the talent and energy of the employees with the company's objectives new people-oriented strategies needed to evolve. The challenge before the HR function therefore was how to transition to a leaner organization while retaining a committed workforce. Transitioning to a slim organization also required enablers in the form of skill enhancement and multi-skilling of the workforce to enable an effective unit-wise and department-wise downsizing.

Performance Systems

Redesigning systems and processes for personnel evaluation, reward and promotions across all levels was a major task under the organization module. The promotion policy in practice had been designed about a decade ago. As promotions, by and large, were delinked from vacancies, over time it had led to a top-heavy organization with bulges at certain levels, combined with dilution and fragmentation of roles, responsibility and accountability.

It was decided to modify the promotion policy so that the growth of personnel did not dilute the structure. Promotions were to be based on merit and optimally spaced to avoid bulges. The executive levels below Head of Works were to be restricted to a maximum of four to five. Intra- and inter-plant rotation on promotions beyond certain levels and the introduction of qualification bars were some other features of the new promotion policy. It was decided to implement the new promotion policy after discussions at various forums, for which a time frame of six months was fixed.

Simultaneously, significant changes/amendments were put in place in SAIL's personnel policy. New policies were introduced covering executive appraisal system, E0 (a grade of executives in SAIL) policy, cluster-based non-executive promotion policy, etc.

The measures to right-size manpower needed policy initiatives to boost manpower productivity. These initiatives were in the form of flexible working arrangements, elimination of unproductive work practices, reduction in contract labour and reduction in CISF manpower. Flexible working arrangements were introduced in operational areas through the gradual merger of various Lines of Promotion (LoPs) in related areas. With a thrust on providing training to workers to enhance their skills in multiple jobs in a particular work area, the need for many LoPs in these areas had decreased. An effort was made to make this initiative more effective by reviewing the non-executive cluster promotion policy and giving it a more productive shape.

Unproductive work practices needed to be eliminated for improvement in manpower productivity. SAIL plants and units did a good job in this area. Success stories like redeployment of manpower from one section/department to another, reduction of crew size for a particular job, reducing the general trend of late-coming at a particular plant, mine, etc., helped in achieving productivity gains. Actions were also taken for better utilization of manpower through the elimination of shift start delays and by ensuring that various maintenance and operation crew took up additional jobs by better time management, thereby enabling employees to attend to non-scheduled jobs, etc.

At the steel plants, a plethora of measures such as ensuring strict adherence to office timings through the regular circulation of office communication and uniform application to encourage punctuality, counselling and disciplining habitual absentees, timely availability of canteen vans, increased use of mobile serving trolleys and staggering tea break timings, regulating exit/entry through a timely renewal of identity card, adherence to exit/entry timing, regular checking and observing discipline etc, contributed to improved manpower productivity and better utilization of manpower. At the stockyards, steps to regulate entry time of trucks/trailers, on-time delivery etc., helped improve customer servicing and avoid delays.

Training and Development

SAIL had been a pioneer for a number of HRD interventions and over the years, some of its personnel policies of SAIL had become industry benchmarks, followed by a large number of companies. 'To train is costly; but not to train is costlier', had been the dictum in SAIL for several years and its training and development system was recognized amongst the best in the country.

However, it was realized later that by its emphasis on managerial training, SAIL had neglected the development of technical training. This need was subsequently addressed to make HRD interventions more effective. Multi-skilling was taken up at almost all levels of operations to provide more flexibility in work practices and to carry out specific jobs utilizing fewer people. Awareness about best practices of different plants was encouraged and effort made to increase the

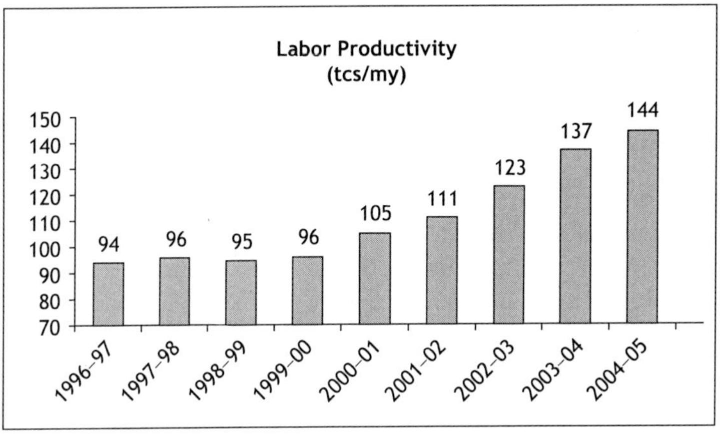

spread of operational excellence, which otherwise would have remained confined to certain pockets.

On the development aspect of human resources, Mr S. N. Upadhayay, General Manager (P&A), DSP, observed that the new age organizations were built upon greater awareness and competence of employees. To achieve this, strategies such as shop floor group interactions, technology awareness programmes and mass communication exercise called 'Rupantaran' were used at DSP. Several problem-solving exercises were taken up and successfully conducted such as fall in the ladle temperature, seepage in the concrete structures, delay analysis in the capital repair of blooming and billet mill, etc.

The effectiveness of measures to boost manpower productivity resulted in the average manpower productivity of the four main plants increasing from 94 tonnes of crude steel/man year in 1995–1996 to a level of 144 tonnes of crude steel/man year by 2004–2005.

There was a change in the service condition of the central government employees in 1998, when the Government of India accepted the recommendation of the Fifth Pay Commission to increase the age of central government employees from 58 to 60 years. In line with the decision of the Government of India, the age of superannuation for SAIL employees was also revised to 60 years.

Incentives, Rewards and Punishment

Incentives set up for employees in the plants and the marketing provided one of the levers to direct efforts of the workforce on those activities, which were most productive. The earliest incentive schemes were designed to achieve rated capacity production and were based on monthly production rates for different departments. Subsequently, focus shifted from production to productivity and weekly group-based motivational schemes were introduced in which techno-economic or operating efficiency parameters were given around 1/3rd of the weight-age. However, due to mixed outcomes, many departments switched back to production-based incentives/rewards schemes.

The incentive/rewards scheme operational at the plants at the time of SAIL's restructuring program had the following design.

Parameters for Incentives/Rewards	*Production (in %)*	*Cost (in %)*	*Quality (in %)*
Executives	40	30	30
Non-executives	50	25	25

Mr Alok Sahay who was associated in various capacities with Steel Executives Federation of India, a representative body representing officers of Public Sector Steel Industry, i.e., SAIL, RINL, NINL and MECON and held the positions of General Secretary and Chairman SEFI, recalled the innovative practices put in place to incentivize marketing personnel on the field. 'SAIL due to the global steel recession started having trouble in meeting the cash requirement. By 1998, we were not sure how to deal with this situation. I suggested to Mr Pande in January 1998 that a quarterly reward, uniform across CMO against cash collection will trigger the desired focus. He readily agreed. A target was set for the quarter. The whole of CMO, including messengers, would take daily updates on the cash situation. This pushed all to increase sales. 'We created a kind of group synergy that was never witnessed. Mr Pande could adopt any good suggestion and had a vision to see the result,' Alok Sahay added.

Subsequently, SAIL's marketing wing CMO went ahead and implemented a redesigned scheme in 2000–2001, based mainly on relevant parameters such as turnover, net sales realization, per tonne handling cost and cash collection; which started yielding positive results.

There was a great need to redesign the incentive/reward scheme in the works area where the higher weight associated with production resulted in a tendency to produce high even at the cost of inventory building without bothering about the market demand. Hence, as a part of the restructuring plan, SAIL with effect from 1 June 2001, implemented a redesigned incentive scheme, which gave higher weight to cost, quality and productivity and also brought in profitability as a distinct parameter for earning incentives and rewards.

Redesigned Incentive/Reward Scheme at Works

Parameters	*Executive (in %)*	*Non-Executive (in %)*
Production	40	50
Cost	17.5	15
Quality	17.5	15
Profitability	25	20

The Managerial Reward scheme applicable to senior/top executives also included parameters like 'product-mix' and 'order fulfilment' to encourage new product development which had linkages both with plants as well as marketing. The redesign of the incentive/reward scheme was further expanded to cover the raw materials area, where the reward schemes for mines encourage the availability of quality raw material.

To identify and implement levers for enhancing organizational performance, a workshop was held in October 2001, where nine thrust areas for enhancing organizational performance were identified. Inter-plant/unit task forces were constituted to work on each of the areas, one of which was strengthening the system of accountability and improving focus on performance orientation through a well-defined reward and punishment (R&P) system.

The taskforce on this issue was headed by the Executive Director (P&A), Corporate Office. The Task Force made a series of recommendations for effective implementation of the R&P system by bringing accountability through the implementation of well-defined qualitative/quantitative performance standards in key performance areas (KPAs), tasks and targets.

The salient features of the new system were as follows. KPAs, tasks and targets were to be identified and finalized for each executive by the second week of March by the Heads of Departments and communicated to the HR department by 31 March. A compilation of tasks and targets was to be submitted to respective General Managers (GM)/ Executive Directors (ED) and the Head of Personnel (HoP). Key performance was to be set for Annual Production Plan (APP), customer focus, cost reduction, quality, safety, profitability, organizational thrust area, etc. Each plant/unit was to constitute a personnel/line team/internal resource person to facilitate identification of tasks and targets wherever necessary. The whole exercise was to be monitored by respective GMs/EDs and Chief Executives. The tasks and targets and performance were to be reviewed after six months and monitored by the Heads of Departments. Appraisal and mid-term review were to be done on identified KPAs/tasks/targets with respect to time-frame, six-monthly progress, etc.

For rewarding exemplary performance, several measures were suggested, which included strengthening of cash reward systems with the provision of specific funds for the purpose, increased use of letters of appreciation, providing selection committee with appreciation letters, commendations, etc. Clearly spelling out of criteria for the outstanding performance of the department/executive/non-executive/group, this was to be a key consideration in the services at the time of promotion and was also for encouraging/facilitating employees to participate in QCs/Suggestions/Vishwakarma/Shram award schemes.

If KPAs/tasks/targets were not met, punishment was to be given. Any negligence of duty/mal-operation, misconduct, etc., was to be immediately acted upon as per Conduct and Appeal/Standing Orders (CDA rules). Action against erring employees was to be taken immediately, viz., letter of reprimand and advisory letters in case of failure to achieve agreed targets on quantity, quality, product-mix, techno-economic factors, cost control targets, etc. Monitoring of disciplinary cases was to be done every month by Chief Executives.

A booklet was prepared with the title 'Accountability for Managers through Identification of KPAs, Tasks and targets, Monitoring, Implementation and Review: A guide-Book' and circulated to help finalize the KPAs, tasks and targets.

Succession Planning

The HR development and management systems and practices of SAIL helped not only in sustaining organizational excellence but also equipped it with means to overcome challenging times. An indication of the effectiveness of this system was that the top positions in SAIL, including Board-level positions, were resourced almost entirely through internal candidates. Additionally, almost all top PSUs in the country resourced their managerial cadre through executives developed in SAIL. Also, all companies in the steel sector that came up post liberalization accessed their managerial and technical cadre from SAIL.

However, the need for a change had come. Over the years, the systems lost their credibility as they became outdated and were no longer in tune with the organizational requirements. This inadequacy was felt most strongly in the area of succession planning for key positions in top levels of the management. To overcome this, the company developed a well-defined structure for key positions, following which, the organization structure with Executive Director positions were finalized and notified in 2001. A mechanism was also developed for succession planning for key positions. Also, to prepare the managers for senior positions, an inter-functional/inter-unit rotation system was put in place.

Communication and Feedback

The company's objectives and goals as well as priority and thrust areas remain mere concepts unless communicated to each employee in the organization. To accomplish it, a communication drive was undertaken, by posting resource persons and teams at unit/department/shop levels with the responsibility of creating awareness among the workers and gaining feedback. Besides, structured weekly meetings with the team leaders, regular meetings with heads of personnel, field visits of SAIL's top-level executives to various plants/units and regular meetings with national trade union leaders, succeeded in establishing a framework for meaningful agenda setting, planning and course correction from time to time. This process helped in creating greater effectiveness of cross-functional teams and a better appreciation of the company's overall objectives.

At Durgapur Steel Plant a unique platform was devised for the resolution of people-related issues and for facilitating the change process by the participation of labour unions. The three major unions operating in DSP at that time—HSEU (CITU), HSWU (INTUC) and DSSU (AITUC), were brought together on a common platform called forum unions. The forum unions acted as workers representatives and helped in a joint effort to arrive at a consensus to resolve the key people related issues. Transferring the contentious issue to the common platform eliminated the incidence of problems taking an unhealthy turn on the shop-floor.

It would be fitting to end the section with a recollection of Sanjay Kumar and Dinesh Likhi from the Business Planning department of SAIL, who had gone to attend a workshop organized by the Department of Public Enterprises (DPE) and Standing Committee on Public Enterprises (SCOPE) at Mumbai in 2001. The workshop was attended by about 20 to 30 Central Public Sector Enterprises. In the course of the workshop, Kumar and Likhi presented SAIL's Turnaround Plan and its implementation to the participants and cautioned that it was a work in progress and the results would be revealed only in due course. At the end of the presentation, an HR manager from MTNL approached the SAIL team and said that SAIL's initiatives in HR engagement were a revelation. 'Suffering similar affliction, SAIL has moved so much ahead compared to other PSUs,' she noted.

CHAPTER 10

In the Interest of Employees

The Turnaround Plan had several interventions, which had a direct bearing on the fortunes of employees, viz., spinning off the non-core assets into JVs, hiving off the loss-making special steel plants, a steep reduction in manpower strength and contract labour, doing away with the restrictive practices, etc.

Furthermore, given the financial situation of the company, there was the curtailment of numerous benefits and perks enjoyed by the employees. Accounting for annualized savings of around ₹170 crore, these austerity measures covered deferment of LTC/LLTC (effective from December 1998), complete stoppage of leave encashment, no payment towards ad-hoc adjustable advance, higher rates for the subsidized services in townships and closure of unviable schools in the townships.

When the recommendations for the Turnaround Plan were communicated to the company at large, there was an expected backlash from the trade unions. Posters were put up by the Centre of Indian Trade Unions (CITU) at SAIL's central marketing office saying that the McKinsey report was meant not for the revival or survival of SAIL but its burial. Hiving off Salem Steel Plant (SSP) in Tamil Nadu, Visvesvaraya Iron and Steel Plant (VISL) in Karnataka and Alloy Steels Plant (ASP) at Durgapur in West Bengal were major issues for the employees engaged in these units. There was resistance even to hiving off power plants to a subsidiary company, with SAIL as the major partner. At SSP, all the TUs had joined hands to form a 'Save Salem Steel Committee' and observed a day's token strike demanding investment in SSP by SAIL, rather than by a private partner. Though TUs had no objection to voluntary retirements, they were worried that employment opportunities were shrinking in the steel industry.

Employee engagement, therefore, posed the single biggest challenge in implementing the turnaround initiatives. A supporting factor in the endeavour to win the trust of the employees was the structure for managing the IR, which evolved in SAIL over many years.

Industrial Relations

Responsibility for maintaining a peaceful, harmonious and productive IR climate lay with dedicated groups of personnel, at the plants/units as well as at the Corporate Office, created for the purpose. The corporate group regularly monitored the overall IR scenario at all SAIL plants/units, besides maintaining close liaison with various statutory and government agencies. At the plants, a team of personnel officers at each shop floor worked to maintain a sound and peaceful IR situation by remaining in constant touch with the employees, enforcing discipline in an unbiased manner, being sensitive to employees' grievances, clarifying their doubts, keeping management informed of any developments and taking suitable proactive actions to prevent any breakdown of the IR machinery.

Responsible trade unionism and a responsive management were the pillars of industrial harmony. SAIL had more than 250 registered unions functioning at its plants/units at the time of restructuring. Despite the multiplicity of unions, a pattern of bargaining had evolved over the years and a recognized union or a forum of bargaining came to exist in each plant/unit. Negotiations, discussions and collective bargaining on employee-related matters took place only with the recognized unions or with the forum unions at the SAIL plants.

By careful nurturing over the years, the company had fostered a bipartite culture. The experience of workers' participation in decision-making was very rich, fruitful and rewarding. Both employees and the management showed a high level of maturity, mutual understanding and active cooperation on all organizational issues and a tradition of resolving conflicts through discussions across the table was established.

The system in the steel plants operated at both formal (committees for major employee-related areas) and informal levels. In the latter, workers' participation in decision-making operated through Quality Circles, Suggestions Scheme, Shop Improvement Groups and direct contribution of employees to production and productivity at the shop floors. These activities enabled harnessing creative talents of individual employees and groups, which received the highest levels of recognition in the country like the PM's Shram awards. Other significant awards being received by workers included the Vishvakarma Award instituted by the Labour Ministry, INSAAN National Award for Suggestion Scheme, National Award on Performance of Quality Circles, etc.

Gradually it was realized in the organization that intervention of external agencies such as the government or judiciary should come only after the self-regulating internal institutions failed to resolve the issues. This understanding brought about a change in the thinking of the unions and management. In spite of differences which invariably cropped up on several issues, both sides agreed to sort out their problems across the table.

Most of the vital collective bargaining issues, including wages and other economic issues at SAIL were dealt with by industry-level consultative machinery, called the National Joint Committee for the Steel Industry (NJCS). The NJCS, comprising employers, central trade unions and the plant level unions, was set up way back in 1969 and was a standing committee. It not only finalized the revision of wages and allowances over a period of five years or more but also involved itself in continuously monitoring the implementation process. All decisions in the committee were by consensus. The long-term settlement of wages and allied issues at the industry level enabled the parties to concentrate on economically productive issues at the plant level.

The Apex Level Consultative machinery dealing with issues pertaining to Executives' salary revision and its implementation was Steel Executive Federation of India (SAIL-SEFI) forum. These Apex Level consultative committees also deliberated on matters pertaining to and steps to be taken for an increase in production, productivity, improvement in quality, reduction of cost and wastages, etc.

Wage Revision Negotiations

A wage revision for the employees had become due on 1 January 1997, after the expiry of the 1992 wage agreement, which covered a period of five years up to 31 December 1996. After receipt of the charter of demands submitted by the workers' representatives for revision of wages and related issues, several rounds of discussion were held at NJCS Forum.

The executives' salary revision was also due from 1 January 1997. They had persistently raised the issue in several consultative meetings. However, due to the difficult financial position of the company, there was a delay in the wage/salary revision.

The Government of India had, in the meantime through the Department of Public Enterprises, issued a directive to make the wage/salary revision henceforth for a period of ten instead of five years.

Due to the delay in wage revision, based on the demand by the workers' representatives, workers in June 1998 were paid varying amounts as ad hoc adjustable advance and also monthly ad hoc adjustable advance from June 1999 onwards, which were to be adjusted against wage revision.

After obtaining approval from the SAIL Board of Directors on 30 January 2001, the proposal for the salary revision for executives was sent to the MOS for approval of the government. However, the approval of the government was taking time, as the MOS consulted concerned ministries on the issue. SAIL's proposal at this critical juncture received timely support, when Mr A. K. Rath, then Joint Secretary DPE, who subsequently became Secretary to the Government of India, recommended in favour of wage revision. Mr Rath was also supportive in another critical area when he recommended the continuation of delegations that SAIL enjoyed under 'Navratna', despite its weak financial performance.

Recalling those times, the then ED (P&A), G Upadhyayaya, reminisced, 'I had joined SAIL, Corporate Office at Delhi on transfer from Bhilai Steel Plant as Executive Director (P&A). While coming to join the office in April 2001, I was surprised to see that the office bearers of SEFI, the association of executives, had gone on an indefinite 'dharna' in SAIL, Corporate Office with effect from 18 April 2001 on account of delay in salary revision of Executives and were demanding that the management should obtain clearance from the Government expeditiously for implementation of salary revision.'

Mr Upadhyaya who had worked at Bhilai Steel Plant knew Mr R. S. Yadav, Chairman of SEFI, who was also the President of the Officers' Association at Bhilai. As the President of the Officers Association at BSP, Mr Yadav had exhibited a very positive approach to various issues. Besides Mr Yadav, Mr Upadhayaya was also familiar with Mr S. K. Hajhra Chaudhuri, General Secretary of SEFI.

Shri Arvind Pande was unhappy with the conduct of SEFI office-bearers and expressed his anguish over the development, in his meeting with Mr Yadav. Mr Yadav said that while he appreciated the efforts of Chairman, SAIL, he wanted to draw the attention of the government for an early clearance of the proposal.

'Since 19 April 2001, I was going to the MOS to follow up with various officers for obtaining clearance of the proposal from

Government SAIL Chairman had also taken up the matter with Secretary, Ministry of Steel,' recalled Mr Upadhyaya.

In a discussion, on 25 April 2001, the SEFI office-bearers were apprised that the proposal for executive salary revision had been approved by the MOS and had been referred to the Department of Public Enterprises. It was conveyed that sincere efforts would be made to get the proposal cleared from DPE at the earliest. Thereafter, the MOS could issue a Presidential Directive on the subject, paving way for implementing the revised pay scales for executives. In view of these positive developments, SEFI Office Bearers lifted 'Dharana' on the same day and thanked Chairman, SAIL for the positive approach and promised to maintain a congenial and healthy climate in the SAIL–SEFI relationship.

The MOS issued the presidential directive on 14 June 2001 for implementation of salary revision of executives in SAIL, with the stipulations that the payment of arrears arising due to revision of pay scales for the period from 1 January 1997 to 31 December 2000 would be considered by the government only when SAIL's financial health improved.

The implementation of salary revision of executives was notified through the office order on 16 June 2001. For the purpose of pay fixation in the revised scales of pay, it was to be done notionally from 1 January 1997, with the actual payment from 1 January 2001. The revised scale of pay was to be operative till 31 December 2006. For the first time, the revision period was to cover a period of ten years, that is, 1 January 1997 to 2006 and without making arrear payment from 1 January 1997 to 31 December 2000 along with the wage revision.

NJCS the first bipartite forum of its kind was set up at the national level in 1969. After the success of this experiment, the idea was emulated and followed by other Public Sector Undertakings. Despite having varying ideologies and varying positions amongst different trade union organizations, the committee functioned in harmony and symbolized unity in diversity. A great deal of success could be attributed to (a) the accepted concept of equality amongst all members, and (b) the fact that all decisions were taken by consensus.

The contribution of Shri Gopeswar, Shri R. C. Arya, Shri Rajendra Prasad Singh from INTUC, Dr M. K. Pandhe and Shri A. Dakhi from CITU, Shri Gaya Singh and Shri Anirudh from AITUC, Dr Shanti Patel and Shri R. K. Samantrai from HMS and Shri S. K. Benjamin from the Tata Workers' Union was unparalleled for the effective functioning of the NJCS.

While the discussion on wage revision for workers was going on, the workers' representatives had divergent views on two issues: (a) the payment of arrears and (b) the coverage of IISCO employees.

Since the salary revision of Executives had been implemented through Circular dated 16 June 2001 without making arrears payments on account of revision, the workers' representatives could not press the point further and signed MoU on 1 July 2001.

While signing the MoU on 1 July 2001, the workers' representatives did not accept the exclusion of IISCO from the wage agreement. It was pointed out by them that IISCO was covered under all previous agreements including the last agreement which expired on 31 December 1996. Accordingly, they insisted that the NJCS Agreement to be arrived at with effect from 1 January 1997 should also cover IISCO. It was clarified to the workers' representatives, however, that as IISCO had been referred to BIFR there were constraints, both legal and financial in covering IISCO.

The workers' representatives desired that the question of coverage of IISCO workers be settled prior to the signing of the final memorandum of settlement. Unless this matter was resolved, they expressed their inability to sign the final memorandum of settlement. The representative of management agreed to take up the matter with the government expeditiously.

For resolving the coverage of IISCO Employees' issue the matter was discussed in a core group consisting of Shri Gopeswar, Shri Arya, Dr M. K. Pandhe, Shri Gaya Singh and Shri R. K. Samantrai. The outcome was the following clause in the final memorandum of agreement: 'The Workers' Representatives pointed out that as per previous agreements, employees of IISCO should be covered by this Agreement also since the revival package could not be finalized during last several years. However, taking into account the financial position of IISCO and in view of the fact that the revival package of IISCO has not yet been finalized, it has been mutually agreed that IISCO employees who were on the rolls of IISCO as of 31 December 2000 will be paid monthly adjustable advance at 12 per cent of their basic pay plus FDA on 31 December 1996. This monthly Adjustable Advance would be paid with effect from 1 January 2001. This advance would not be counted for any other purpose and would be adjusted against future wage revision benefits. The extension of other provisions of this agreement and payment and adjustment of Adhoc Adjustable Advance for the period 1 January 1997 to 31 December 2000 will be considered separately at the time of revival package which management agrees to submit at an early date. The other benefits enjoyed by IISCO employees before signing this agreement would continue.'

Finally, the memorandum of agreement was signed on 23 July 2001 in the presence of Minister of Steel, Shri B. K. Tripathy, Secretary, MOS, Shri A. K. Agarwal, Chairman, SAIL, Shri Arvind Pande and other Directors of SAIL. In line with the executives' salary revision, for the first time, the revision period for workers was also for ten years from 1 January 1997 to 31 December 2006, however without making arrear payment from 1 January 1997to 31 December 2000 along with wage revision.

True to the commitment of SAIL Management and the Government, the arrears for the period from 1 January 1997to 31 December 2000 were paid both to the executives and the workers in July 2004 when the SAIL had turned around and made good profits based on the steps taken in the preceding years.

Wage revision in SAIL at a time the company was under acute financial stress was no easy feat. Mr Alok Sahay, who had held different positions in SEFI, said that the credit for wage revision should go entirely to Mr Pande who was people-centric and enjoyed the implicit trust of employees.

'In July 2000, I returned after a year from Oxford. I was still in SEFI. Upon my return, I found SAILNews carried an interview of the then ED I/c (P&A) that he was highly grateful to SAIL officers who understood the company's condition and had accepted the reality of missing the pay revision. The next day, I went to meet Mr Pande very briefly. I asked him about the interview and informed him that SAIL will have to give the pay revision. He wanted to know who will give the pay revision. I said Mr Arvind Pande; he didn't say anything, as I left,' said Sahay.

He continued, 'Next day I called for a SEFI internal meeting, which was held at Durgapur. We discussed the wage revision in the internal meeting held on 23 July 2000. I suggested that we should agree to divestment of power plants through the JV route as it will be with the more efficient hands of NTPC and will generate resources. The DSP Officers Association opposed it by arguing that it meant selling family jewels. SEFI then decided to go for a form of protest called 'work to rule' which basically meant that the officers would not partake in any work in addition to that provided under the rules. I was convinced that we were being unfair to the Chairman who was favourable to wage revision but was helpless as the NTPC team that visited Rourkela for due diligence was attacked. All this had resulted in a situation where SAIL had no surplus cash for the pay revision.'

Alok Sahay added, 'A meeting of one representative from each unit was called by Chairman, SAIL on 8 August 2000 to resolve the 'work to rule' call of SEFI. SEFI office bearers demanded pay revision to stop their work to rule call and Chairman mentioned that if SEFI ensured smooth due diligence of power plants, he would immediately agree for the pay revision. Finally, when SEFI office bearers kept going round and round, I intervened and assured the Chairman that we would ensure safe due diligence and that he could organize for the same. Chairman immediately committed for the pay revision.'

'Interestingly, he wanted SEFI to also talk to Union Leaders. We did that the very next day and went to meet Dr Pandhe of CITU. With help of Mr Tapan Sen, we could convince Dr Pandhe. We finally got pay revision within a year. This changed the morale of the entire workforce and created a sense of trust in SAIL management. Mr Pande knew that people were the strength of the organization. SAIL came back in black within a few years,' concluded Sahay.

The Age for Superannuation

While approving the restructuring package for SAIL, some of the Government agencies wanted the age of superannuation at SAIL to be rolled back from 60 to 58 years. This point had been raised while according approval to SAIL's restructuring package in 2000 and it came again when SAIL's performance was reviewed by the Committee of Secretaries in 2002.

The issue was analysed at SAIL, and it was concluded that it may not be in the best interest of the company. The total number of employees above 58 years on 1 April 2002 numbered to around 8,000. In case the superannuation age was reduced to 58 years, it would have resulted in an immediate cash outflow of around ₹300 crore on account of gratuity, earned leave and half pay leave. This amount was over and above expenditure towards the other terminal benefits. Further, in case of separation through VRS, there were savings for a longer period as about 30 per cent of the total emolument for the employee opting for VRS need not be paid.

Other than the financial numbers, there were other reasons that made the roll-back a difficult decision at SAIL. The roll-back of the age of superannuation was likely to be resisted by employees, trade unions and officers associations, resulting in an IR problem. Also, it would have been a de-motivator for employees. At the organizational level, the roll-back would have resulted in a vacuum in the top management structure of the organization—especially at the level of general managers and executive directors where about 40 per cent and 55 per cent of the executives would have separated immediately. A lack of continuity at such senior positions did not appear prudent at a time when the company was working towards accomplishing stiff targets in the operational and business parameters. Sudden reduction in the superannuation age would also have resulted in the separation of skilled and experienced employees in key operating areas such as machine operators, melters, smelters, certified boiler operators, high-pressure welders, etc., which would have impacted the operations of manufacturing plants and mines. Further, recruitment for some of the key positions would also have upset the manpower reduction plan of SAIL.

Further, the superannuation age in SAIL was revised upwards in May 1998. Since then, around 3,000 fresh employees had joined SAIL for whom the age of retirement as per the service terms was 60 years. The change of superannuation age for other employees would have resulted in carrying two sets of employees with attendant complexity. Finally, in view of the difficult financial situation faced by the company SAIL had already taken up several austerity measures, which resulted in a reduction of perks and facilities to its employees such as stoppage of leave encashment, cancellation of LTC/LLTC, stoppage of all loans and advances, discontinuation of recoverable advances against bonus, non-payment of arrears of wage revision, etc.

Given the above complexities, it was decided by the company to use a judicious mix of VRS and natural separations to reach manpower rightsizing targets, then rollback the age for superannuation.

Alok Sahay recollected an anecdote related to the age of superannuation, 'In 1998, when Central Government extended retirement age from 58 to 60, SAIL Board in May 1998, also decided to extend the age of retirement which was communicated during the Chief Executives meeting to all CEOs. It was also decided parallelly to withhold all promotions for two years. I was Chairman SEFI and I felt this was bound to create a major upheaval among the entire executive collective. I requested Mr Pande for a meeting with SEFI. We presented our perspective that the company gives promotion only to a small percentage of total eligible executives. By announcing nil promotion, 100 per cent of executives would be demoralized. If promotions continued, though in small numbers, even those who were not promoted would have hope of future progress. Much to the dismay of Personal Directorate, Mr Pande reversed the decision of withholding promotions there and then.'

Own Your House Scheme

At a time when SAIL was in the midst of responding to the challenges posed in the divestment of loss-making units, an interesting opportunity to improve the liquidity position came from an area not conceived in the original restructuring plan. Lying outside the arena of the 'Turnaround and Transformation Plan', monetization of the company houses had a linkage with the restructuring plan and also a strategic relevance beyond the immediate future.

To keep the morale of the employees high despite financial constraints, the SAIL Board approved and implemented wage revision for the company in the year 2001. The increased wages, along with the VRS already in place under which around 10,000 separations were targeted every year required substantial cash outgo.

During an internal brainstorming session convened by SAIL Chairman, all avenues of enhancing cash generation for the company were explored afresh. As an outcome of the meeting, flats and houses in the steel townships of SAIL were identified as assets, which could be monetized for cash generation for sustaining operations.

SAIL's steel townships were well planned and equipped with good civic infrastructures such as wide roads, parks, well-planned shopping complex and civic amenities for education and health services and were a favoured location for judges and bureaucrats amongst others to reside in.

'Own Your House' in SAIL Steel Townships

The steel plants at Bhilai, Rourkela, Durgapur and Bokaro, set up during the fifties and sixties came up mostly in the tribal areas, had no urban space in the vicinity of the steel plants for the employees to live in. As the workforce was very large, it became necessary to develop dedicated townships to provide employees and their families with a life a modicum of comfort. A good township was also necessary to attract well-qualified professionals and engineers required in the steel plants, setup at remote and distant locations.

SAIL's steel township at Bhilai, Bokaro, Durgapur, Rourkela, Ranchi, Salem and Bhadrawati had about 1.2 lakh apartments and houses spread across the steel cities. Over the years steel townships developed in a manner so as to have no dearth of living space in the surrounding areas. Also, in due course SAIL employees developed co-operative housing societies or their own houses around the steel townships. The company's house allotment rule did not make such employees eligible for allotment of company accommodation in the steel townships.

SAIL's manpower rightsizing plan under the MoU signed with the Government of India was to reduce manpower strength from 1.6 lakh in 2000 to a level of 1.0 lakh over a period of 5 years, by a combination of VRS and natural separations. Therefore, by the end of 5 years, approximately 20,000 houses and apartments were likely to be surplus even after meeting the 100 per cent residential requirement of the employees. Unless maintained properly, such premises were likely to be encroached upon or occupied by unsolicited and locally influential and powerful people. It was also apprehended that over time, the condition of the vacant and unused premises would decay making them uninhabitable. The HEC Township at Ranchi was a living example where the company had lost control over its own township which at one time was one of the most valued assets at Ranchi.

Against this background, a new concept cropped up to lease various categories of residential flats to the employees on a long-term lease basis. The proposal was non-conventional and had never been attempted or introduced in any of the public sector enterprises. Moreover, it also required clarity from a legal perspective.

The proposal was very attractive to SAIL employees who had lived in the steel townships for several years but could never imagine having their own house within the township. However, as the idea had originated outside the personnel department of the company which traditionally looked after the management of townships, the initial response to this innovative idea was only lukewarm. When the views of Managing Directors and CEOs of the steel plants were solicited, as ultimately steel townships fell in their area of control, if indeed such a scheme was to be introduced; some of them expressed their apprehension about its implementation.

The employee-friendly 'own your home scheme' was conceptualized at a time when SAIL's wage agreement was under finalization. It helped create a conducive environment for the discussions and made the trade union leaders happy and supportive. However, some MDs expressed their genuine concern from a legal perspective. What bothered them was that as the land for setting up steel plants had been acquired by the government for a public purpose, could SAIL lease the houses and flats to its employees and ex-employees who were private individuals? It was a relevant point and needed addressing before seeking approval from the SAIL Board.

The long-term lease housing scheme of SAIL was aimed primarily to improve the company's liquidity, provide beneficial use of an asset likely to be rendered idle and find favour with the employees in general. However, there was a possibility that the move would be objected to by the state governments. Hence, it was imperative for the management to move only after fortifying the concept legally.

The task, therefore, was entrusted to Mr A. K. Shahi, ED Law and the then Principal Law Officer of SAIL. A point supportive of the concept was that it aimed to shore up the revenue of the company, thereby providing it with a means to prevent from becoming sick.

Mr Shahi reasoned that this could also be construed as a public purpose, given the fact that there would have been a huge social cost were SAIL to become sick. Not only it would have had a devastating impact on the employees who would have lost their job but the economic activity dependent on the steel plant operations, both direct and indirect, would have been badly hit, besides depriving the government of taxes. It would also have been catastrophic for numerous small entrepreneurs who operated in the nearby markets and owned shops in and around the steel townships, providing livelihood to a large number of workers.

Based on the above reasoning, Mr Shahi contended that leasing of houses to its employees and the use of the lease premium to revive the company was equally a public purpose. He was also of the view that employees or ex-employees who had contributed in setting up, developing, operating and maintaining the steel plants over the last 30–40 years constituted a class by themselves and could not be compared to any other private entity. However, these views needed to be supported and confirmed by the acknowledged legal professionals.

Looking into the importance of the matter, the opinion of eminent Senior Counsels Mr Harish Salve, Mr Ashwani Kumar and others was sought on the issue. All of them supported the reasoning evolved at SAIL and dispelled the concern that such a move would be contrary to public purpose.

Mr Salve was of the firm view that public purpose is not static but a dynamic concept which changes with time. When the steel plants were being set up, the public purpose was to acquire the land for the construction of the steel plants. Subsequently, the public purpose was to operate and maintain the steel plants. When the company was facing a serious financial crisis and there was a recession in the global markets, any step including leasing of houses and using the premia so received for the revival of the company was a bona fide public purpose. Mr Ashwani Kumar endorsed the opinion of Mr Salve. Both gave their written opinion on the subject. Mr P. Chidambaram, Senior Legal Counsel, was also consulted who affirmed the view of Mr Salve and Mr Kumar.

There were no problems anticipated in the case of Durgapur Steel Plant in West Bengal and Rourkela Steel Plant in Odisha, where the state governments were supportive. However, there were some apprehensions regarding Bokaro and Bhilai Steel Plants located in the states of Jharkhand and Chhattisgarh, respectively.

In view of the concerns raised and to ward off any future embarrassment, Mr Shahi met and briefed the Advocate Generals of the states of Jharkhand and Chhattisgarh. He impressed upon them that the scheme was in furtherance to the interest of the states and the employees of SAIL's steel plants. The Advocate Generals of the two states were also apprised of the opinions of the leading senior counsels of the Supreme Court on the subject.

Armed with the legal opinions and in view of the associated benefits, the scheme for long-term housing lease was placed before the SAIL Board and after their obtaining approval rolled across SAIL Plants. Mr Shahi was confident that in the event of any court case on the issue, there was enough merit to defend the scheme.

'Own Your House Scheme' was widely welcomed by the employees, trade unions and officers' associations. The scheme was designed in such a manner so as to find acceptance at each of the plants and at the same time not to create any inconvenience for the working employees and their families. It was important that SAIL received money from the long-term leasing scheme without any delay. To ensure its smooth implementation, a separate outfit was created in the corporate office and in each of the steel plants where the scheme was to be rolled out. Nodal officers in the plants and at the corporate office were identified with full responsibility and accountability for implementing the scheme. Some plants suggested creating a separate zone or sector for leasing the flats and houses, however, getting houses and flats vacated immediately was neither practical nor feasible.

To design the scheme within the given timeframe, discussions were held in the groups formed at the corporate office and in the plants. SAIL had clear title and leases over lands under its possession at Bhilai,

Durgapur and Rourkela. However, although the steel plant had been operational for 30 years and the company in complete possession of land handed over by the state government, Bokaro Steel Plant possessed neither the conveyance deed nor the lease deed executed by the state government despite paying the compensation amount in full.

To assess lease premium and the rent at each of the steel cities which had different types of houses and flats, HDFC was appointed as the valuer. Also, in order to facilitate quicker settlement, employees who were ready to opt for VRS were allowed to avail set-off towards the lease premium against the amount to be received from the company for the VRS. For the other employees/ex-employees opting for long-term lease, SAIL arranged services of banks for 'on the spot' availability of home loans. SAIL also provided the required comfort to the lending banks at Bokaro where there was a lack of clarity on ownership over the land.

The 'Own your House Scheme' was well designed and its implementation did not face any hurdle thereby ensuring a quick receipt of the lease premia. Entitlement for long-term lease of flats and houses were based on the seniority and length of service of the employees. The existing occupants of the flats/houses who had opted for the long-term lease were kept at the top of the list for entitled employees and were required to do only the paperwork as no shifting was required. Next in the hierarchy were the employees working in the plant. Employees working in a plant but opting for a flat in another plant had a lower priority.

An attendant benefit flowing from the scheme was that it enabled the steel plants to reduce their expenditure in maintaining the leased flats. The scheme for long-term lease continued to operate till SAIL's financial position became sound, after which it was discontinued. SAIL's total receipt under the scheme was more than ₹400 crore.

The long-term lease scheme benefited SAIL and its employees in several ways. It was a win-win situation for all stakeholders. The company could access an additional revenue stream when its need was most felt and at the same time, its employees got a house/flat in a steel township having all amenities, which they could enjoy even after their superannuation.

On a visit to steel townships of SAIL today one can observe certain flats/houses better maintained than the rest. These after a reflection, are the flats/houses taken under 'Own your house scheme'. It is no gainsaying that with a little care and attention of the local Town Management Departments of the steel plants the appearance of the townships can be improved.

There have been some unintended consequences of the scheme. Some long-term lessees occupying ground floor flats have built compound walls of their own choices and design. Others have added one or two additional rooms and bathrooms in an unauthorized manner with the usual alibi—'personal need' as justification for these unauthorized constructions. However, had the Town Administration Department been more vigilant it could have prevented such unauthorized construction to take place. Alternatively, with the approval of respective local management, an additional plan of uniform design for adding one extra room and a bathroom could have been thought of in lieu of additional premium payable to the company. For adding a boundary wall or fencing, town administration could have approved a uniform design and helped by engaging a suitable agency for construction. This would have maintained uniformity and also earned more money for SAIL.

Before concluding it would be worth mentioning that a solitary Writ Petition was filed in the Madras High Court challenging the scheme. With the homework already done, SAIL was able to defend its position effectively. The Madras High Court after examining different aspects of the matter found nothing wrong in the scheme and dismissed the Writ Petition.

SBU Structure

A task to be accomplished under the restructuring program of SAIL dealt with the implementation of an organizational structure whereby SAIL was to be divided under a long products SBU and flat products SBU.

The product-based SBUs were to be headed by SBU heads who would have been responsible for production, marketing, mines management and profits of the respective SBUs. It involved the separation of marketing and Raw Materials Division to Longs and Flats units along with a change in the Board structure and reporting relationship at the top level of the company.

A rationale for the SBU structure was that under the functional structure operated by the company no one other than the Chairman was responsible for the profits. The MDs heading the plant was looking primarily after operations and projects in their respective units. The SBU structure was expected to lead to greater synergy between the production and marketing functions and take the responsibility of profit one level lower than that of the SBU heads. As a consequence, the MDs of integrated steel plants would have ceased to be the Board members. The Raw Materials Division was also to be bifurcated with separations of the mines to organizationally integrate with flat or long SBU.

The implementation of SBU structure was split into two phases. The first phase dealt with changes in the operating level. This was implemented in the marketing function up to the level of Executive Director by separating the warehouses of SAIL from the branches and by creating product-based marketing whereby two separate groups were created for the marketing of the longs and the flats.

The second phase dealing with the Board-level changes required clearance from the government. The matter was taken up for a detailed deliberation in 2004, where it emerged that many of the pre-conditions to the SBU structure had undergone a change.

The most critical amongst these related to mines and the envisaged growth strategy. The SBU structure envisaged the decentralization of mines. However raw materials in the steel industry had gained enormous significance after the upturn in the market beginning in the second half of 2002–2003. It was, therefore, felt desirable to develop expertise in the area through a central function, especially as substantial investments were foreseen in mining. Moreover, it was recognized that there would be greater flexibility with respect to distributing the materials to plants with a centralized function.

As further implementation of SBU structure would have involved major reorganization and relocation of staff and such a shock was not warranted when the plants, the units and the mines were functioning smoothly. A decision, therefore, was taken to drop the implementation of the SBU structure.

Conclusion

What was remarkable about SAIL restructuring was that such a massive intervention could be carried out without any major labour strife. The credit for this is largely attributable to the way the company engaged with its employees and the trust employees held in the management. Mr Pande in a way personified this trust and made it a point to involve the unions and the associations at each stage to win their confidence.

Never to delay taking decisions where genuine interests of employees were involved, Mr Pande was a willing empathizer. The 1994 batch of Management Trainee (Administration) had joined SAIL on 9 October 1994 instead of September 1994 as there were issues with the Trainee Hostel. The promotion policy of the company, however, allowed the promotion of these trainees in 1998, only if they joined by 30 September 1994. When presented with the facts of the case Mr Pande instantly approved the exception and the batch got promoted in time in 1998.

The trust Mr Pande enjoyed amongst the employees enabled him to take difficult steps. One day, Mr V. S. Jain, the then Director (Finance) called Alok Sahay, President SEFI in the presence of

Mr Arvind Pande and showed him the Company's Balance Sheet. Mr Jain urged on behalf of the Chairman that if SEFI agreed to give up Leave Encashment as a prerequisite, it would save SAIL from getting declared a sick company. He also mentioned that the next pay revision can come only if SAIL avoided getting declared a sick company. 'Considering the situation, I agreed as I was sure Mr Pande would never betray our faith,' said Sahay. Mr Pande could then persuade the unions also to agree.

CHAPTER 11

Perspective from the Units

The RSP Challenge

SAIL restructuring was akin to a war within which each of its steel plants engaged in their own battles. The integrated steel plants, over the years, had grown their own histories, cultures and traditions. Differentiated on the basis of product-mix, the scale of operations and by the stage of modernization, the four integrated steel plants of SAIL faced unique challenges within the company's overall turnaround and transformation process.

Some of the actions were common to all the plants. For example, as the company was cash starved, the foremost priority was to identify areas, which could be monetized. Varying from plant to plant, the inventory of ingots, semis, finished and in-process materials at the plants had grown to almost one and a half million tonnes, many times the normal level.

Overstocking of finished steel at plants resulted in overstocking in marketing yards, which were open yards. Some plants also stocked finished materials in the open to create space in the works area. Unsold material lying in the open often led to damage and downgradation of materials, resulting in a loss in realization.

The high stocks of steel also resulted in a big dilemma in production planning. In view of the high inventory, the Operations Directorate at the Corporate Office decided to reduce the annual production plan for saleable steel by almost a million tonne and make it up by the supply of the saleable steel from stocks. Since traditional planning was always for growth, SAIL had to take the government in confidence to set a lower production target. The reduced time for operations was planned to be utilized for capital repairs of the blast furnace and other units in a coordinated manner. By implementing this approach, the company was able to realize not only the money locked in the stocks, but also conserve expenses towards raw materials purchase.

In some plants, steel scrap arising surplus after the in-house melting had not been disposed of for decades. An important avenue for secondary cash generation, it was found at BSL that whenever an effort was made to sell steel scrap, the mafia took over the auction, resulting in the cancellation of the auction process. A way around, however, was found by using the e-auction system to sell steel scrap.

Amongst all integrated steel plants under SAIL, RSP posed a unique challenge. The overall investment at RSP during the modernization at an initial estimated cost of ₹3,955 crore, was much higher than the investments at DSP and BSL. With the impact of cost and time overrun during the project execution phase, the financial charges on RSP's books spiked significantly, further exacerbating the plant's abysmal physical performance. At the helm at RSP as Managing Directors during the turnaround plan period 1997 to 2004, were Mr A. K. Singh, followed by Mr R. C. Jha, and from 2002 onwards Dr Sanak Mishra.

Financial Express on 25 October 2002, reported how SAIL, which was struggling to come out of the red, was banking on the laggard RSP to improve its performance. Afflicted by poor labour productivity, RSP was acknowledged as the worst performing amongst SAIL's four integrated steel plants. The in-house prepared Turnaround and Transformation Plans had recommended RSP's divestment if its performance continued to remain unchanged.

It was at this juncture that Dr Sanak Mishra who was heading the Office of Restructuring at the corporate office and was Executive Director, Corporate Planning, was transferred to RSP as its CEO to lead its transformation.

In about two years, 2002–2004, the Rourkela Steel Plant (RSP) achieved one of the most dramatic turnarounds. What happened there was unique. While turnarounds in industry and business are not uncommon, the process through which it was achieved at Rourkela was not commonly observed. For an insight, it is worthwhile to begin with the circumstances that led the steel plant into the stranglehold and the hopeless situation it found itself in.

The Rourkela Steel Plant (RSP) was the torchbearer for the Public Sector Steel Industry in India and carried the banner of the industrial revolution in the nascent Republic of India. The construction of the steel plant, then a part of the erstwhile Hindustan Steel Limited (HSL) and subsequently a unit of the Steel Authority of India Limited (SAIL), was started during the mid fifties of the 20th century, in collaboration with a consortium of leading steel plant designers from the Federal Republic of Germany.

The units at the 1.0 MT stage were commissioned during December 1958 and the early part of 1962. To meet the additional demand for flat products in the country, it was decided to increase the capacity of the blooming and slabbing mill, hot strip mill and plate mill at RSP. Accordingly, the capacity of ingot steel was increased from 1.0 MT to 1.8 MT between the years 1965 and 1969. Besides the expansion of the capacity of the existing units, the scheme also envisaged the addition of new units like electrical sheet mill (for dynamo and transformer grade steel) and galvanizing lines (for corrugated and plain galvanized sheets). Subsequent to the expansion of the steel plant, a number of units were added to enhance the production productivity and product quality to meet the market needs. These units included spiral weld pipe plant, captive power plant-II, mechanical shop, structural and fabrication shop, heavy loco repair shop, slag granulation plant and coke ovens battery number 5.

These additional facilities made Rourkela Steel Plant one of the unique steel plants under the SAIL umbrella with a wide variety of special purpose steels. The uses of its plates in ship building and high pressure vessels, silicon steel in electrical industries, corrugated galvanized sheets for roofing including industrial roofing, pipes in the oil and gas sectors, tin plates in the packaging industries and special plates in the defence of the nation were well recognized.

In order to overcome technological obsolescence and to remain competitive, RSP went in for modernization, which was conceived in the year 1988. Phase-I of modernization focused on improving the quality of raw materials and comprised a new oxygen plant, upgradation schemes for blast furnaces, a dolomite brick plant, a cast house slag granulation plant at blast furnace-4, a raw material handling system, a coal handling plant (in coke ovens) and a power distribution system. It was completed in the year 1994.

Phase-II consisted of a new Sinter Plant, sinter plant, basic oxygen furnace and slab casting shop in SMS-II, modification of plate mill and hot strip mill and installation of slab casting shop in SMS-I. Except for Hot Strip Mill, which was completed in the year 1999, all the other areas were completed in the year 1997.

RSP had been continuously incurring losses year after year, since the nineties. While a part of this could be explained due to the overcapacity in the steel industry and the consequential decline in steel prices, there were other contributing factors that did not meet the eye and had been taken for granted.

The facilities that had been introduced during the modernization at a cost of more than ₹4,000 crores were financed with borrowings mostly from financial institutions and carried a huge burden of interest. The equipment and facilities installed in the modernization also entailed a high depreciation. The only way out for the plant was to utilize this equipment and facilities fully for generating sufficient revenue to cover the financial burden. Low capacity utilization both in the modernized units as well as the pre-existing units added to the fixed cost and contributed to the losses.

Poor equipment health that led to frequent breakdowns and interruption in production was one of the main reasons for the low capacity utilization in the plant. Fires and 'mal-operations' occurred frequently and contributed to breakdowns and production interruptions. The state of health of equipment in the critical areas such as coke ovens, blast furnaces, SMS, power plants, and other downstream areas was far from satisfactory; stifling any effort to hike up the production.

Another phenomenon visible was the general acceptance of low standards. It manifested in low efficiency and poor techno-economics which added to the production cost on one hand, and poor quality of products on the other, leading to piling up of the unsold stocks.

It appeared that a significant quantity of production was targeted to the volumes only to earn incentives, unrelated to any end-use need of the market. Also, the level of discipline in the steel plant was far below the acceptable mark, thereby making any effort to come out of the situation a difficult exercise. There was a perceptible fear among the employees due to the dominance of pressure groups, which resisted even an incremental improvement at the shop floor.

The result was that the steel plant was accumulating losses year after year. Instead of working towards improving the situation, the employees were more concerned about finding reasons that had led to the mess, and blaming everything of the past as the cause of the problem. The confidence of employees, both Executives and Non-Executives, had been shaken and no one believed that any improvement was possible. Most employees were already expecting the closure of the plant, hence morale was very low. The other problematic thing was a visible absence of any leadership throughout the organization. No one seemed to be in a position to understand the implications of this phenomenon, and Rourkela Steel Plant was incurring a loss of around ₹3 crore a day.

Experiments in Courage

It was against this background that in May 2001, Dr Sanak Mishra was given the responsibility to head the Rourkela Steel Plant as its Chief Executive, relinquishing his position as the Executive Director of Corporate Planning and Head of the Office of Restructuring.

On arriving at Rourkela, the first thing he did was to have an intensive examination of the ground realities to comprehend what actually was wrong. It became clear with some homework, that although there were some external factors common for every player in the steel industry emanating from the depressed market; there were many woes specific to the steel plant—the 'internal factors', which had nothing to do with the outside world. Low capacity utilization, poor equipment health, breakdowns, mal-operation, fires, poor techno-economics, poor quality of finished products, etc., were all the consequences of the actions of the Management and employees of the steel plant. It was, therefore, the employees who had to undo it, working hand in hand with the Management.

Recapping the situation Dr Mishra said, 'Throughout my life, I have firmly believed that the human resources are the most powerful force in taking any organization forward, even if the organization is highly technology centred. So any effort that was to be made had to have employees at the centre. Considering the industrial relations situation and a lack of employee faith in the Management, largely the creation of shop floor pressure groups, many had cautioned me on the steps to be taken where the employees were concerned. But it was clear that if things at Rourkela Steel Plant had to improve then steps were needed right away and we simply did not have the luxury of an unlimited time frame.'

Dr Mishra, added, 'I also told myself that if the steel plant had to improve its lot primarily through internal actions, then it had to be isolated and insulated from any form of interference from political masters and bureaucrats. I understood clearly that this was an onerous responsibility, which was solely mine, and I also understood that in doing so, there was a very real risk to my own position and continuance as the Chief Executive of the Steel Plant. I decided to take that risk, telling myself that if the plant had to survive and revive, that was the least I should be doing!'

'Oblivious to the words of caution of my well-wishers, then, I decided to listen to the voice of my own conviction and move on. In fact, I took the unprecedented step of visiting the shop floors in an exercise that was internal "Reaching Out", within a week of taking the charge of Rourkela Steel Plant. This was actually a clear deviation from the protocol of hierarchy, broken very consciously. My idea of doing things keeping in mind the interest of Rourkela Steel Plant was in effect aimed at engaging the attention of each and every employee in the process of revival of Rourkela Steel Plant. While my colleagues on the shop floor were somewhat surprised and taken aback seeing the Chief Executive right at the workplace, I chose to speak directly to the employees who operated machines and equipment.'

In about a month, or so, having travelled the length and breadth of the steel plant, Dr Mishra got the opportunity of meeting thousands of employees. He began by telling each group the truth regarding the prevailing state of affairs at Rourkela Steel Plant. Describing the unenviable situation before the organization in clear terms he explained that unless each employee understood and worked for the steel plant, the future could no more be taken for granted. At the same time, he welcomed them to voice their feelings about the situation. It became obvious that several people had no clue about the importance of their individual roles; many did not know how their own performance affected others and how the performance of others affected their own. Dr Mishra had a straightforward question to each section of employees, 'Are you prepared to take up the challenge for the future of the steel plant or are you going to sit and watch the situation go out of hand?'

Happily many were willing to provide an honest effort to make things better. Most of the employees found the MD's approach of speaking his heart out an unusual one and they also spoke from their heart telling, 'Give us challenges and we will achieve', and, 'Give us the resources and we will produce at record level.'

Another thing Dr Mishra did during this time was taking a god look at the critical and key positions at the Senior Management and General Manager Level; and making a complete reshuffle of many incumbents, giving them new areas for delivering results instead of continuing in departments where they had grown. These senior executives were posted with clear cut responsibility for results. Similarly, non-performers were also eased out to the sidelines, making way for potential performers in key positions. One of the purposes behind these actions was to demonstrate to the employees that there had to be a paradigm shift through visible initiatives directed towards bringing improvements.

The Ten Priorities

During his interactions with the employees, Dr Mishra took the time to make a note of different aspects of the organization, keeping in view the ultimate objective of turning around the steel plant from loss-making to a vibrant one. He introduced and energetically engaged employees in 'Ten Priorities'. To convey the seriousness of the initiatives, crack teams were formed with senior executives to monitor each one of them.

1. Employee motivation and employee pride
2. Leadership practice
3. Environmental relations and organizational change
4. Plant maintenance and equipment health
5. Small investment schemes for maintaining current operations
6. Sustained operation and consistent production
7. Strengthening secondary streams of cash generation
8. Operation and purchase cost reduction
9. Sustaining the benefits of any Improvement Projects already carried out
10. Enhancing gross margin and net sales realization

Bringing Closeness: Reducing the Distance between Minds

Dr Mishra had decided to bring about a turnaround through a mass movement that involved each and every employee of Rourkela Steel Plant; a movement that would reduce the distance between minds. One of the difficulties was that in any interaction, employees always came up with the blame game and kept pointing out the responsibility of the management to bring about improvements and its failures; besides failure of equipment performance and other shortfalls. This was a mindset that had crept in over many years of working in a casual manner and had put the Management and Managers on the defensive. It had become an accepted position that Managers would listen to allegations from the employees and it was their responsibility and the responsibility of top management for all failures.

The other thing was to blame the upstream units and downstream units besides blaming maintenance by operation and vice-versa. Moreover, most employees, be it Executives or Non-Executives, thought that they were working very hard and not getting enough reward or recognition. The interactions, therefore, were focused on all aspects other rather than how to make things better. This had to be overcome by a paradigm shift. It needed some straight talking and some courageous actions. It was of paramount importance that the employees understood that turning around the loss-making steel plant was not the sole responsibility of the Managing Director only and that each employee had to accept responsibility in his/her respective place and sphere of work.

A New Credo: Regenerating Strength with People (R-S-P)

It was against this backdrop that a string of interaction sessions was started by Dr Mishra within a few months of taking over the charge of the Rourkela Steel plant. Named Workshops for 'Sharing Concern', it involved nearly 120 employees at a time from key operational (production) departments in the beginning; and subsequently from the centralized services and maintenance departments. In each of these Workshops, 70 per cent of participants were non-executives. Dr Mishra sat through each and every workshop and set the tone with some plain talking. He explained the areas of concern, which had been identified and repeatedly reminded the participants, 'We ourselves are responsible for the situation in which the steel plant finds itself. While things were bad, improvements could not come from actions by anyone from outside or the Managing Director alone.' On the other hand, solutions to Rourkela Steel Plant's problems could come only through internal physical actions to be performed by the employees themselves on the shop floor. The deliberations, process and expected outcomes in these Workshops are shown in the chart below.

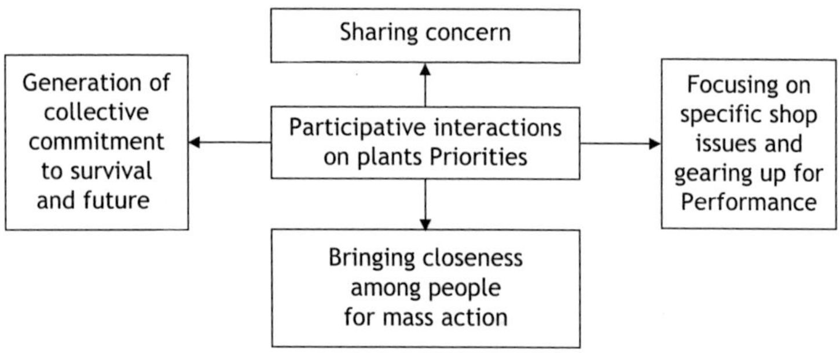

For the first time, the financial figures of the steel plant were placed before the employees who got a feel of where RSP stood financially. Although there was a downside of employees getting demoralized due to was sharing of this information, it was decided to go ahead, so that there could be a sharing of concern through this knowledge.

Components like gross margin, revenue realization, fixed cost, variable cost, contribution and net margin (or profitability), relevant to the department, were also presented and discussed in detail. Through this type of presentation, one thing was made clear: the focus had to be on 'profit-related working' and each one needed to understand whether a particular action was contributing to more cost, or, to more revenue. Accordingly, employees, a member of a collective, or, a department, had to be careful and carry out actions in a manner that there was an addition to revenue rather than cost. Mr S. C. Nayak, who at that time was GM (HRM & Power Plant) said, 'People till recently did not know from where revenue was being generated, how it was being spent, and the cash flow position. Today they are fully aware of the economics of RSP.'

Employees were encouraged to explain their understanding of the problems and what according to them could be a solution. Their views were taken seriously, but it was emphasized during the interactions that there was no use in blaming others for the faults because everyone was accountable for results. It was, therefore, necessary to sit with the people of the agency blamed, as they were also a part of us, so that the job was done in a manner that met expectations. During the Workshops, it was reiterated again and again that, 'the future of the steel plant lay in the hands of the employees themselves'. It was, therefore, important that each employee did what was expected from him/her and not what was convenient to him or her.

On several occasions when employees felt the pressure of hard work, they would talk of rewards, but Dr Mishra was prompt in conveying to them, 'No one is doing Rourkela Steel Plant a favour by working hard. And I frankly cannot tell you not to work hard. The process of reviving the Rourkela Steel Plant involves hard work like never before, and I cannot promise you anything for this hard work. But the one thing I can assure you of at the end is a sense of accomplishment. I can tell with confidence that it will be much more satisfying than any reward that you may get.'

Seeing subsequently, the impact brought about by this interaction in the plant, Mr K. S. Sokhi, GM I/c, (Services), said, 'There is a visible change in the last one year, not only in production but in RSP's work culture. The systems today are being jointly evolved, rather than being imposed.'

Because of the adverse market conditions, RSP had been operating only three out of its four blast furnaces. The plant, because of the low capacity utilization in its primary units, had evolved a system of importing slabs from other sister units to keep its finishing mills running. While low capacity utilization added to the fixed cost, the import of slabs also inflated the costs. For RSP's profitability, it had to produce slabs from its own hot metal and then convert it into finished products against firm orders.

Dr Mishra took two important decisions in the early days to counter the situation. The first was to absolutely minimize the import of slabs from sister units, and, the second was to reintroduce the four-blast-furnace operation. Since the market conditions had not improved this was a risky decision. But he decided that instead of importing slabs it was better to focus on cost reduction through capacity utilization which should result in improving profitability, the ultimate objective. This entailed putting pressure on blast furnaces and SMS, both of which at that time had a poor track record in continuous operations. At the same time, he issued clear instructions that the finishing mills shall not produce except against firm orders. He made it clear that it was better to keep the finishing units idle and carry out maintenance activities than to make steel which ultimately was not sold.

He impressed upon his colleagues that while it was the job of the Central Marketing Organization to organize orders, RSP had many unique products for which the customers were known and it was important for them to believe that the plant was capable of fulfilling their needs. A strategy of organizing customer contact was also put in place by which the requirements of quality in the market were understood and met.

Simultaneously all concerned were asked to explore ways and means to meet customer requirements in terms of quality, packaging, chemistry, etc. Innovations were encouraged in all units, right from the sinter making up to the finishing mills.

The health of blast furnace (specifically BF-3) was in very bad shape. During November 2001 when pressure on production was very high, it was decided to carry out its shell repairs in banked condition and a target of 21 days was fixed for the same. The MD did some straight-talking with the concerned agencies and those involved to achieve the result. As a consequence, for the first time in four decades, a major job at RSP was finished before time.

Side by side, the problems of frequent breakdowns and mal-operations were addressed. Dr Mishra was quick to realize that it was a people and systems interaction problem, not so much related to technicalities, as to the issue of the mind. Employees numbering 100 to 120 at a time from departments involved in these practices were called and spoken to. These employees were asked to diagnose the cause of the breakdowns and mal-operation and come out with their own suggestions for preventing them. Surprisingly, after initial heart burning they came out with solutions and some departments even took oaths to not do anything that will cause mal-operations.

To meet the challenges being built, it was essential that there was adherence to discipline throughout the organization. Also, it was essential that everyone joined in. It was made clear through disciplinary actions that those who did not take the duties at the shop floor seriously would not be tolerated. The background or level of the person ceased to matter in cases of a breach of discipline. Several executives and non-executives were proceeded against in a very transparent and fair manner to set examples of the seriousness to set things right at the steel plant.

Mr G. Jagannathan, who at that time was the ED (P&A), admitted that the communication exercise across the plant had made a big difference in the perception of employees, resulting in better industrial harmony and higher productivity. Following the MD's lead of a consistent approach, standardization was brought about even for dealing wit IR-related issues.

Initial Results of the Turnaround Strategy

Gradually the results started coming, in the beginning in trickles, but later on, gathering momentum. Monthly production and sales figures surpassed all earlier levels in almost every area. Stocks were brought down to a manageable level. Innovations enabled the smooth operation of production units even in the worst of monsoon conditions. Hot strip mill took up rolling of longer slabs for better customer satisfaction. Packaging of HR coils, cold rolled products and silicon steel reached a level that customers began to acknowledge. Employees were able to recognize the potential they and the steel plant possessed and began to speak of targeting higher levels of performance. For the first time many of the units like sinter plant, SMS-II, hot strip mill and silicon mill simultaneously performed at rated capacity giving employees tremendous confidence. Other departments also smashed their existing records and began to look for further improvements.

What had been achieved was termed by Dr Mishra as a 'reduction in the distance between the minds' of people, and a spirit of working to help each other in their respective departments. Employees began to see themselves as members of a family on a single platform with a common purpose.

'All This gave me a great deal of confidence,' said Dr Mishra, 'In fact, by now the resistance among the employees to work hard for results seemed to be significantly less. They had tasted success and felt a sense of accomplishment like never before. This led to targets that were nearly 20 per cent higher for the financial years 2002–2003 and 2003–2004.'

Engaging Large Groups for Securing the Future: The Mass Contact Exercise

With steep growth plans, there was a need to involve the entire collective in larger groups so that the combined effort could be brought about through synergy.

'We began what is unprecedented in corporate history. Starting from 1 April 2002, each Wednesday, I, along with the Executive Director (Works) interacted with 500 different employees of different levels belonging to departments cut across the steel plant, sitting at the Gopabandhu Auditorium inside the Plant premises,' recalled

Dr Mishra. Popularly known as Managing Director's weekly Mass Contact Exercise, it was regularly held, making it perhaps the longest-lasting large group intervention anywhere in the world.

The tone in these mass contact exercises was set by the MD by spelling out issues, which impacted the 'Survival and Future of Rourkela Steel Plant'. The information shared with the employees covered the priorities, achievements, performance against potential, what prevented the plant from doing better, etc. The presentations on each topic were made by non-executive employees from different shop-floors who communicated in either Oriya or Hindi. These were backed up by Departmental level discussion programmes called 'Performance Excellence Workshops' which focused on the kind of performance expected from the departments for RSP's growth targets. In both kinds of programmes the presentations were followed by interactive sessions where the idea was to enable individual employees to come out with their action plan, as to what they would like to do individually, and as members of their department, to bring about actions for achieving the steep targets.

As would be expected, the interaction programmes began with the question of low earnings in some units due to low production, which was not always the fault of workmen. People also complained of a lack of resources and lack of planning, etc.

'I took it as an opportunity to tell people that we had to address customer needs. For example, unless the pipe plant collective produced shorter lengths there would be fewer orders. Similarly, I told employees that attention to maintenance and ensuring proper maintenance was the responsibility of the department's employees as the maintenance was also under the same head of department. If they did not sit together and sort out then things could not improve. While answering and responding to suggestions of employees I made it amply clear that we should better stop the production if there is any risk to the safety of our employees, or if the health of the equipment is not up to the mark. I also emphasized that all employees would have to report in time and stay till the end of the shift so that we got continuous production and output,' narrated Dr Mishra, 'Similarly, on occasion, I informed an employee, who was trying to shirk his responsibility and pass it on to his superiors, that I did not see any difference between executives and non-executives and that we are all equally responsible for the job assigned to us.'

The positive vibrations unleashed by the initiatives in employee engagement were reciprocated by the executive association and the unions. Mr Bramha Mishra, the President of RSP Executives' Association said, 'At RSP we are seeing a definite change in the mindset. There is transparency in top management. The mass communication exercise has dispelled many distorted views in the minds of employees. People now know the priorities, survive or perish.' Acknowledging the part played by the company for employee benefit, he added, 'Despite the massive cash crunch, the company has given its employees a salary revision. It is now time for us to reciprocate. It is upon us to take RSP out of the red permanently. The task is Herculean, but the level of exuberance among the employees is very high and one sees hope.'

Similar was the sentiment expressed by Mr D. N. Panicker, General Secretary, Rourkela Shramik Sangh, RSP's recognized trade union. In an interview with the in-house magazine, SAILNews Mr Panicker said, 'We will have to go for a new work culture for the prosperity of the plant. I have been advocating this to the workers and even in the joint forums. My slogan is 'Own to earn'. Poverty multiplies problems, when benefits are cut workers are demoralized. But prosperity solves problems automatically. I tell workers to work together, channelize time and energy and utilize skills and talents to make the company prosperous so that all can share the prosperity.'

New Systems in Place

Standard operating practices were put in place for dealing with cases of indiscipline. Irrespective of their being executives or non-executives, RSP came down very heavily on each case of indiscipline by employees, sending out a clear message that those who did not respect the plant were not going to be tolerated. Exemplary punishment orders were passed to convey this.

The distinction between workers and officers was removed and each employee was responsible for the result in his area of work. While the transfer of officers for improving working was routine, for the first time, workers were transferred to other departments when required. The redeployment of employees was seen purely to meet work needs and not to satisfy pressure groups or personal preferences.

Direct reporting system was introduced to get over the wasteful practice of reporting through Zonal Time Offices, and also to give dignity to the employees who now signed 'in' and 'out' in attendance registers at their respective workplaces.

A new system of gate pass and identity cards for contract labourers and other visitors was introduced. The plant refused to issue Gate Pass to those who had a criminal background and withdrew gate pass from the existing contract labourers who were found to have a criminal background. The purpose was to protect the sanctity and security of the steel plant and its employees.

A check-out system for membership of unions was made open to all trade unions so that employees got the freedom of choice in union affiliation.

Safety standards were overhauled and reset, keeping in mind the 'Safety First of Employees', and employees without basic protective equipment were routinely turned back from work. Two-wheeler drivers without helmets were not allowed entry.

Departments were encouraged to organize campaigns like safety and environment with melas involving large groups and also rewards were given every month to the departmental collectives for achievements like zero accident, zero absenteeism, 100 per cent production performance, etc.

Results for Financial Year 2004–2005: Confirmation of the Model

The Steel Plant continued to perform at high volumes. What was significant was that the steel plant not only produced more than 1.50 million tonnes of saleable steel, but also dispatched identical quantity to the market for a record third year in a row, establishing the acceptability of RSP's products among the customers.

Mr M. Prasad, GM (Quality), mentioned, 'The quality of steel produced is absolutely first class. There is no occurrence of lamination and chemistry homogeneity, etc. The problem the inconsistency of physical tolerance has been substantially reduced.' Elaborating some measures taken to improve product quality, he added, 'For HR coils pass-through for coils up to 0.45 mm through coil box has been made mandatory, work roll changes made consistent, preventive maintenance taken up at coilers to eliminate telescopicity. RSP has become the first flat steel producer in the country to provide end protection for coils. As for plates, today 100 per cent of the plates produced are tested ultrasonically, even if not specified,' mentioned Mr Prasad.

An important feature in the steel plant's success was the operation of many of the production units at more than 100 per cent capacity utilization for months together, overcoming the problem of capacity utilization that had plagued its progress since inception. Besides this, RSP improved significantly in its techno-economic parameters with unprecedented improvements in various items like energy consumption, consumption of water, consumption of stores and spares, etc., per tonne of crude steel; besides significant improvement in the lining life of Converters in both SMS-I and SMS-II, which brought down the cost of production, thus contributing immensely to the profitability of the steel plant.

With this performance, the steel plant, which had entered the net profit made from January 2004, was able to move into a net profit for every quarter of the financial year 2004–2005 and ended the year with an astounding net profit figure of ₹1045 crore. The net profit achieved was not only the highest ever in the plant's history, but was also higher than the sum total of profit earned during all the previous years put together. The Rourkela Steel Plant, thus, had come up from a level of ₹3 crore loss per day to a level of ₹3 crore profit a day; a remarkable recovery achieved in exactly three years.

A very important aspect of this performance was the restoration of confidence in the employees, their ability to break away from the shackles of fear and low performance and a growing belief that there was no limit to their abilities once people start working together as the members of a family.

Making Rourkela Steel City 'A Place to Live and Work'

Somewhere along the line, as the Steel Plant marched ahead on a path of prosperity, the residents of Rourkela (known as 'Steel City' and by 2001, labelled as a 'Dead City'), started dreaming of renovating the town and rejuvenating life and living.

It all began with re-emphasizing the Annual Vanamahatsov, which involved schoolchildren, followed soon by a revival of Rose and Chrysanthemum shows, boating facilities and toy train in the Indira Gandhi Park, making the Annual Horticulture and Flower show more popular and several such steps.

As a starter, with a view to fighting the menace posed by plastic bags, a campaign was launched in the State in the year 2003, when nearly 14000 participants belonging to schools, colleges besides citizens, socio-cultural organizations and employees of RSP formed a human chain stretching more than 8 kilometres to create awareness and discouraging the use of plastic and polythene bags. RSP then banned the use of polythene and plastic bags in all its establishments.

The entire city was given a massive facelift, roads were given fresh carpeting, drains rebuilt, chowks were made wider in many places, all walls cleansed of graffiti, etc. Playgrounds and facilities for games and sports were revamped, attracting the sports-loving school and college students to these locations with new enthusiasm.

Rourkela then pioneered 'City Architecture in Steel' by building monuments in welded and painted steel to reinforce the commitment of the steel plant to various social purposes and the vision for the future. Some examples were: 'Water for Life' at the Water Supply Department, 'Ring of Well Being' at the Ispat General Hospital, 'Steel for Harmony' dedicated to the citizens of Rourkela at the Birsa Munda Chowk, 'Steel for Safety' at the Traffic Chowk, 'Steel for Prosperity' inaugurated by His Excellency the then President of India, 'Guru-Shishya Sampradaya' in Ispat English Medium School, etc. All these were conceived, designed, fabricated and installed from Rourkela Steel Plant's own steel by its own employees. This truly represents the creativity and enthusiasm of the RSP collective who wanted to fulfil their dream of a new prosperous Rourkela.

Corporate Social Responsibility

The Rourkela Steel Plant started some developmental activities in its peripheral villages in the 1970s. Activities like providing roads, bore wells, and some health care activities used to be carried out and managed by a section of the Town services department of RSP. The funds for these activities were allocated by SAIL under the peripheral development.

During 2003, it was decided to intensify the corporate social responsibility (CSR) programmes. A separate department was created to manage the programs and projects. In order to create a road map for the implementation of CSR activities, RSP engaged an expert agency named Society for Rural Industrialization (SRI) based in Ranchi. SRI after carrying out a detailed survey and the study of the peripheral area and the people residing there submitted a report called Shankhadhwani, which provided the direction for implementation of various developmental projects and programmes.

One of the primary suggestions in Shankhadhwani was to set up an institute, which could be the centre for planning, designing and implementation of RSP's CSR programmes and projects.

With the objective of institutionalizing the activities related to CSR by RSP, the Institute for Peripheral Development (IPD) was formed. An MoU was entered into with BAIF Development Research Foundation, Pune, to ensure continual professional inputs. One of a handful of such institutes in India, IPD is the nerve centre of RSP's drive on CSR. It is interesting to note that the above CSR programs of Rourkela came well before the 2013 CSR guidelines enacted by the Parliament of India.

CHAPTER 12

Battles within Battle

Perspective from the Plants

Each of the integrated steel plants of SAIL faced unique challenges. In some cases the competition magnified manifolds; in others, the extant efficiencies and cost of production no longer guaranteed survival. A sluggish market was common to all the steel plants, but the product-mix and manpower issues posed varying degrees of challenges.

BSL and RSP were producers of 'flat products', which had not faced much competition in the protected markets of the pre-reform era. This situation changed dramatically after the mid-1990s. Competition magnified both from domestic as well as overseas sources. DSP and BSP were predominantly long product plants—dependent on dynamics of the domestic market, although each had one flat product in its portfolio—plates in BSP and skelp in the case of DSP.

BSP had seen relatively harmonious and peaceful industrial relations over the years, a phenomenon not shared by the steel plants in the eastern states of Jharkhand, Orissa and West Bengal, where union militancy was more frequently observed.

The steel plants also differed in technology and scale of operation. BSP and BSL had a capacity of around 4 MTPA of crude steel, whereas DSP and RSP operated with a capacity of less than 2 MTPA of crude steel.

Three of the integrated steel plants, DSP, RSP and BSL, underwent modernization to address the backlog of technological obsolescence. While it provided the plants with the technical capability to compete, it posed additional challenges by way of project execution and stabilization of production from the new facilities, as well as its integration with the existing older facilities. Also, the inevitable delay in project implementation pushed up the project cost and inflated the capital-related expenses.

It needs to be reiterated that SAIL's modernization of the three of its integrated steel plants at a cost of around ₹12,650 crore was humongous. By far the biggest investment undertaken by any steel company in India in the 1990s, it put huge stress on the project management and resource mobilization capacity of the company. The megaprojects were dealt with simultaneously at three different locations, and in addition, another big project, Steckel mill was implemented and commissioned at SSP. The cost overrun of modernization was partially offset following the financial restructuring, but a big charge towards interest and depreciation persisted.

BSP and BSL were the plants under the SAIL umbrella, which remained profitable after mid 1990s. BSP remained in the black throughout the years 1997–1998 to 2003–2004, albeit with reduced profits. The same was true for BSL, which remained profitable except for 2 years, 1998–1999 and 2001–2002, but saw a sharp decline in its level of net profit.

The sharp variation in the performance across individual units resulted in an underlying current of resentment in the workforce of the profit-making plants, as they realized that their efforts were dragged down by the loss-making units. At the company level, it became clear that cross-subsidizing the loss-making units was no longer tenable, and that each of the units had to become viable and sustainable on its own.

The competitive pressures and the do-or-die situation resulted in many innovations in the processes and products across SAIL units, signalling a break from the past. It also led to a breakthrough in the organizational climate, which had existed in the past. Cost reduction took primacy in the operations as the falling price line provided no respite; and quality and customer orientation became the means of retaining and expanding on a customer base, where the customers had become very choosy.

Bhilai Steel Plant

BSP, traditionally known as the flagship steel plant for SAIL, was the winner of the coveted Prime Minister's Trophy for the best operating steel plant in India for a record number of years. Recognized as the most efficient under the SAIL umbrella, BSP's performance came under acute pressure from 1998–1999 onwards. Its profits, which had touched a record of ₹819 crore in 1995–1996, came down to ₹301 crore in 1998–1999, and in the succeeding year 1999–2000, it barely managed to keep afloat with a profit of ₹92 crore. Urgent measures were required to reverse the plant's performance. At the helm, as Managing Directors at BSP during these turbulent years, were Mr V. Gujral till the year 2000, followed by Mr B. K. Singh.

Set up with an initial crude steel capacity of 1 million tonne with Russian assistance, steel was tapped for the first time at BSP on 12 October 1959. The plant went through two stages of expansion whereby its capacity increased to 2.5 million tonnes in 1967, and then to 4 million tonnes in 1988. After completion of the 4 MTPA stage, BSP had seven blast furnaces, two SMS, of which SMS-I operated with the traditional open hearth/twin hearth route and had a crude steel capacity of 2.5 MTPA, while SMS-II was a modern shop of 1.5 MTPA of crude steel capacity equipped with LD Converters and continuous casting facilities. BSP's rolling mill complex comprised blooming mill, billet mill, wire rod mill, merchant mill, rail and heavy structural mill, and plate mill. Its product mix had bars and rods, light and heavy structurals, rails, plates and semi-finished steel in the form of blooms, billets and slabs.

The depressed steel market from the mid 1990s, led to a number of shop floor innovations at BSP. These operational improvements and in-house innovations enabled the plant to counter the challenges posed by factors external to it. Many of the changes carried out were done for the first time in India, and within SAIL many of BSP's achievements were designated as benchmarks.

Cost Reduction Drive

One such innovation was a modification carried out in the sintering plant so that the exact weight of nut coke could be mixed in the sinter. This mix of sinter with nut coke, when charged in blast furnaces, gave impressive results and became a subject of publication in the technical journals by SAIL's Research and Development Centre. Another innovation was to bring modification in coke ovens to charge 50 mm coke in the centre of blast furnaces. Also a first in India was slag splashing of treated slag with calcined dolomite in LD Converters, which increased its lining life from 350 heats to 10,000 heats. Later this practice was adopted by all steel plants in India.

Mr Suresh Pandey, who was ED (Works) at BSP and later became the MD of BSL, recollected some measures taken up at BSP, 'A deeper analysis helped us in identifying and eliminating costs related to some materials which did not merit use but were being used traditionally. One such item was the low-grade manganese ore in the Blast Furnace charge to maintain a certain percentage of manganese as demanded by the LD shop. This was in addition to the high-grade manganese ore, which was used in the LD shop. There was apprehension in the LD shop that low manganese percentage in the heat caused lance jams. During the blowing operation for processing the heat into liquid steel in the LD shop, almost all of the manganese went out as slag, which appeared a total waste of material. In a joint brainstorming between BF and LD shops, it was decided that for 15 days BF would produce metal without manganese ore addition. Since Indian iron ore contains a small percentage of manganese, the hot metal produced by BF was expected to have a small amount of manganese any way.'

'During the 15 days trial period, instances of jamming of the lances were no different than the earlier occasions. A decision hence was taken to stop manganese ore charging in the blast furnaces. A similar exercise was done by LD shop where also the use of manganese ore was discontinued. Also discontinued was the usage of calcined bauxite,' explained Mr Pandey.

Mr Pandey cited another example of ingenuity by BSP, 'An area of increasing sales margin was by minimizing rejection and enhancing the production of high contribution items. Rails for BSP were the best margin product, but production from the ingot route was leading to a higher rate of rejection. Production capacity from the continuous casting route was limited due to the limitation of the bloom casters' production capacity. Railways, on the other hand, was demanding all rails from the bloom caster route. Both the problems were overcome by converting one of the slab casters as a slab-cum-bloom caster capable of casting both slab and blooms. This was done with the in-house expertise and resources without any capital expenditure or outside help.'

Coking coal in SAIL was a key cost element in the cost of production of steel-making, not only because of its high value, but also as being an import item it required payment in foreign exchange, and any adverse fluctuation in the rate made it even more costly. Economizing on coking coal consumption was, therefore, a key thrust area in the cost reduction drive.

Further reduction in the cost of hot metal at Bhilai was brought about by increasing the blast temperature and utilizing the coal dust injection in furnaces that had the facilities but was idling for significant time due to technical problems. These systems were put back to service using in-house experts, which enabled access to low-cost heat inputs and thereby lower cost and cash savings.

Rails for Indian Railways

While there were incremental gains by way of cost reduction in various shops, the biggest breakthrough by far at BSP happened in the area of rails production. Being a primarily long products plant, Bhilai catered to the requirement of construction and the infrastructure segments. In its product offerings, it had only rails and plates as premier products. Its other products such as bars and rods and structurals had limited use in high-end applications. Plates produced in its plate mill had good acceptance in the domestic as well as export markets, but the hostile environment for international trade had narrowed its market scope drastically. Against this background, all of a sudden, the demand for rails by India railways increased by more than 100 per cent, to the tune of 7 lakh tonnes per annum, from a level of around 3.3 lakh tonnes that the plant had been supplying.

Bhilai was the sole supplier of rails to the Indian railways. A meeting, therefore, was called by the railway minister to assess the capability of BSP to supply the enhanced requirement of rails. Mr B. K. Singh, the MD of BSP, asked for two months' time to prepare the finishing side of the rail mill to augment rail production at the plant.

'Original design capacity of BSP's rail and the structural mill was 500,000 tonnes of rails and 250,000 tonnes of heavy structurals. After about a month, the Chairman Railway Board came to Bhilai to see the progress of the work and was suitably impressed. Having done the preparatory work, BSP started improving the monthly rate of production. It operated at the rate of 4 lakh tonnes per annum in the first month, 5 lakh tonnes per annum in the second and 6 lakh tonnes per annum in the third month. The production of finished rails which was 3,71,000 tonnes in 1999–2000 increased to 7,69,000 tonnes in 2002–2003 and to 8,09,000 tonnes in 2003–2004, significantly above the original design capacity!' recalled Mr B. K. Singh.

N. N. Sachitanand, reporting for *the Hindu*, wrote in the newspaper on 4 December 2003, 'The Steel Authority of India's integrated steel plant at Bhilai in Chhattisgarh is the world's largest producer of rails. With the addition of secondary refining facilities such as an

RH degasser and a ladle furnace in its SMS-II, Bhilai is now able to enhance the safety of rail travel by producing rail steel with hydrogen content below one ppm (parts per million), although Railway specification permits hydrogen in liquid steel up to 2.5 ppm. Dissolved hydrogen in steel is one of the factors contributing to the failure of rails in the long run. The RH degasser also reduces the aluminium and silicon oxide inclusions in steel to almost nil. This enhances the fatigue life of the rails.

Expressing its complete satisfaction and confidence in Bhilai rails, the Indian Railways have ordered over 7 lakh tonnes of prime rails for the current fiscal year including 2 lakh tonnes in 26-metre length. The plant's rail and structural mill is now dispatching prime UTS 90 rails in 13 and 26 metre lengths at the rate of over 60,000 tonnes of rails every month.

Bhilai has also taken up a project costing ₹350 crores to manufacture long rails of 240-metre and 260-metre lengths. Concerns of safety and economy of operations have necessitated rail companies the world over to switch to long rails with very few weld joints. The longer the length of the rail, the lesser the number of welds per kilometre length. The commuter enjoys a safe and bump-less ride and the rail company saves on track life and maintenance. Production of long rails was slated to start in late 2004 but work on the project has been so fast that production may commence four months earlier.

Bhilai has plans for enhancing the rail production facilities with the installation of walking beam furnaces and enhancement of rolled-rail length. Extensive and modern automation and control systems envisaged will further improve productivity and product quality.'

About the rails production at BSP, Mr B. K. Singh said, 'We have a long experience of rail making and we are today producing world-class quality rails with hydrogen content less than 2 ppm. Germany is the only other country which has achieved this. Bhilai has the backing of a full-fledged research unit. All this gives Bhilai a cutting edge over any competitor.'

Redundancy of the Nameplate Capacity

After a dip in profits in 1999–2000, there was a steady improvement in the performance of BSP. In 2001–2002, one of the worst years for the steel industry, all steel plants except Tata Steel and BSP made losses. So acute was the crisis that some steel companies were forced to down their shutters. It was remarkable that under such a market BSP's profits increased over the previous year, a unique distinction in India's entire steel industry.

BSP was able to improve its profitability in 2001–2002 by continuously improving its energy consumption, coke rate and other techno-economic parameters which were the best by any steel plant in the country. Despite a sluggish demand and anti-dumping measures which restricted exports, the plant was able to reorient its product-mix to the needs of domestic demand. Production of plates, bars and rounds, heavy structural, heavy blooms was regulated and a thrust given to the production of wire rods and light structural which maintained consistency in demand. BSP was also able to push the production of UTS 90 rails to a whopping 519,000 tonnes to meet the demand of Indian Railways.

To prop up sales realization in a market where prices were headed southwards, BSP made a special effort to increase the component of high-value steel. As a result, nearly 25 per cent of the total saleable steel produced in the plant comprised special and value-added steel, viz., API 5L, X 60 and X 65-grade plates, boron bearing structural plates for export to the European market, UTS 90 rails, EQ wire rods, etc.

Mr B. K. Singh said, 'The work culture of Bhilai has supported consistent profitability of operations. While only an aware workforce can be expected to deliver results, the resilience of its workforce to respond to any changed scenario has enabled its management leadership to take on and meet any change successfully.'

Indeed the workforce at BSP was constantly creative, seeking cost-effective solutions for the problems faced. More often than not, the hands-on workers took the initiative in the area, with the executives and the supervisors playing a facilitating role for implementation. This innovative approach to problem-solving encompassed all areas of the plants and mines. The results were evident as recycling of solid waste reached the highest ever level of 68 per cent. Slag cut-off systems were introduced in the twin hearth furnaces to improve the quality of steel and enhance the recovery of ferroalloys. Bottom pouring of ingots started in SMS-I to improve yield in rolling and reduce steel defects. Argon rinsing was started on a regular basis to improve the homogeneity of steel. Ladle covers were introduced at SMS-I and SMS-II to reduce temperature drop, reduce heat loss and improve shop logistics. Innovative use of waste limestone chips at Nandini mines was taken up by installing dry screening and washing at the mine, using in-house resources. It took the plant only two months and expenditure of ₹1.4 crore to set up beneficiation facilities for 9 million tonnes of waste limestone chips available at Nandini, a major leap forward for waste reduction and utilization.

Turnaround years catapulted BSP into a new orbit of performance excellence, as the design capacities were exceeded in almost all the shops. Merchant mill with an original capacity of 500,000 tonnes produced 550,000 tonnes of finished products in 2003–2004. Wire rod mill with an original capacity of 420,000 tonnes produced 563,000 tonnes of wire rods and the plates production crossed 1 million tonne in 2003–2004, exceeding its capacity of 950,000 tonnes.

New records were set in the areas of operating efficiency. Energy consumption reduced from a level of 7.3 Gcal per tonnes of crude steel in 1997–1998 to 6.8 Gcal per tonne of crude steel by 2003–2004. BF productivity improved from a level of 1.61 THM/m^3/day to 1.74 THM/m^3/day and the coke rate reduced from 596 kg/THM to 503 kg/THM in 2003–2004. Saleable steel production at BSP for the first time crossed the 4 million tonnes mark in 2003–2004.

Buoyed by a strong overall performance - especially in rails, BSP's profits bounced back. From a non-existent profit in 1999–2000, the plant recorded a profit of ₹477 crore in 2001–2002, which improved to ₹735 crore in 2002–2003, only to be overtaken by a record profit of ₹1932 crore in 2003–2004!

Durgapur Steel Plant (DSP)

In the battle for survival set in motion by SAIL in 1997, the company's key to survival hinged on improving the performance of two of its weaker integrated steel plants—Durgapur and Rourkela Steel Plants. While both the plants showed strong signals of transformation, DSP made a spectacular resurgence against its chequered history spanning more than four decades.

DSP, the third of the integrated steel plants under SAIL, was set up in the early 1960s with an initial capacity of 1 million tonne of crude steel. By 1967, the crude steel capacity of the plant was enhanced to 1.6 million tonnes. DSP used the traditional technology of the Open Hearth Route of crude steel production. Its rolling mill complex in 1967 comprised of blooming mill, billet mill, merchant mill, section mill, skelp mill, fish plate plant, sleeper plant and wheel and axle plant

The plant's production, which had peaked in the mid-sixties, started declining in subsequent years, and a prolonged period of indifferent performance followed up to the eighties, when the government accorded approval for modernizing facilities at DSP.

Durgapur Steel Plant was a perennial loss-making plant under SAIL. To modernize its facilities and take care of the technological backlog, a modernization package worth ₹2,887 crore was conceived in 1989. However, the commissioning of a number of facilities under modernization saw inordinate delay ranging anything between 3 to 5 years compared to the initially envisaged target dates. By the time the modernization was completed in 1996, the total project cost had ballooned to ₹5,075 crore, an increase of more than 75 per cent over the initial project estimate.

According to Mr Seth, Executive Director (Projects), DSP, 'The delay and rise in cost were mainly due to unexpected international events which directly affected the pace of the modernization program, and the devaluation of the Indian rupee. The breakup of the Soviet Union was the major factor contributing to the delay as Tyazpromexport, a premier Russian company, was the consortium leader in the modernization packages in two major areas, sinter plant and blast furnaces, and was also involved in other packages. The breakup of the USSR resulted in disruption of material supplies and other related problems.'

Slow but Steady

The ramping up of production from the new facilities brought about its own challenges, and the overall improvement took place gradually. Commenting on the gradual ramping up of capacity, Mr S. B. Singh, the then MD, DSP, said in 1999, 'It took some time for the modernized units at DSP to homogenize interphase with the old units. The DSP steel collective also took some time to acclimatize to the newly modernized and automated setup. The psyche of the collective which was tuned to the old technologies had to be moulded to the latest where timely action is a must and response time least. Extensive theoretical and on the job training helped in a big way to bring about change in the mindset. We have taken a major communication exercise to make the employees fully aware of their immediate and long-term goals.'

Mr S. B. Singh added, 'If you take the case of BOF and CC the two shops we acquired under modernization, we have been setting monthly production records every month and are presently at just over 90 per cent of the rated capacity. Modernization has enabled us to possess the latest steel-making technology. Our BOF and CCP could be the envy of any integrated steel plant. We have set up the latest facilities for raw materials handling and sinter production. We have two modernized blast furnaces which have been performing exceedingly well. Operations have become simpler and efficient by adequate automation in our merchant mill and wheel and axle plant which were partly modernized.'

Mr U. P. Singh, who at that time was ED (Works), DSP said, 'DSP will reach the rated capacity of production by March 1999.

But we have to exceed our capacity level of production substantially to achieve cash profit. Our SMS collective is fully geared to surpass the rated level of production. We are planning to produce 1 million tonne of concast steel from our CC machines progressively with small modifications.'

The products of DSP were received very well in the market. In 1998–1999 DSP exported around 78,000 tonnes of billets. TMT bars produced by DSP using Thermex quenching technology acquired under modernization allowed savings in steel to the tune of 8 to 12 per cent. DSP's TMT bars did very well despite the sluggish market, and the plant had the distinction of being the first plant in the country to roll out extra strength thermo-mechanically treated (TMT) bars.

From July 1998, DSP started supplying Indian Railways with BG wheels of IR 1993 specification, comparable with the best in the world. The specifications which were introduced from 1 July 1998, required stringent control on the percentage of carbon, manganese, silicon, chromium, nickel, molybdenum, copper and vanadium in the wheels. These wheels which were to be used for high-speed passenger trains, at that time were being imported and Railways had formulated specifications at par with the best in the world. The wheel and axle plant during this period also developed diesel loco wheels, an import substitution item.

Dr S. K. Bhattacharyya, who took over the reins of DSP as MD in 2001, said, 'In physical performance, DSP had been posting a growth of 5 to 6 per cent every year. Some of the units have operated beyond rated capacity. The techno-economic are at all-time best levels. The benefits of modernization have come slowly but progressively through increased production volumes, technological improvements, and better techno-economic parameters leading to lower cost of production and development of new products.'

'With 50 per cent of the products being semis which fetch low prices in the market, DSP's net sales realization has traditionally been low. We can only overcome this problem by increasing the component of value-added products,' he added.

When the Momentum Built

The improvement in the performance of DSP had started showing as the plant achieved a record campaign life of 2508 blows in one of its converters in 2001, which then was the best in any steel plant in India. Another area of improvement was the significant reduction in the metallic input per tonnes of crude steel, which reduced its cost of production and made it a leader amongst SAIL plants in producing more with fewer inputs. Also, DSP was second only to BSP in energy and water consumption efficiency.

The turnaround of DSP was orchestrated with the stabilization of BF-BOF-CCP units. As the hot metal production of the plant surged, it put pressure on BOF, which increased its number of heats processed per day ranging from 35 to 37 to 45 to 47. To match the BOF, CCP started operating at 130 per cent of the rated capacity.

'More production through BF-BOF-CCP route also means more production of semis, because the downstream units can only consume about 45 per cent of total crude steel production of the rated capacity,' said Nilotpal Roy, Executive Director (Works) in 2003. 'Rest of the billets are sold in the market which is currently very lucrative. Therefore, there is a thrust in exploiting the full potential of billet caster. Thankfully the billet caster has the potential to go beyond its rated capacity.'

The improvement in DSP's performance was across units. Starting with crude steel production of 1.25 million tonnes in 1996–1997, DSP improved its performance every year to reach a level of 1.76 million tonnes by 2003–2004 reflecting a capacity utilization rate of 98 per cent. Hot metal, which barely touched 1.3 million tonnes before 1996–1997 rose progressively to 2 million tonnes in 2003–2004. The CCP unit attained 100 per cent capacity (773,000 tonnes) in continuously cast billets in 2000–2001 and exceeded it to reach a production of 1 million tonne in 2003–2004.

A new record was set in DSP's merchant mill, which reached its rated capacity in 2000–2001 and exceeded it every year thereafter to produce 330,000 tonnes in 2003–2004, capacity utilization of 118 per cent. The merchant mill enhanced DSP's market share in bars with the branding of its TMT bars 'SAIL Shakti', a product which was amongst the best available in the country.

The Wheel and Axle plant responded to Railways' requirement of high-speed wheels, by adding a new product S-profile wheels to its product mix.

The section mill throbbed with activity for meeting a surge in the demand for structural. The mill, which was not modernized, achieved dimensional accuracy in the production of angles, channels and joists. It boasted of a prestigious clientele like Indian Railways, BHEL, L&T, NTPC, etc. Its products also met the stringent requirement of high tensile and higher ductile properties of TLT sectors.

There was a marked improvement in DSP's operational efficiency parameters, as its energy consumption came down from a level of 8.9 Gcal/tcs in 1996–1997 to 7.4 Gcal/tcs in 2003–2004, and the BF productivity improved from 1.11 THM/m^3/day to 1.45 THM/m^3/day for the same time period. There was a visible improvement in coke rate, which reduced to 560 kg/thm by 2003–2004, from a level of 679 kg/thm in 1996–1997.

All the above changes happened at a time when the manpower numbers reduced from a level of 30,000 in 1994–1995 to around 17,000 by 2004. DSP's story truly was mediocrity metamorphosing into excellence.

Elusive Profits

Starting from inception the plant had made a net profit only three times in 1965–1966, 1978–1979 and 1981–1982. It made cash profits for two years before breaking into the net profit zone in 2003–2004 after a gap of 23 years.

The improved financial performance according to Executive Director, (Finance and Accounts), Mr S. N. Srivsatava, was attributable to, 'The increasing cost-consciousness amongst the employees, which turned out to be a major turning point.' This viewpoint was reinforced by Mr B. M. K. Singh, Executive Director, Materials Management, who said, 'While the production boomed, the plant inventory came down significantly from a level of ₹270 crore to around ₹100 crore in six years. In the same period, the consumption of stores and spares reduced from ₹1,900/tonne of saleable steel to ₹1,250/tonne, effecting a savings of ₹90 crore per year.'

Business Standard, published on 12 April 2004, reported that the Durgapur Steel Plant (DSP) of Steel Authority of India Ltd (SAIL) is set to post its first net profit in the present millennium. The plant registered net profit once each in the sixties, seventies and eighties. 'The three-figure net profit, which the plant is expected to net in 2003–2004 will be the highest ever achieved by the plant as yet.'

DSP closed the year 2003–2004 with saleable steel production of 1.61 million tonnes of saleable steel, which surpassed the previous best of 1.58 million tonnes achieved in the year before. It also recorded the highest ever hot metal production at 1.98 million tonnes surpassing the previous best of 1.94 million tonnes achieved the year before. Similarly, the crude steel production at 1.76 million tonnes was the best surpassing the previous best of 1.71 million tonnes. The continuous casting plant produced over one million tonne of billets at 130 per cent of the rated capacity setting up a growth rate of 3.3 per cent over the previous best figures achieved in the year before.

Organization Matters

One of the key contributors to the transformation of DSP was the change in the organizational climate. The employees at DSP, for most of the prior two decades, had been victims of the industrial and social unrest in the state, leading to militant trade unionism in the industrial belt of Durgapur. The plant's increasing sickness was attributed to a large extent to the indifference of the workforce, which inured with years of low performance, felt that DSP could not be revived despite the injection of new technology.

The turnaround in the attitude of the employees was gradually brought about by providing them with extensive training abroad and in the Centre for Human Resource Development of DSP. Armed with the new skills, the employees were able to see the benefits of modernization first hand when they put the learning into practice on the shop floors. The workers benefited from a reduction in physical labour, higher production resulting in higher incentives, and the ability to enjoy a better life.

A totally new culture came about in DSP through an extensive communication campaign aimed at creating awareness amongst employees and sensitizing them to the realities of the business environment. Regular interaction sessions at the shop floor level did wonders. The unions also matured and everybody understood that the only way to survive was by generating one's own resources. Looking at the condition of companies facing closure all around, the workers felt that they had certain strengths at their command to reverse the loss-making situation.

Dr S. K. Bhattacharyya, MD, DSP, gave his insight into the transformation, 'Mind is always more powerful than the machine. The company-wide communication exercise has worked wonders in instilling an intense desire among the employees to excel.'

'The single most motivating factor is the recognition from the family, friends and the society at large, that we work for a plant that makes a profit. They have realized that the current spate of success has come through their hard work and commitment. The mental barrier regarding rated capacity has also been broken. The DSP collective is today a confident and vibrant lot which believes in itself,' elaborated Dr Bhattacharyya, adding, 'DSP's revival had a great impact on employees to boost their morale and self-esteem. A major share of Durgapur's population is directly or indirectly dependent on the fortunes of DSP. The turnaround of DSP has rejuvenated the entire region.'

The sentiments were seconded by Mr V. K. Gulhati, Executive Director (Personnel and Administration), 'After seeing the tangible results and benefits of their hard work, the employees are now determined to repeat performance. The employees now find pleasure in their performance. The new-found confidence was exemplified in 2002–2003 when the plant completed the capital repair of BF-2 one day ahead of schedule.'

Explaining the changes introduced, Mr Gulhati said, 'The Company took a major HR initiative to improve age mix and skill mix in tune with the advancement of technology. The number of lines of promotion (LOP) was reduced to improve the flexibility of working. Simultaneously the competence mapping exercise was undertaken to identify and reduce skill gaps. At the Wheel and Axle plant, for instance, 17 LOPs were merged into four. In the townships, the LOPs have been planned to be brought down from 13 to a single. The existence of too many LOPs and their impermeable demarcation fostered operational delays earlier. These were merged within functional orientation, resulting in the strengthening of interpersonal relationships and productivity enhancement.'

'With a reduction of manpower, it became essential to improve the competence level of employees. But what added a different hue was the massive communication programme. Persistent flow of information on different issues through different media triggered an awakening among the employees.'

'There is another perceptible change in the air. There is a tranquillity in the air. Gone are the intermittent assemblage, the groups of people thronging the roads, and canteens and swarming near the gates discussing plant problems and at times filling the air with a cacophony of slogans. Labour unrest has become a thing of the past and the steady hum of operations unbroken. Labour productivity has doubled from 65 tpmy in 1996–1997 to 131 tpmy in 2003–2004.'

The most revealing comment came from a leader of the workers' union, 'In a free market economy, we have to remain competitive and commercially viable. The workers have to take equal responsibility for this along with management because their fortunes are closely linked with the profitability position of the company. No good can come in an environment of strife and antipathy. Instead, we have to work hand in hand, while ensuring that the welfare of employees is never compromised. This has been clearly understood by both the management and the workers.'

Bokaro Steel Plant

Being youngest amongst all integrated steel plants in SAIL, BSL started production in 1972, and over time became the largest producer of flat products in the country. It produced HR coils/sheets and plates, CR coils/sheets, galvanised plain and corrugated sheets and tin mill black plates.

BSL's facilities comprised five blast furnaces and two SMS, of which SMS-I had a crude steel capacity of 2.5 MTPA and SMS-II a capacity of 1.5 MTPA. Prior to modernization, the production of crude steel in the plant was in the form of ingots, as BSL did not have continuous casting facilities. Its mills included a slabbing mill, hot strip mill and two cold rolling mills, CRM 1 and CRM2.

Prior to 1991, BSL had the advantage of being the producer of HR coils, a product reserved for the government-owned companies. However, following the liberalization of a number of domestic players entered the field with the latest technology, and its products came under acute competition both from domestic producers as well as from imports. Tata Steel, Essar, Jindals and Bhushan Steel emerged as the key competitors in the domestic arena, at a time when cheap imports, particularly from CIS countries, flooded the market.

During the era of controls, BSL was the highest profit earning steel plant under SAIL and considered its cash cow. The dropping price lines and intensification of competition saw BSL's fortunes transform rapidly. A record profit of ₹806 crore in 1995–1996 declined year after year to a loss of ₹165 crore in 1998–1999. The financials of the unit were also impacted by the high capital-related expenses as an investment of nearly ₹2500 crore was undertaken in the plant in the nineties towards modernization of its hot strip mill, the introduction of continuous casting in its SMS-II, and other related schemes.

The modernization programme undertaken by BSL was to provide the plant with the requisite means to compete in a market, which had become increasingly competitive. For BSL not only was the market impacted by excess supply; the customers became choosier and their requirements more stringent.

The entire steel making process of BSL was based on the ingot casting route, technology prevalent in the late sixties. Considering the various advantages of continuous casting towards yield improvement, conservation of energy and improved quality, the Government of India sanctioned Stage I modernization of BSL in July 1993 with a commissioning schedule of July 1997. All major contracts were awarded in 12 months. Trials for the steel refining unit were started in September 1997 and the first continuous casting machine started its trial runs in November 1997. Subsequently, all units of Stage I modernization was completed by January 2000.

After the modernization, the saleable steel capacity of BSL went up to 3.8 million tonnes from a pre-modernization capacity of 3.2 million tonnes. The concast slab production capacity increased to 2.2 million tonnes from nil, and the capacity for production of HR coils increased to 3.95 million tonnes from a level of 3.36 million tonnes. Other than an increase in production capacity, the modernization of hardware provided BSL with the wherewithal to compete in an intensely competitive market, by the superior quality of finished products, improvement in yield and labour productivity; reduced energy consumption and cost of production, and better pollution control and overall environmental management.

During the period 1997 to 2004, BSL was headed by a number of very good technocrats, Mr K. A. P. Singh, Mr B. K. Singh, Mr Suresh Pandey and Mr U. P. Singh. After completion of the modernization, various efficiency parameters in the plant started showing improvement.

Products and Processes

Other than reducing the cost of production of HR coils which had a reference benchmark rate of US$200/tonne, the modernization helped BSL develop and commercialize a number of new grades such as SAILÇOR for Railway coaches, SAE 1020 for propeller shafts of automobiles, SAE 1541 for cycle chains, API for petroleum pipelines, WTCR for cold reducers, E34 for chassis of light vehicles, etc.

After completion of the modernization, Mr Barun Ghoshal, Executive Director (Works), of BSL said, 'Our products are now rated to be the highest quality even by the most discerning of customers. The confidence reposed both by domestic and foreign customers is borne out by massive orders of high-quality steel.'

Elaborating on the benefits of the newly commissioned continuous cast shop, Mr B. K. Singh, MD BSL commented, 'Our aim was to achieve 100 per cent of rated capacity in the quickest possible time. The continuous cast route slabs yield a benefit of 9 per cent in the cost of production, vis-à-vis the rolled slabs. Further, the quality of products made from concast slabs is superior.'

Mr V. K. Srivastava, who at the time of modernization was AGM, hot strip mill, and subsequently became MD of the plant, said in October 2000, 'On an average BSL is exporting 25,000 tonnes of HR coils every month. Due to the reliable working of the modernized units equipment availability and mill utilization has gone up by 10 to 15 per cent and the diversions on account of product quality reduced to 1.5 per cent.'

The SAIL restructuring program forced every steel plant to investigate at the micro-level opportunities to improve processes parameters. As a result, a number of technical improvements were introduced in the plant during the period.

In the area of Coke Ovens, all doors were made airtight, and due attention paid to cleaning the doors from both sides as well as surrounding areas. In the by-products, area a nitrogen line was laid for purging as a replacement for steam. For undertaking any mechanical job, purging was done using nitrogen which nullified chances of explosions in case of any sparking. This practice was later introduced in all the other sister plants.

A change in the practice of crushing was introduced in the sinter plant by introducing flip flap screen which screened out coke of less than 3 mm size, which helped in a significant reduction in the generation of micro fines. As a consequence sinter production increased, and the coke consumption reduced.

The initial design of blast furnace had a two-bell system with a throat armour plate made of steel box filled with bricks, which used to give problems after capital repairs. This design was modified, and after changes in the steel casting around the periphery, no problems were further encountered. Other improvements were carried out related to the tap holes and monkey holes and in the stack area, which improved the overall performance of the blast furnaces.

In the hot strip mill, automation in the roughing and the finishing areas improved the product tolerance with respect to width and thickness, thereby improving customer acceptance and realization for the plant.

Managing a Crisis

Notable crisis management for BSL was with respect to its water system. The plant had a reservoir with a capacity to hold seven days of water consumption only. The supply of water to the reservoir was from Tenu Ghat through a canal, which was 34 km long. The supply of water from the canal got disrupted when a bridge, which was built over the river that fed water to the canal collapsed.

Recalling the incident Mr B. K. Singh, MD, BSL, said, 'The plant was faced with an onerous challenge of reactivating the water system so that water supply resumed within seven days. Work had to be undertaken in an area, which was so remote that there was no power supply and DG sets were used for lighting and welding. The officers had to work in the temporary tents set up for resting and taking food. The entire job was completed in six and a half days and the plant operations did not stop even for an hour!'

Back with a Bang

By leveraging the benefits of modernization, BSL could bring in an all-round improvement, which enabled a record production of 3.75 million tonnes of crude steel in 2003–2004. A major milestone for BSL was achieving the rated capacity of continuous cast slabs, a facility set up under the modernization, in 2002–2003, and exceeding it in 2003–2004. With an upturn in the market, BSL posted a record profit of ₹1120 crore in 2003–2004.

Financial Express reported on 3 June 2004,

> Bokaro Steel Plant of government-owned Steel Authority of India Ltd (SAIL) has posted a record net profit of ₹1,120 crore for the 2003–2004 fiscal on a turnover of over ₹7,743 crore to become the third-largest profit-making steel plant in the country after Bhilai Steel Plant and Tata Iron and Steel Company. This is not only more than three-and-a-half times the previous fiscals net profit of ₹311 crore, but is also nearly 40 per cent higher than the previous best figure of ₹806 crore achieved by this flat product making plant in Jharkhand in 1995–1996.

A number of pro-active and vibrant human resource initiatives, such as the interaction of the management team, unions and employees in various cross-sectional interface forums like Sujhaav Aapke 2004 and interaction with young managers, were the contributing factors in achieving excellence in the plant's performance. The newspaper quoted a senior official of the company, saying, 'Bokaro's performance is marked by all-round improvement, viz., production and productivity, new in-house maintenance initiatives, cost reduction, inventory control and techno-economic improvement. A growth of 17 per cent in sales, coupled with 33 per cent reduction in interest, and cost reduction of over ₹110 crore catapulted Bokaro to this level of excellence. Production of crude steel, saleable steel and hot rolled products posted all-time best figures. Overall saleable steel production stood at over 3.45 million tonnes.'

The official further added, 'What makes this achievement all the more remarkable is the external odds overcome by the employees of the BSL to post this result. With careful planning, innovative solutions and well-organized teamwork, Bokaroites defied the constraint of coal shortage almost throughout the last quarter to exceed the targets for the fiscal.'

CHAPTER 13

How the Market Was Won

The steel markets were in turmoil during the years 1997–1998 to 2003–2004, experiencing huge swings, the markets plummeted and rose only to go down again. Double-digit demand growth which had given an expectation of take-off for the steel sector in India during 1994–1995 and 1995–1996, appeared a flash in the pan, as the markets became hostage to a number of adverse factors attributable to both international as well as domestic sources.

A recessionary trend prevailed in most of the steel user segments—capital goods, consumer durables, construction, which with a lack of investment in the infrastructure sector, led to virtual stagnation in the demand. The growth in steel consumption fell to 2 per cent in 1997–1998, from a level of 14 per cent in 1995–1996 and 21 per cent in 1994–1995.

The growth in demand was very meagre in subsequent years. A recovery appeared imminent in the first half of the year 2000–2001, but the market suffered immediately after, on account of trade sanctions imposed by the USA, Canada and the EU. Fiscal 2002 was the worst year in the memory, as regards steel pricing. Almost all steel companies globally including India bled. The market had to wait till the second half of the calendar year 2002, for the normalcy to return. The year 2003–2004 signalled a break from the past, as the domestic demand rebounded with a growth of 8 per cent.

During this turbulent period, the consumption of finished steel in India went up from 24 million tonnes in 1997–1998 to around 33 million tonnes by 2003–2004 at an annual average growth of less than 5 per cent. The devastation in the industry, in fact, was much more evident in the domestic crude steel production, which registered a negative growth of 4 per cent in calendar 1998 and a negligible growth of 1.5 per cent in 2001.

HR coils price traded in Mumbai, quoted in metric tonne, went down sequentially from around ₹18,300 in the financial year 1998 to less than 18,000 in the financial year 1999, and further fell to ₹17,500 in the financial year 2000. It rallied to ₹18,500 in the financial year 2001 only to crash down to ₹16,200 in the financial year 2002. The recovery in earnest started only in the financial year 2003 when price surged to a level of around ₹19,000 per tonnes.

In India, several green-field capacities had come up under Essar, Lloyds, Jindal Vijaynagar, Ispat industries, etc., mainly for producing HR coils and the downstream products in the flat steel categories. The drop in domestic demand led to significant excess capacity in the flat products. The trade restriction that came about after 2000, closed the external markets and magnified the distress faced by the industry to unprecedented levels.

International Market for Steel

The international steel market had gone into a tailspin following the Asian Currency Crisis. As a fall out of the crisis, the global trade experienced a reverse inflow of steel into the international markets resulting in a glut. This led to a sharp fall in the international prices; and with the imports becoming cheaper, the domestic steel markets went down as well. Capacities for the production of steel outstripped global consumption and significant regional imbalances in steelmaking capacity and consumption emerged. The financial turmoil in the South Asian economies led by Thailand and Indonesia, followed by Japan and South Korea, and the drastic currency devaluation led to a continuous decline in the export prices in dollar terms.

With the USA remaining a major steel importing region, significant flows of cheap imports were routed towards it. To protect the domestic steel industry, the USA and EU raised trade barriers by way of anti-dumping and countervailing duties as well as safeguard measures. EU-15 countries which had substantial intra-regional trade in steel did not even require many imports to sustain internal demand. These markets were thus effectively shut for imports.

Global consumption saw negative growth in 1998, followed by a meek recovery in 1999. There was a pick up in the steel consumption in China in the year 2001, which was almost entirely nullified by the drop in consumption in the rest of the world. After 2001 as the markets gained normalcy, the surge in Chinese demand broke the trend the industry had become used to over the previous five years.

Prices of steel reflected the abnormal shifts and surge in demand during this period. The price of HR coils, a product traded most by volume, saw huge swings. The HR coils prices which were in the range of around US$265 in the first quarter of 1997, saw a continuous declining trend which brought it to a low of US$180 by mid-1999. There appeared to be a rally in the prices thereafter, only for the prices to hit rock bottom in the third quarter of calendar 2000. The period was characterized by the world spot prices dropping to the levels below marginal costs.

The US Government had initiated anti-dumping investigations, on complaints from four US producers, against 11 countries including India. Countervailing duty investigations were proceeding against Argentina, India, Indonesia, South Africa and Thailand. The US Congress had passed the anti-dumping bill, which enabled the US administration to help the domestic steel-makers hurt by foreign competition by sharing anti-dumping and compensatory costs.

This encouraged even small steel manufacturers in the USA to file anti-dumping cases.

Towards the end of the decade, steel demand from China started increasing exponentially. The Chinese economy was in the process of globalization and foreign investment was being wooed. Huge investments were carried out towards infrastructure building which was further buoyed by construction activities as a part of the Olympics to be hosted by the country in 2008. As a consequence, despite being the leading producer globally, China's imports crossed a level of 25 million tonnes per annum in 2001 and eventually led to a recovery of the global steel industry.

From a level of 111 million tonnes in 1998, steel consumption in China zoomed to 232 million tonnes in 2003. The China-led growth in demand for steel since the beginning of 2002, brought about a 7 per cent growth in the world steel consumption and helped eliminate the oversupply situation in the international market. It also boosted the price from the rock bottom levels of 2001–2002. The evacuation of steel from the over-supplied domestic market helped in firming up the prices in the home market. This was a welcome relief for the Indian steel companies which had been reeling under the impact of demand recession for over five years.

In the mid-year in 2002, there was still an apprehension amongst the steel producers whether the improved steel prices would continue to persist. Mr N. N. Sachitanand, reporting for *The Hindu*, on 18 July 2002, wrote,

> Just when the Indian steel companies, as well as their creditors and shareholders, were beginning to breathe easy consequent to the firming up of steel prices during the last six months, J. J. Irani, President of the Steel Alliance, set the cat among the pigeons by stating that the international price rise may peter out by the beginning of next year. The Steel Alliance, incidentally, is a cluster of five of the biggest hot rolled coil (HRC) producers in the country. The HRC market was the worst hit in 2001, as can be seen in the

price trend graph. The prices in 2001 were half of the reigning prices in the mid 1990s, when the new HRC plants in India were conceived.

'The veteran steel man, J. Mehra of Essar Steel, is inclined to agree with Dr Irani. According to his reading of the situation, the economic downturn in the USA and the EU, which began in early 2000, caused a mismatch between global supply and demand of steel, particularly in the flat products segment that caters to consumer goods such as automobiles and white goods. This caused a slide in steel prices during the latter half of 2000, which cascaded into an avalanche by early 2001 when the depressed CIS countries, desperate for hard currency, started flooding the globe with their steel at rock bottom prices. In a time of dropping prices,' explains Mr Mehra, 'the tendency of consumers is to postpone purchase and wait for a further price drop. When steel consumers shied away from buying, the desperate and panicky producers further dropped their prices, thus worsening the situation.'

'The end result was that considerable steel capacity in the USA, EU and Japan got mothballed or taken out due to bankruptcies. According to figures provided by the International Iron and Steel Institute, the average annual growth rate of world crude steel production was plus 2.4 per cent between 1995 and 2000 but a negative 0.1 per cent in 2000–2001. Finished steel consumption in the USA dropped to 103 mt during 2001 from 115 million tonnes in 2000. Similarly, the consumption in the EU dropped from 145 million tonnes in 2000 to 142 million tonnes in 2001.'

'The sole exception to this trend was China, where a vigorous growth in the automobile market and heavy investment in infrastructure led to a consumption of 170 million tonnes of steel in 2001, compared to 141 million tonnes in 2000. But for Chinese imports, the steel market in 2001 would have further plummeted.'

Sachitanand wrote in his article that Mr A. K. Singh, Director (commercial) of SAIL, differed in his outlook of the steel market. He reasoned that not much of the capacity in the USA shut down during the past 18 months could be brought back into production, due to financial and technical reasons. Second, with the improvement of the Russian economy, the steel from the CIS countries was being absorbed in that region itself, leaving little for export to the rest of the world. Third, China was expected to substantially increase its imports as it had started colossal construction projects in preparation for the Olympics to be hosted by 2008. Mr Singh was confident that the scenario in India would be even better. While steel consumption was growing slowly, no investment in fresh capacity had been forthcoming in the country for the past four years.

The steel market, in fact, continued to hold. Mr A. K. Varma, Executive Director (ITD), SAIL, commented in 2003, 'China is the single most important factor that has changed the course of the entire global economy. A net exporter of steel till a couple of years ago, the country has become a net importer. The sheer tonnage is staggering. In the first seven months of the current calendar year alone, China has imported 23 million tonnes of steel. India with its geographic proximity to the world's largest steel market has a distinct advantage in trading with China.'

As the domestic prices surged in line with the international prices, there was a clamour from the steel users who accused domestic steel producers of raising prices by restricting domestic supplies in favour of exports. Mr B. K. Tripathy, Union Minister for Steel, said in a steel Consumers Council in August 2003 that after deregulating the sector, the Government was in no position to regulate the price movement. 'Prices in a liberal economy are determined by market forces alone, and the government has little to say,' he stated.

Sail's Domestic Sales

During the crisis years, the post of Director (Commercial) of SAIL, responsible for its marketing division, was held by Mr U. K. Mittal, followed by Mr K. A. P. Singh, Mr M. K. Moitra, and Mr A. K. Singh; when the marketing of steel was extremely tough.

Nevertheless, SAIL's marketing performance was sterling during the years of depressed demand. Growing at an average rate of 5 per cent per annum, the overall sales increased by around 40 per cent to reach a level of 10.7 million tonnes in 2003–2004, from a level of 7.5 million tonnes in 1996–1997. Except for a blip in 2000–2001, when the sales registered negative growth, the sales volume improved year after year. There was only a marginal dip in the market share of the company despite intense competition from 27 per cent in 1997–1998 to 25 per cent in 2003–2004. Its share in HR coils, in fact, went up from 30 per cent in 1997–1998 to 34 per cent in 2003–2004. There was, however, a fall in the market share of CR coils and sheets and galvanized sheets, where SAIL had not added capacity under modernization, by 11 per cent and 6 per cent, respectively.

Sales turnover growth was dismal in the earlier years despite a relatively good performance in sales volume. Clocking an average growth of around 2 per cent from 1997–1998 to 2001–2002, the surge in turnover only came in 2002–2003 and 2003–2004. However, it was to the credit of SAIL that it posted a growth of 5 per cent in sales volume in 2001–2002 when the market was at its weakest.

Marketing Initiatives

Key Account Management and reorganization of SAIL's marketing division in flats and longs product groups, were two of the most important interventions in marketing under SAIL's restructuring plan.

Key Accounts Management (KAM) which was introduced in early 2000 had envisaged benefits in terms of enhanced customer share and better NSR. Two years after its implementation, it was observed that while information flow to the customer and feedback had improved manifold, the process was yet to be uniformly internalized and required fine-tuning for successful implementation.

One of the measures decided to be introduced was that while the KA managers reported to their respective branch managers, the branch managers were to be made KA managers for certain major key accounts. At the plant level, ED (Works) had been given the main responsibility for the KA orders received. The Heads of PPC (Plant Production Control) were given the charge as Plant Information Coordinators (PICS) and were to act as the interface between marketing and the plant. The PICS were to ensure coordination from steelmaking to dispatch of materials, as projected by product accounts coordinators (PAC) the counterpart of KA managers in the plant.

The KAM of CMO was also given the responsibility of generating a monthly Customer Satisfaction Index (CSI), which was introduced for continuous improvement of SAIL's relationship with its customers.

SAIL's ability to compete in the marketplace was evidenced by its performance in the year 2001–2002, the worst year for the steel industry in terms of prices. Despite continuously severe adverse market conditions, SAIL notched up a record sales of 8.1 million tonnes in the domestic market in 2001–2002, a growth of 10 per cent growth in carbon steel sales in a market that grew only by 2.6 per cent in apparent consumption. Moreover, this performance came about when globally a combination of oversupply and low demand, had pushed prices to an unprecedented low. Trade barriers imposed by several countries had closed the markets for many products. At home, the capital goods sector saw negative growth during the year. In such a market, the domestic sales of steel by SAIL increased by 4 lakh tonnes!

The reorganization of SAIL's marketing division had been an event covered by the media. A news item on 3 June 2000, reported,

> The Steel Authority of India (SAIL) restructured its marketing set up in all the regions in accordance with its plan to bifurcate the organization under two broad product categories of flat and long. Under the new arrangement, the regional headquarters at the four metros will be headed by two different regional managers looking after flat and long products separately. (*The Hindu*, 2000, June 3)

'Two more groups—one dealing with specialized products such as pipes, tin plates and electrical sheets and the other for value-added mild steels, rural marketing and distribution channels—are also being created. Since SAIL markets a large range of steel items ranging from semi-finished to the most sophisticated categories, the move will ensure a higher degree of specialization and familiarity with the products at the regional level.'

SAIL's marketing performance benefitted immensely from the product orientation of the marketing activities. The reorganization of the marketing into flat and long product lines, led to a focus in each market segment in a more intensified manner, resulting in selling more, expanding the customer base and getting a better price in a competitive market space. It also imparted better product knowledge and specialization to the sales force.

Mr A. K. Singh, Director Commercial of the company said in an interview to SAILNews in 2002, 'Product based market is a more effective system in the present very highly competitive market. It helps to provide a sharper focus to our customers in various product segments as well as an integrated market-oriented approach between Central Marketing Organization (CMO) and the plants. Besides, the accountability of every individual is also maximized. Comparing the performance of competitors also becomes easier, as the task of identification of competitors for every product at any location is also simpler.'

Agreeing to the benefits of product-based marketing, Dr S. Dubey, Executive Director heading the Long Products group noted that, 'Product based marketing is an international practice, followed by all leading steel producers in the world. SAIL was the first company in India to adopt this practice. The fact that today our competitors like Tata Steel have also been inspired to follow the suit, speaks strongly of the benefits that product based marketing brings.'

Mr S. K. Roongta, who at that time was Executive Director, Flat Products, and later became Director Commercial and Chairman of the company, felt that with each of the groups dealing primarily only with two plants, the marketing plant interaction and coordination had become more effective. This aspect was to be seen in a context where all the competitors of SAIL had a single unit plant, producing a limited number of products. SAIL on the other hand a number of plants, producing a vast range of products. Earlier the Regional Manager of CMO had to handle the entire range of products right from pig iron to high-value Cold Rolled steel from the four plants of SAIL. He was also to keep track of the market dynamics and take quick marketing decisions. This was a humongous task and as a consequence, effective coordination both with the plants and customers suffered, as did market monitoring and operations control. The setting up of segment wise targets enabled concentration of efforts leading to a more proactive and responsive sales force.

Mr J. P. Agarwal, Vice Chairman of Surya Roshni, a customer with whom SAIL had more than 20 years of relationship, said, 'We as customers welcome the reorganization of SAIL's market set-up along product lines. The measures adopted are more in tune with the requirements of each product group. For instance policies and procedures relating to HR coils have been fine-tuned for the user segments like pipe manufacturing and cold rolling industries.'

'Marketing executives have become more approachable, customer-friendly and less bureaucratic. Besides, the closer marketing-plant coordination has brought about a better appreciation of each other's strengths and weaknesses and willingness to cooperate for customer satisfaction,' was the view of Mr A. K. Mukerjee, Executive Director (Personnel & Admin.), CMO.

Mr A. N. Majumdar who was General Manager, Rural Marketing and Distribution Channels, pointed out that the product planning had vastly improved because of higher exchange of information with the customer under the new system. 'With the identified personnel dealing with each account (customer), information is exchanged on more familiar terms and both sides have much closer,' he added.

Mr A. K. Jain, who was Regional Manager (Flat Products), Northern Region, acknowledged that with the area of responsibility brought down to fewer customers, it became possible to formulate better strategies for each of them as well as resolve issues faster. 'We could focus on each product, identify the requirements of different user segments, concentrate on the customer needs, including technical delivery conditions, take up each case with the concerned plant, and reach the materials on time to customers. Seeing the efficiency of the system the customers also started to show higher dependence on us in comparison to our competitors.'

Narrowing down operational areas of each executive to specific product lines, provided scope to strategize more effectively. Mr A. K. Jain formulated a fixed price scheme suiting smaller customers that elicited an excellent response. In fact, the smaller customers were the ones who contributed to the surge in sales in flat products.

Mr Vipin Puri, GM (F&A), CMO explained how greater accountability at each level with specific responsibilities had shown the results. The inventory level was reduced drastically. Cash collection saw growth and the realization of sundry debtors was faster.

An important intervention that helped SAIL to compete effectively in the marketplace was empowering the field force with greater authority and powers for taking the competition head-on. The PSU culture typically stymies bold and aggressive action. In order to find solutions to the problem, Chairman Pande had direct interaction with ten top branch managers in the absence of their regional and zonal heads, unusual in a highly hierarchical oriented company.

It became clear that the operating sales team did not have the powers to sell the entire production at SAIL, which often led to high inventory holding and stress on finances. There was a constant fear of the vigilance administration agencies, viz., CVC, CAG and CBI, and everyone felt safe in an environment of a limited delegation of powers.

Identifying it as a limiting factor, a handful of Branch Managers (BM) were asked to frame the delegation of powers that they needed to fulfil the aspirational sales targets beyond 100 per cent. Initially the BMs were reluctant in getting the powers, as it was safer to push files up for approvals. However, they were persuaded into framing a charter of a delegation of powers that would empower them to respond to quick market changes, without any delay. This implied an assurance that they would be given protection from unnecessary and unwarranted victimization.

SAIL's marketing performance also received a boost from the technological up-gradation of its production units. In the flat products categories, which saw maximum competition, a special thrust was given to the sales of value-added products. As a measure to improve the net sales realization, increased offerings were made in grades such as API, medium carbon E-34/38 steels, SAE 1020 sheets for auto components and hi-tensile plates. In the long products categories, additional sales were generated from products such as high carbon wire rods, spring steels and high-quality semis.

Export Performance

During the course of seven years starting from 1997–1998 to 2003–2004, SAIL exported an average of around 7 lakh tonnes every year. Starting from a level of around 7 lakh tonnes in 1997–1998, the exports zoomed to 1.1 million tonnes in 2003–2004, a record that still has not been breached. During this period the company had to contend with the closure of the markets it had traditionally exported to, and reorient both its product basket as well as export destinations.

The year 1999–2000 had been a good year for the company in export sales. Its mild steel exports had grown to a record 7.6 lakh tonnes, and pig iron exports 85,000 tonnes. However, the subsequent years proved troublesome. Traditionally, SAIL's exports were directed to the USA, Europe and Japan. Following the imposition of anti-dumping duty and countervailing duty (AD/CVD) on SAIL's cut to length plates and HR coils by the USA, and by EU and Canada, steel exports of the company faced a setback.

New markets needed to be explored to sustain the exports which ranged between 5 lakh to a million tonnes, in the overall sales.

Fortunately, around that time many of the modernized units of SAIL had started producing superior world-class products. As a result, SAIL started exporting to a host of Southeast Asian countries as well as neighbouring countries such as Myanmar and Sri Lanka in addition to new destinations such as Mauritius and Madagascar. Although the volume of steel exports came down to around 5 lakh tonnes in 2000–2001 and 2001–2002, it picked up again to a new record of 8.5 lakh tonnes in 2002–2003. Buoyed and confident after exporting 0.85 million tonnes in 2002–2003, SAIL aggressively kept an export target of more than a million tonnes of steel exports for 2003–2004, with 19 products, 21 markets as its goal.

Explaining the export performance of the company Dr Anil Dhawan, who in 2003 was Deputy General Manager in SAIL's International Trade Division (ITD), said, 'Over the years SAIL has established for itself the reputation of a reliable supplier of quality materials. Offering quick shipping and adhering to delivery schedules are our strong points. It is a tribute to our professionalism that SAIL exports shipments have never faced rejection till date.'

For SAIL, China had emerged as a major destination during 2002–2003, where 0.34 million tonnes of steel plates, HR/CR coils and sheets and galvanized products were exported. Substantial quantities were also exported to the Philippines, South Korea, Thailand, Vietnam and Malaysia. Nepal emerged as a major destination of steel exports, and more than 50,000 tonnes of materials were also exported to the European countries.

Dr Dhawan informed, 'As a policy, we encourage shipments to new markets, even if the quantity is small. We do not back out of the contract if the market improves elsewhere. This increases trust in SAIL and our customers do not leave us when the market slides.'

Globally, the world trade in steel was maximum in products such as HR coils, semi-finished steel, CR products, plates, and galvanized products in flat products followed by long products such as wire rods and rebars, structural, etc.

Plates from BSP were SAIL's oldest established export product, accepted in the markets worldwide. It reached a peak volume of 361,000 tonnes in 1997–1998, with the major destinations being the USA, Europe, Canada and Japan. However, stiff tariff barriers imposed on SAIL plates by the USA in 1999 and then by the EU, closed these markets, and SAIL's exports of plates to these markets virtually became zero in 2000–2001, and the overall exports of plates declined almost to a half to 149,000 tonnes.

Under such a scenario, SAIL shifted its focus to new markets such as Korea, Taiwan, Philippines and Singapore. SAIL also struck a deal with Europe that allowed exports of plates at a reduced rate of duty. This enabled the exports of plates to bounce back to a level of 2.8 lakh tonnes in 2002–2003.

BSP plates had an advantage over their Indian competitors as it was the only company from India supplying plate mill plates. Tata Steel, Essar and Ispat exported plates made from their hot strip mill. The BSP plates had an advantage in quality with better physical and chemical properties. Being available in thicker and wider dimensions and produced as per international standards—ASTM 831, SS 400, British, German and Japanese standards, gave it an added advantage.

Trade Disputes

The steel crisis of the 1990s where HRC was traded at an unimaginable price of less than US$200, led to a near collapse of the steel industry worldwide. Many companies went out of business and job cuts became rampant. As a consequence, a number of new capacities that had been set up in the nineties became uneconomical and surplus. Financial institutions started withdrawing support to the sector, and an excess supply overhang persisted for the whole industry.

The USA, which was facing its own price war between big and mini mills, had to contend with cheap imports emanating out of excess production in countries with cheaper cost of production. The developed economies where the cost of production was higher because of local costs were the main targets for the cheap flow of steel. The situation was such that even consumers, the main beneficiaries of cheap steel, felt cheated owing to a continued fall in prices, even after transacting at a relatively low price. With cheap imports flooding the market, the local steel producers put pressure on their respective governments to enforce protective measures in the form of tariff or non-tariff barriers within the WTO framework. These measures took the form of safeguard measures, technical restrictions, anti-dumping investigations and countervailing actions.

The crisis years for steel, which saw a prolonged overhang of excess supply in the global market intensified trade disputes. Against a background of sharp upturns and downturns, the US president came to the aid of the ailing American steel industry by invoking a 'safeguard agreement' under WTO rules, which was adopted in US Law as Section 201.

Like the USA, EU and Canada also took trade actions such as AD/CVD investigation and imposition of duties to check imports and go for safeguard actions when required. Trade actions for restricting imports against any country or group of countries required undertaking extensive preparation for launching and conducting investigations. Besides causing disruption to trade, it was a costly process involving time, money and resources. It also created an unfavourable environment for the exporting countries which had to undertake wide-ranging coordination efforts with several organizations/agencies involved in domestic production, sales and exports, as well as their governments to defend the charge of dumping/subsidization.

The spurt of trade-related cases that started in the late 1990s continued up to 2002. Trade actions were launched by the USA, EU-15 countries, Canada, Thailand on exporting countries like CIS, Korea, Japan, India, China, etc. After the USA invoked Section 201, others such as the EU and Canada followed with their own safeguard measures. The main products targeted were HR sheets/plates/coils, cold rolled and stainless steel products.

As a follow up of anti-dumping duty against HR coils, the USA had entered into a Suspension Agreement with Russia and Brazil for both quota and minimum price restriction for next 5 years. The imposition of AD and CVD duties against the import of cut to length plates from India, however was in violation of the WTO rules. Nonetheless, it forced the stoppage of export of plates in the near term. Further, cases on plates and HR coils initiated by USA, Canada and EU required a huge record-keping by individual exporters in India, which was highly time-consuming and necessitated significant changes in accounting methods.

A number of export schemes including DEPB, which were primarily linked to duty-free imports allowed by the GoI, were viewed as subsidies by the USA, EU and Canada. There was thus a need to re-examine these schemes to ensure their compatibility with WTO and avoid the CVD.

Under the above scenario, SAIL developed its in-house expertise and set up a Task Force to handle trade-related cases. The most important case for the Task Force was that of cut to length plates or CTL plates of BSP.

The Case of CTL Plates

BSPs cut to length plates were very popular in the USA and Japan. SAIL was utilizing one full shift of operation at BSP's plate mill for exports. Given the domestic demand, it was necessary to keep loading export orders for the plate mill to keep its capacity utilization at a reasonable level, and engage the workforce productively. SAIL's export division, called the International Trade Division (ITD) had the responsibility to book orders on a continuous basis for the plate mill. It was widely acknowledged that SAIL plates were the first choice for plates in sizes 12 mm to 40 mm and grade A36 (American standard for basic grade for plates and construction steel in general). The orders were being booked in lots of 10 to 20,000 tonnes or even higher.

Seeing the popularity of SAIL plates, the domestic producers in the USA filed an Anti-Dumping Duty petition on SAIL, India, along with other exporting countries to the USA, with the US authorities, USDOC (United States Department of Commerce) in 1999. It was followed by a Countervailing Duty petition on SAIL, India, which challenged the export subsidies of the Department of Commerce, GoI, particularly the DEPB (Duty Entitlement Pass Book) scheme.

The AD/CVD measures initiated by USDOC not only jeopardized Plate exports to the US but it also threatened closure of at least one shift of operations of Bhilai's plate mill. There were additional concerns from the Government of India because of the CVD case.

ITD had no machinery or expertise to handle such cases. In view of this, Mr Arvind Pande, Chairman SAIL, directed Dr Anil Dhawan, then DGM (ITD), to handle this area exclusively. Given its significance, the case was monitored by Chairman, SAIL, himself regularly, and was also looked into by the Secretaries of Steel and Commerce, GoI. One of the reasons for this was the bearing it had on the export incentives schemes of the Government of India, which were under attack. The US steel producers wanted a very heavy CVD on import of plates to the USA; the export incentive schemes particularly DEPB was to be defended by the Ministry of Commerce, Government of India, directly.

In a joint meeting of Secretary (Steel), Secretary (Commerce) and Chairman SAIL, which was attended by Dr Dhawan, it was decided that the case will be fought by SAIL for AD (Anti-Dumping), as it was company specific; and Commerce Ministry, GOI, along with SAIL, (as SAIL had been made party to CVD case) for the Anti-Subsidy case, which was applicable to all export schemes. The Commerce Ministry advised that since SAIL will be engaging lawyers (American Lawyers) for the AD case the same lawyers will be engaged to cover the CVD case of the GOI, as well.

Based on the recommendations by the Indian Embassy in the USA, SAIL engaged one of the best known legal firms M/s. Wilmer, Cutler & Pickering, which was based in Washington, USA, to handle the case.

All the notices by USDOC were dealt with systematically in a time-bound manner. A series of meetings were held at Delhi, BSP, Commerce and Steel ministries. All data and information were collected and compiled. The consultants from the legal firm visited BSP, SAIL Corporate office (Finance Department), India. The consultants, after carrying out their analysis, concluded that it was not dumping and that the Export Incentive Schemes were well defined, thereby refuting both the allegations of dumping as well as subsidization.

The most important area which came to light in the process was that the USA needed T-By-T (transaction by transaction) data for each export consignment, with cost tracking right from raw material on an 'On-line' system. SAIL did not have this 'WTO Compliant' system and was operating mostly on manual systems. SAIL's consultants 'constructed' the T-by-T data, based on the manual data they had collected and presented the same to USDOC.

The consultants were very confident that based on analysis of data, it would fall under De Minimis, that is, negligible, which would not attract any dumping duty. There was, thus, no case of dumping. The submission ran into thousands of pages and had several thousand pages of data. As per the practice, the USDOC team came for verification of data and found that SAIL's submission complied in all respects.

However, after a series of meetings with ITD, Finance and Accounts section of SAIL's Corporate Office, domestic sales branches of CMO and BSP, they went back and declared that instead of SAIL data, they will depend on the 'facts available' from the petitioners. Based on the facts available from petitioners, the USDOC imposed an anti-dumping duty of 72.49 per cent and a countervailing duty of 12.82 per cent respectively on CTL plates imported from India, which was confirmed by US International Trade Commission (USITC) in January 2000.

Narrating the event, Dr Dhawan recalled, 'Our lawyers were shocked and wanted SAIL to take the issue to WTO. They were willing to help SAIL in the case without any charges. Chairman, SAIL after consultation with the Ministry of Steel, gave a directive to the ITD to file a case in WTO against the US ruling.'

SAIL filed a complaint with the US Court of International Trade against the ruling as USDOC had arrived at duties disregarding the data of SAIL. Also, the matter was taken up by the GoI through the Permanent Mission of India (PMI) to World Trade Organization (WTO), Geneva for panel formation at WTO to look into the violation of WTO provisions by the USA.

The developments of the case were reported by PTI, on 20 March 2002, quoting an official agency, 'The Dispute Settlement Body of the World Trade Organization would decide next June on the dispute arising out of the anti-dumping duties that the USA imposed on Indian cut-to-length carbon steel (CTL) exports to that country. The US Department of Commerce imposed anti-dumping and countervailing duties of 72.49 per cent and 12.82 per cent respectively on CTL plate imports from India. The investigations were initiated in February 1999 and the final duties were imposed in February 2000. India sought formal consultations with the U.S. under the dispute settlement mechanism of the WTO which was held in November, 2000. At India's request, the Dispute Settlement Body on 24 July 2001 established a panel to examine the issues raised in the dispute. As per the time-table for the panel, the final report would be circulated to the WTO members by June.'

The ITD team comprising Dr Anil Dhawan and Mr B. N. Jha, who was the Executive Director (ITD), went to WTO, and with the help of the consultants, argued the case against the USA for deciding the case on a 'Facts available basis', when SAIL had fully cooperated with the US Authorities, and the data verified by the USDOC team by visiting India. Several Hearings took place at WTO Headquarters in Geneva, attended by the SAIL, ITD team.

SAIL's stand was proved correct, as the WTO gave the ruling that USDOC had been wrong in deciding the case on a 'Facts Available' basis and directed USDOC, to take SAIL data into account for calculating AD duties. USDOC contested the decision, but WTO stuck to its ruling and USDOC had to comply and recalculate the duties, and issue the AD order for SAIL again.

The BSP CTL Plate case is considered a landmark in the Trade Dispute Cases, as it was a rare case in steel trade at WTO, where the USA had been advised to review its AD orders. Following the WTO order, USDOC came out with a revised rate which brought down AD duty to around 42 per cent. Although the duty on CTL plates continued to be very high, the entire process brought about other benefits in terms of the data management in SAIL becoming WTO compliant and the export incentive schemes of GoI revised to conform to WTO compliance.

The CTL Plate case also helped SAIL's ITD in gaining expertise related to trade disputes. It subsequently successfully countered AD cases against the EU and Canada in CTL plates, and Thailand in the HRC anti-dumping case. SAIL also became a coordinating company for the Indian companies fighting the AD and CVD case against the EU and guided the rest of the industry in fighting the AD cases successfully.

Competition for Rails

Rails were a prime product for SAIL. Produced in SAIL's flagship, BSP, it was a product that along with plates was the main determinant of profits for the plant. BSP produced rails conforming to Indian Railway specifications as well as various foreign specifications such as British, Japanese, Egyptian and Union of International Railways Standards. Indian Railways was the customer for rails from SAIL, although some small quantities had been exported to South Korea, Argentina, New Zealand, Sweden, Turkey and Bangladesh, etc., whenever export opportunities arose. In the late 1990s, Bhilai rails came under intensive competitive pressure, when Indian Railways explored opportunities for alternate sources of supply.

BSP's rail and structural mill was set up in 1960 with a capacity of 5 lakh tonnes per year of rails and 2.5 lakh tonnes per year of heavy structurals. There was an implicit agreement between SAIL and the Indian Railways that BSP would continue to meet the requirement of rails so long it was able to fulfil the order quantities and maintain quality standards stipulated by the Indian Railways. BSP at that time was the only supplier of rail in India. Rails were, however, of shorter length of 13 metres.

Under liberalized policies of the 1990s, the Railways embarked on an ambitious plan of track replacement and network expansion. The 9th Five Year Plan in 1997 acknowledged infrastructure as a limiting factor for growth and laid down ambitious targets for new rail lines as well as track requirements, which resulted in a four fold increase in the physical targets set for the years 1997–2002.

The Ministry of Railways was not confident about the ability of BSP's rail mill to augment supplies while maintaining quality. Also, there had been a series of accidents which led to implementation of more stringent specifications by way of (a) lower hydrogen content in rails to make them less brittle, and (b) use longer rails so that tracks had fewer joints. Research Design and Standard Organization (RDSO), which functioned under the Ministry of Railways as the Technical Advisor and provider of services related to design, new technology standards, testing, inspection and safety; announced a major shift in specifications for rails in 1996. Under the new specification 'end straightness' and overall straightness requirements were specified which required production of longer rails to help meet the stringent standards.

Indian Railways floated a global tender on 6 October 1997 to create another domestic source of rails supply to help meet its total requirement of 7 million tonnes of rails for the 9th Five Year Plan. Although 16 parties responded to the tender, none was found acceptable by the Indian Railways. Subsequently, it was decided to hold a pre-bid meeting before floating another tender.

The Indian Railways on 28 April 1998, held a pre-bid meeting attended by about 25 firms. The prospective bidders, however, wanted an increase in the off-take assurance stipulated by the Indian Railways at 1 lakh tonne to 2 lakh tonnes. They also wanted the period of off-take commitment to increase to 15 to 20 years instead of 5 years, envisaged by the Indian Railways. As none of these conditions was acceptable to Indian Railways, a decision was taken at the inter-ministerial level to augment the rails production at BSP to meet the enhanced requirement of rails.

It may be said that the ministers for railways, Mr Nitish Kumar and later Ms Mamta Banerjee, were very encouraging to the idea of SAIL expanding its capabilities to meet the requirements of Indian Railways both quantitatively as well as qualitatively. Mr Nitish Kumar, Minister of Railways and Mr Naveen Patnaik, the Minister of Steel, visited BSP accompanied by SAIL Chairman Mr Arvind Pande to have a first-hand assessment of Bhilai Steel Plant's readiness to meet the requirement of Indian Railways.

BSP realized that in absence of significant quantity and quality improvements, its market share for rails would be severely threatened. As rails were one of the most profitable products in SAIL's portfolio, the loss of market share would have dragged down the financial performance of not only the plant but the company as a whole. It was obvious that unless BSP met the larger orders and the new quality standards of Railways, it could not continue to remain the sole supplier of rails to the Indian Railways. To accomplish the newer quantity and quality targets, a variety of programmes were initiated between the years 1999 to 2003, whereby the supply of rails to Indian Railways increased from 3.2 lakh tonnes in 1999–2000 to 7.1 lakh tonnes in 2003–2004

A part of the increase in production was achieved by shifting the composition of rail and structural mill away from structurals towards rails. However, there were also substantial improvements in the utilization of capacity and worker productivity. The total shifts worked went up by 15 per cent and the average output per rail shift increased by 28 per cent. Also, the number of defects were cut down by 50 per cent and delays caused by employee errors reduced by 43 per cent. Some of the improvements originated in departments outside the rail mill, for example, higher production of rail blooms in the SMS, but the majority came from changes within the rail and structural mill.

Training had the most systematic influence on output per worker for rails production. It was revealed that the training programme, 'acceptance of rails' held in 2001, resulted in 50 per cent of the improvement in additional blooms processed per shift for rail manufacturing. Another major initiative for enhancing productivity was by reducing the delays caused by employee mistakes and malfunctioning of machinery.

Indian Railways in 2001 indicated their requirement of a long rail of 65/78-metre length, at about 1,50,000 tonnes per annum and desired that SAIL should go ahead with the investment planning decision for production of longer rails. Consequently, SAIL decided to upgrade BSP rail structural mill to produce around 1,50,000 tonnes per annum of longer rails. It undertook a project to manufacture 65/78-metre long rails which were to be welded in rail panels 240–260 meter long at BSP itself. These long, welded rail panels were to be directly transported from Bhilai Steel Plant to the track renewal sites. The entire expenditure of the long rail project related to manufacturing of long rail, welding into the rail panels was to be borne by SAIL. The approximate expenditure on the long rail project was estimated at ₹320 crore with commissioning in December 2003.

Keeping in view the investment of this magnitude to cater to the needs of the Indian Railways exclusively, SAIL requested the Railways to enter into a general understanding so as to ensure that the railway requirement of long rails were met by SAIL and also the investment made by SAIL was gainfully utilized. An MOU was signed between SAIL and Indian Railways on 1 February 2003 whereby Railways committed to buy its total requirement of long rails from SAIL and also the other lengths, subject to annual review within the overall policies of the Government of India.

In the meantime, Jindal Steel and Power Limited (JSPL) had acquired a second-hand rail and structural mill from South Africa and was desirous of entering the market for rails.

However, JSPL had to wait for a few years as it did not have RH degasser mandated by railways for secondary refining of steel; and became eligible to be a potential supplier for rails only after installing RH degasser in 2008. The MoU between SAIL and IR, however, provided BSP to be the supplier of rails till it was able to meet the quantity and the quality requirements of the Indian Railways. Consequently, JSPL filed a case before the Competition Commission of India with a plea that the MOU signed by SAIL for supply of rails to the Indian Railways was anti-competitive and resulted in an entry barrier and denial of market access.

The case came up for the decision of the Competition Commission of India (CCI) during December 2011. The critical issue to be decided was whether the MOU, an exclusive supply agreement, was anti-competitive and foreclosed the completion. The CCI in its judgement saw the economic rationale of the Indian Railways to enter into an MoU to ensure a steady and secure supply of domestically produced rails. It stated that the MoU between SAIL and Indian Railways was an outcome of a bargaining where both SAIL as well as Indian Railways were monopolistic. In cases such as these, called bilateral monopolies, the joint maximization of the surplus from the agreement resulted in an economically efficient outcome. The Commission also examined the case with a perspective of 'Completeness of Contracts' and other relevant aspects for competition. In its judgement the Commission found no substance in the claim that the MoU between SAIL and Indian Railways was non-competitive and pronounced the case as closed.

mjunction

At the time SAIL was in the midst of implementing the Turnaround Plan, an interesting business opportunity emerged for the company. Lying outside the arena of the 'Turnaround and Transformation Plan', this opportunity had a strategic relevance, beyond the immediate future, and a potential to transform the manner in which SAIL had engaged with the market.

Online business, a commonplace occurrence today, was a different world in 1999, when businesses based on the internet and e-commerce had just started emerging. An opportunity came up when Dr J. J. Irani of Tata Steel and Baba Kalyani, promoter of Kalyani Steel, approached Chairman Arvind Pande to join hands to collaborate on setting up an online marketplace for primary and secondary steel through e-auctions. Both TATA Steel and SAIL were major steel players in the domestic steel industry. Although SAIL and Tata Steel were competitors in the domestic market, this initiative was undertaken to take advantage of the internet and e-commerce.

There was a good business rationale for SAIL and TATA Steel to collaborate. As the alliance enabled a larger range of complementary products, the new economy platform could gain by driving larger volume and becoming more efficient. An independent digital marketplace was viewed both by Tata Steel and SAIL as a future oriented business opportunity.

Teams from SAIL, Tata Steel and Kalyani Steel started working out the modalities. The teams had members directly reporting to the Chairman/CEO's of their respective companies who backed them completely. For a brick and mortar company like SAIL, a typical public sector undertaking, working in the dot.com space was something far ahead of its time.

An international consultant engaged to draw the business plan, came up with a plan that envisaged ₹20 crore of share capital and the venture sustaining losses in the initial four years before turning profitable. The initial proposal was to set up a Joint venture company by the name of metaljunction.com which would have equity contributions of ₹8 crore each from SAIL and TATA Steel and ₹4 crore from Kalyani Steel.

With this kind of a business plan, it was not easy for SAIL to invest in a futuristic venture especially as the company was facing a severe cash crunch. To compound the matters further, it was around this time that the dot.com bubble burst, making things even more difficult. The NASDAQ composite index which included many internet-based companies peaked in value on 10 March 2000, before crashing. A major reason for this was that analysts at the time focused on aspects of individual business rather than on cash flows and revenue generation. Suddenly e-marketplaces were out of fashion. Six months after the dot com bubble burst, Kalyani Steel opted out of the venture. It was hence decided that SAIL and Tata steel would have a 50:50 partnership and halve their contributions to ₹4 crore each in the JV. Along the way, it was also decided that the name of the venture would be changed to mjunction to allow it a wider mandate rather than being confined to only metals.

There were enough pessimists in SAIL who believed that any investment in the venture would be a complete waste of resources. As SAIL at that time had a high debt burden and limited resources, one of the directors on the Board prophesied the venture to be disastrous for the Company. This was to be seen in the context of acute cash crunch faced by SAIL, which at times was so severe that cash was unavailable even for the excise duty on steel dispatches.

That the venture could finally see the light of the day was only because it was completely backed by Chairman Arvind Pande who had the foresight to see its potential of developing into something big. Hence, in February 2001, metaljunction.com finally came into being—a B2B e-commerce platform promoted by two of the major steel rivals, SAIL and Tata Steel. It also became India's earliest public-private sector joint venture.

In those days the business environment for the internet companies was not particularly good with a number of them winding up. However, with ₹8 crore of paid up equity under its belt, the CEO of mjunction, Mr Viresh Oberoi, who was from Tata Steel started operations, charting a phenomenal growth path. Within 10 years of its existence the market value of the company skyrocketed from ₹8 crore to ₹800 crore. The business volume for mjunction in terms of transactions value soared from ₹94 crore in 2002–2003 to ₹41,134 crore in 2012–2013, a compounded annual growth rate of 74 per cent!

There was in fact a compelling business case for e-marketplaces of creating value by re-engineering of business processes for reduced total cost of ownership of goods and services, and higher realization for saleable products. mjunction exploited this opportunity by providing procurement and selling services. The buyers benefitted through lower price and negotiation cost, access to extended supplier base, economised search and processing costs, and optimization of the inventory holding cost. Sellers on the other hand benefited from higher volumes and profits, expanded their customer base, lowered their negotiation, processing and customer acquisition costs, and improved the overall inventory management.

mjunction started by selling 'secondary steel' or non-prime grade steel, of its promoters, which gave it the volume to succeed in its initial years. SAIL had a system whereby all secondary materials/arisings and diversions of steel were directly auctioned off by the steel plants. But with the setting up of mjunction, the plant arisings were auctioned on this platform, fetching a better price through an online price discovery mechanism. It may not be out of place to mention that had SAIL not given its support to this fledgling organization in its critical years, mjunction may not have had the fortune to script its history.

In 2011, mjunction completed 10 years of its existence with its financial year 2011 revenues touching ₹1 billion. During this period, it earned from its online transactions worth ₹248 billion, consummated on its electronic trading platform. mjunction pioneered the concept of e-auctions for steel by moving the entire process of auctions to the internet. Since then mjunction has returned more than ₹200 crore to each of its promoters in dividend. It emerged as not only India's largest e-commerce company, but also the world's largest e-marketplace for steel. Significantly, when the NDA government went for spectrum auction, it chose the mjunction platform. The government earned over ₹1 lakh crore from the auction, paying an undisclosed fee for its services.

mjunction has radically transformed the steel and coal supply chain in India by ushering in transparency, efficiency and convenience to the way steel and coal is bought and sold in the country. mjunction is now India's largest e-commerce company. Having transacted business over

₹8 lakh crore up to financial year 2019, it has clearly emerged as one of the most successful public-private partnerships in India.

Overcoming PSU Limitations

In 1999, a time when the concept of mjunction was being conceived, PSUs were not allowed to conduct any business online, be it procurement of raw materials/stores and spares, or sale of its products. Traditionally, in the case of PSUs, suppliers had to be empanelled for procurement of any maintenance, repairs and operations (MRO) items and then offers received through limited or open tenders. There were Central Vigilance Commission (CVC) guidelines which did not allow PSUs to deviate from the specified process.

The concept for mjunction came up during the challenging times when SAIL was looking at all possible avenues for cost reduction. Reduction in the cost of raw materials which formed a substantial part of overall expenses was under intense scrutiny in the company. There was a growing realization that new phenomena of online auctions, be it reverse auctions or forward auctions—with an all-encompassing market-making exercise, invariably resulted in a transparent and efficient process, yielding financial benefits. Accordingly, like any private sector steel players, SAIL needed the freedom to decide whether to conduct its business—procurement or sales—offline or online. However, as the PSUs at that time did not have the mandate, it was decided to approach the CVC for taking approval.

Chairman SAIL wrote to the then Chairman CVC Shri N. Vittal, seeking time to discuss the issue. This was immediately given by Shri Vittal who had high personal regard for Chairman Arvind Pande. As expected, the going was not good when the SAIL team made a presentation to Mr Vittal and the entire CVC set-up, seeking approval for e-procurement and reverse auctions. Some members of CVC voiced their concerns and were in no mood to relent. But Mr Vittal, who by then was convinced of the benefits of e-procurement overruled them. He then did something-quite unusual in government circles. He called for his secretary and dictated the approval of the CVC there and then in the meeting itself. Thus, SAIL became the first PSU to get approval for e-procurement through reverse auctions.

At SAIL it was decided to have the first trial for procurement of materials through online reverse auction, involving one buyer and many sellers pre-qualified by the buying agency. The reverse auction process was expected to provide the company several advantages. It was a transparent process where all bidders would have been aware of the lowest price during the bidding as well as the closing price. Second, it was expected to reduce the procurement cost, as the intensely competitive environment would lead to efficient price discovery. Third, it was to reduce the lead time thereby improving the process efficiency of the buyer.

The auction bid was to be designed by using an IT tool called Auction-Engine for incorporating the key aspects related to item specifications, techno-commercial terms as well as bidding rules. Savings both in money and time was expected on account of improved efficiencies in the system.

The heads of the material of SAIL Plant and Unit met in December 2001 where a decision was taken that the requirement of four integrated steel plants would be aggregated in order to maximize benefits. In 2002, SAIL used an online reverse auction process for procuring four commodities, calcium carbide, wire ropes, cables and caustic soda. With this, it became the first Public Sector of India to conduct the reverse auction for procurement of materials over the internet.

The e-procurement services were provided by mjunction whose responsibilities included designing the auction bids, market-making services, including market analysis, new vendor discovery, validating credentials of vendors and e-enablement of eligible vendors participating in the auction events.

The first reverse auction for calcium carbide took off in February 2002 and the process for procurement of wire ropes and cables on 4 March and 5 March 2002, respectively. The process for caustic soda was taken up in April 2002. Savings ranging from 5 per cent to 19 per cent were obtained across the four items over their last purchase price. Based on the experience a detailed report was submitted to the CVC.

Based on the experience of SAIL, CVC allowed the change in a procedure whereby e-procurement and reverse auction was made applicable to all PSUs. In September 2003, CVC clarified that government departments/organizations may themselves decide on e-procurement/reverse auctions for purchase or sales and work out the detailed procedure themselves subject to it being transparent and fair.

CHAPTER 14

Communication Holds the Key

SAIL restructuring was one of the biggest interventions in the history of corporate India. It targeted deep fundamental changes in one of the largest manufacturing enterprises, which had employee strength of more than 180,000. Many of the interventions impacted the employees directly. The manpower numbers were to be brought down by almost 45 per cent. Austerity measures, such as suspension of leave encashment, LTC/LLTC, house building, vehicle and other advances, hit the pay packets directly. Other measures introduced, which impacted the workforce, included changes in the incentives and rewards systems, closing down of uneconomic units at different plants and units, viz., sleeper and fishplate plant at DSP, bar mill at ASP, blooming and slabbing mill and fertilizer plant at RSP, Kulti Works at IISCO and the uneconomic warehouses of CMO. Also, there was curtailment in the unstated benefits given to the employees in the form of subsidized water and power in the SAIL townships.

The implementation of the above measures was to be taken up in parallel at a time when the production and productivity levels were planned to reach record levels. The newly commissioned facilities needed to be ramped up fast. There was a big focus on cost and quality.

Exports that demanded strict adherence to quality and committed timelines, had gained considerable significance in the overall sales plan. The company planned an aggressive reduction in the deployment of contract labour and merging departments with related activities, with their duties taken over by the reduced manpower on permanent rolls by multi-skilling. It was clear that a transformation of this magnitude could not succeed without the active support of the employees and the stakeholders in the change process.

There was a huge challenge of communicating the concerns, the strategies and the goals of the company to a geographically dispersed, multi-layered target audience, which had the biggest stake in the planned transformation. It goes to the credit of SAIL leadership that it sought the involvement of employees and stakeholders at each stage of implementing the restructuring plan. Nothing was hidden from the employees and no hard decisions were shied away from.

The single biggest contributor to the company's transformation was its communication drive, which was all-encompassing. It covered the employees, the trade unions, the officers' associations, the government functionaries, the investors, the media and the politicians. The fact that such a massive transformation could be carried out without a breakout of any major protest in the organization, bears testimony to its skill and communication strategy.

In the pre-reform era, SAIL had enjoyed an unchallenged position in the market. It was large, its size impacted the nature of the market, it had seen low but more or less steady profits over the years, and its larger mission was defined by the national ideology and national goals.

SAIL was perceived as a national benefactor rather than a company with corporate goals. In the era of controls, customers had to come to SAIL, and the key audience for the company was the government, Parliament and the government watchdogs. SAIL could afford to carry the burden of assets that provided negative returns. People came before profits.

A PSU was expected to both serve and profit, with the primacy on serving. It was the social responsibility of SAIL to create jobs. Internally, the social objective of providing jobs combined with the strong trade union presence to shape the environment. The management and the workers were seen as antagonists. Salaries were time-linked and seniority-linked. Profits were a management concern and promotions and performance had little to do with each other.

This paradigm changed dramatically post-liberalization. SAIL no longer enjoyed an unchallenged position in the market. It was seen as a corporate whose job was to make profits, and its contribution to the national development assessed in financial returns on the assets deployed. With the profits turning into losses, the company faced reverse discrimination, where it was perceived as a dinosaur of the days when the government was in the business of doing business.

The role of the Government had ostensibly transformed to that of the principal shareholder in a steel company. Customers no longer needed to come to SAIL. The company's social responsibility now turned into an unwanted burden. Prices were decided by the market. A large number of committed free marketers believed that PSUs like SAIL were an anomaly and the private sector did a better job. Externally, SAIL was seen to be a Public Sector Unit that epitomized all that was classically wrong with state-owned enterprise, which had been set up, to not only meet the needs of nascent India but also provide jobs, take care of the community around and meet the national productivity goals.

In such an environment, pruning rather than protecting jobs became the priority for the company. Salaries and promotions needed to be profit, efficiency and performance linked, and both the management and the workers needed to work towards a common goal.

The changed paradigm needed a fresh orientation in how the company was communicating about itself. Much of the external communication in SAIL was about corporate, financial and inter-plant issues. Most of these issues were seen by the private companies as being matters that did not need to be in the public realm at all.

SAIL had a complex medley of audiences that spanned right across the bandwidth of the government, ministry, Parliamentarians, Parliamentary committees, business partners, local communities, a huge employee base and a media that had fed off SAIL's travails and travesties over an extended period of time. The government that had supported a massive expenditure on modernizing the steel plants was increasingly irritable at the constant barrage of media criticism. It resonated in a rising crescendo of criticism in the Parliament fuelled as much by vested interests within the system as by the competitors.

As the Navratnas, the PSU giants had been bequeathed the title of being super performers, in the greater glory of economy. Government-owned power, steel, oil, telecom companies were hounded mercilessly by the media, as the country hurtled towards free market through economic reforms, which stripped all PSUs and traditional Indian private sector giants of their virtual monopoly positions.

Most companies engaged external audiences in the talk about their products, their presence in the market, marketing strategies, innovations, achievements in products and markets and service offerings. They wanted to present their best face to customers and stakeholders, supplement advertising, build a reputation and even influence the government. But the practice at SAIL was to believe that, 'Everything that happens in SAIL is news. Therefore, we should talk about everything. The media is not interested in the marketing of products unless it is about discounts, in marketing strategies—unless it is about raising and lowering prices, in products—unless it is about rejections, about our achievements—and unless there is a cost over-run!'

The time was ripe for a change in the mindset. Communication needed a reorientation to accomplish the company objectives, by gearing up internally to project a good exterior. The direction of the change was to use the information and the interest in the company to project a professional organization with superior products, fighting a battle where it was disadvantaged by a legacy of old plants, huge social burdens, and yet was a proud mantle-bearer of Indian industrial progress over the years.

An internal group that worked on the new communication policy summed it as, 'It was time to handle the abundance of information with panache and time to start moulding internal audiences to the change. It was time to get the media interested in what we wanted to project rather than pander to their demands.'

Corporate Communications at SAIL

Communications at SAIL was traditionally seen as the responsibility of the Corporate Affairs Division (CAD) at SAIL headquarters, and the Chiefs of Communication at respective plants and units. Communicate, the company did, but in an unorganized and haphazard manner. It was not uncommon to send out a message which reached several employees but left out the intended target group. More often than not, communication was seen as a routine matter, not worthy of becoming an effective tool for management intervention.

Also, over time, Public Relations (the 'PR job') had become the domain of the Personnel department where select personnel executives, wishing for a change from the dreary personnel chores, came to have a cushy PR job. The Head of PR reported to the Head of Personnel who stood as a barrier between him and the Chief Executive, fending off any attempt at establishing direct communication.

Apart from duplication of effort and overlapping of interests, there was neither accountability nor credibility of messages transmitted. In the absence of a clear external communicator, whosoever saw it fit communicated directly with the media, which at times led to utter confusion. The net result was that instead of a structured professional interaction, personal contacts and ad-hoc actions had become the order of the day.

Another facet of the traditional 'PR setup' was that the Chief Executive or Head of the Department was unable to communicate with all employees under his charge in a planned or systematic manner. To make matters worse, the Public Relations department of each plant and unit conformed to the working style of the respective

Chief Executive of the day. Thus, communication channels and modes of communication differed from plant to plant and from one unit to another.

Given the importance of communication in reaching the message of the Chairman to the last person on the shop floor, there was a need to develop an effective communication policy. In light of the above, SAIL formulated a new communication policy which aimed to communicate and facilitate a clear and undiluted flow of communication across the organization, to the employees as well as the stakeholders, and to undertake planned and timely action to pre-empt the emergence of misunderstanding and conflict in any segment of the organization. Further, systems and networks were developed for the dissemination of information through nodal centres to avoid overlapping, establish credibility and maintain a sense of urgency. The new communication policy was to ensure an all-around synergy in SAIL and develop a positive climate of appreciation for the Turnaround Plan and the policies of the organization.

To put the communication policy into action a workshop was organized at SAIL's Management Training Institute (MTI) at Ranchi, where the veterans of Corporate Communication of SAIL plants and units met along with the new recruits. It was to be the responsibility of this team to ensure uniform implementation of the new policy across the company.

To begin with, it was decided that a comprehensive communication drive would be started covering all layers of the organization. This was important, as despite the warning signals on the company's prospects, there was a feeling amongst large sections of the employees that government intervention ultimately will save the day. Low awareness also led to low involvement in the affairs of the company, a situation that needed to be reversed.

An action plan was put in place to implement the new communication policy with turnaround as the key message. The main elements of this intervention were: first, to separate the communication activities from other activities handled by PR such as liaison, hospitality, guest house, etc. Second, a change in reporting relationship whereby all Chiefs of Communication were to report to their respective Chief Executives directly. Third, it was decided to develop a rapport with the local press and the vernacular media; information was to be released regularly to local language dailies. Fourth, each plant/unit was to merge all publications to a single house journal to cover the business environment, production targets and fulfilment,. achievements of sister units, accomplishment of employees and their family members, interviews of shop floor employees, and profiles of customer organizations and competitors activities. Fifth, outdoor communication was to be intensified. Hoardings were to be updated regularly and used inside plants and within townships for wider exposure and dissemination of key messages. Sixth, bulletin boards/ wall sheets were to be displayed on the shop floors which were to contain benchmarks, achievements, slogans and financial impact of steps taken. Finally, cable TV networks were to be used to spread timely information and provide a platform to employees and their family members to showcase their talent.

The First Steps to Reinventing SAIL's Image

At the core of the new team who led the communication effort were Chairman Arvind Pande, Chief of Corporate Affairs Shoeb Ahmed, who later went on to become Director (Commercial), and Arti Luniya in the office of the Chairman, who later headed the Coal Import Group of SAIL; along with the Corporate Communications teams spread across the corporate office and the plants. Supriyo Gupta and his team from Rediff PR, an agency picked to advise SAIL, provided professional guidance in an engagement that lasted over a period of 18 months, and helped re-created the profile of SAIL from the steel giant on its knees to one that roared back to life.

The Agency, Rediff PR, played the role of a catalyst in identifying issues of concern, suggesting solutions and charting out blueprints for implementation. At the core of the media strategy was the necessity to start the work from within, to shape opinions of the internal audience towards the realization of a change in environment, and thereby working together for a larger goal.

The task of restoring SAIL's image was to be done against the background of some harsh realities. Quarter on quarter losses were inevitable at least in the short run and it was not possible to put a date on when the company would make a profit. Also, it was not simply an issue of completing the modernization. In fact, the numbers tended to hide real progress on the ground, as more the investment in modernization progressed, the worse the numbers tended to look with the costs adding up. Further, the ministry, CAG and other assorted government officials were happy to give a sound bite that made SAIL look like a ship yet to get its act together. By October 1998, however, there were enough green shoots to start making a fight of it.

A simple strategy was put in place to get the story right. First, much of the writing on SAIL was either uninformed or mildly malicious. Hardcore steel journalists were more likely to take a negative view of the company simply because they were unable, or unwilling, to observe the changes in a company they had covered for long, and for which they had a deep attachment. They thought the new dispensation was too market-driven, too bent on making SAIL a very different animal from what it was. So the first step was to get across to them systematically constructed arguments, based on facts and figures that showed that SAIL had become a far stronger and efficient company than before.

Second, a lot of the bad press of SAIL was a result of the disgruntled inside the company left out from the transformation or competition. It was important to build a personal bridge with every correspondent with an interest in steel, with the simple proposition of 'take our response' before you file.

Third, SAIL stopped shying away from bad news. The crux of the strategy was to defang bad news by pre-empting it and sharing it in a manner that the full picture came through. So, instead of waiting for the financial performance to become the news of the day, the Chairman started sharing a continuous status report that more or less indicated the expected performance right through the quarter. By the time the company prepared to announce its financial results, the actual news of the results had become a bit of a damp squib. One of the consequences was that SAIL-driven communication started grabbing more space than those coming in from unofficial sources from within the company.

The biggest burden of telling the story well fell on the shoulders of the Chairman, both internally and externally. He had to put a big picture that employees internally could see and relate to. Narrating an incident, Supriyo Gupta, ex-Rediff PR and currently CEO Torque communication said, 'When an exasperated Chairman Arvind Pande told a pestering journalist wanting to feast on yet another "bad story" on losses—"I want to stay away from the front pages of the *Economic Times*," the daily dutifully put that story on the front page right below the masthead.'

Despite a formidable corporate communication setup that had weathered much of the vicissitudes of the decades past, it was clear that a new steer was required and fresh thinking had to be brought into engaging externally. Chairman Arvind Pande had a rather easy and disarming way of engaging the media, which was a matter of fact, without flourish and where he called a spade a spade. That more or less took away the sting of correspondents who had come in to meet with him with a pile of research on how things were going bad, only to be stunned by the discussion that pointed out that the situation was probably worse in some aspects and then given the big picture that drove home a much better story.

In the meantime, the Chief of Corporate Affairs worked with Rediff PR to diligently not only connect with every single journalist but a conscious decision was taken to enlarge the media space as the conversations moved from Calcutta to Delhi with more stories rolling out from the headquarters of the company at Ispat Bhawan,

New Delhi. The Communications team in Kolkata and the Plants too stepped up their engagement and slowly the discourse began to change from 'any gossip goes' to a more informed understanding of the massive changes that were underway in the company.

A very effective strategy that was rolled out was to bring journalists to the plants for them to see the transformation that was taking place. Over the period of a year-and-a-half, correspondents saw for themselves the gigantic transformation taking place in Bokaro, Durgapur and Rourkela. A medley of senior and junior journalists from different cities got a first-hand feel of the activities at the plant.

The quick result was to dispel the myth-making that had taken place earlier of these steel plants dying slowly with a disgruntled, unhappy workforce, poor work ethic, squabbling bosses and a general picture of entitled 'babus' running the show. The picture they took away was one of the hard taskmasters who had the full backing of their unions in making the steel giant turn around.

A plant is always a great place for communicating action on the ground and the journalists invariably went back with a picture that was much at odds with what they had been fed earlier. They saw new machines, focus on waste reduction, clear timelines for completing a whole menu of products, run by a group of men who were competent, superbly confident that they would deliver and machinery that was gigantic in scale and yet ran smoothly. Suddenly the sheen of their earlier visits to the smaller plants of new operators began to wear thin and they started buying back into the story of SAIL.

The plant visits were a good opportunity to focus on the modernization of the plants and create a positive storyline about the direction in which SAIL was headed. The troubled financial results were countered by demonstrating that the fundamentals of the company, its products and its techno-economics were in a far better position than the numbers reflected. But the biggest windfall from these visits was invariably the goodwill. A steel plant visit is a memorable visit for anyone and the mammoth machines in a large-scale plant do their own talking!

The team also broadened the conversation from SAIL being the steel in India, to SAIL being a participant in the ecosystem of steel in India. The company started expressing its views on public policy. Or, how SAIL saw steel industry trends in the coming months, its views on anti-dumping commissions, coal purchase negotiations that were setting precedents, etc. The company began stepping out to critique credit-rating agencies and banks funding steel projects, who were missing out on the essential soundness of the steel majors while downgrading them.

A huge exercise was taken to get people within the company to understand the consequences of sharing commercially sensitive information in a market that was no longer a duopoly. Insights were shared with employees on how rumours were being used against SAIL at a time when there was an unusual level of uncertainty in the world markets, and many reporters and financial analysts were vigorously looking for 'inside' information from unofficial sources.

What was clearly being disseminated was that internally a cultural transformation was being effected to change from a public sector mindset to a competitive mind-set, notwithstanding the nature of ownership. An intensive communication programme was planned to bring about a behavioural change in employees resulting in a cost-cutting exercise of the like never seen before at SAIL.

There was, thus, a large scale exercise for aligning internal audiences with the company objectives, and creating new engagements with the media while keeping a straightforward approach. No favours were done, no one got a freebie, no elaborate junkets or entertainment was dished out. At the end of it, the game was played the old fashioned way—tell a good story and tell it well, tell it the way you want to and don't shy away from the bad news because by putting a bigger picture to it, the story stays yours rather than that told by someone else about you.

As a result of the process adopted, the company increasingly started changing its communication stance from defending, dodging and watching from the sidelines, to developing a coherent argument of achievement, well before it showed up in its financial results. Amazingly, the company was able to steer the story in its direction in a very short period of time. The storyline that came to play was simple and forward looking. It consumed and eliminated the petty reporting that had earlier characterized reporting on SAIL and supposed warfare between various divisions, competition for positions, tussles between government and the company, etc.

The storyline, put across in a rather simple manner read thus, 'These are challenging times. The emergence of new players in the market, change in the character of the market, new products and a new economic milieu have created an environment to which an old giant must adapt quickly and adequately. Today, after many decades of existence, SAIL is faced with a mix of opportunities and risks. Opportunities must be encashed by taking strategic business decisions, and risk must be minimized through the ongoing internal restructuring process and a turnaround strategy.'

The message was bold and clear. It forced the people shaping narratives on the imminent demise of SAIL to look at a much bigger vision and take into account real achievements. By the end of 2002, it became clear that SAIL had transformed itself into a customer-centred, financially aware, synchronized team facing competition headlong and outsmarting the best on many occasions.

Communicating with the Stakeholders

While communication with the media formed a fulcrum of SAIL's new communication strategy, an equally important area of concern was communicating with the internal stakeholders. After the formulation of the Turnaround and Transformation Plan and its acceptance in the SAIL Board, Chairman SAIL invited the national leaders of trade unions to SAIL Corporate Office, where a detailed presentation was made on the crisis confronting the company and the strategies evolved to overcome it. It was conveyed that the interest of the employees would be foremost, but the turnaround needed some bold steps without which the company itself may not survive.

Similarly, when the efforts to revive IISCO under a joint venture route did not fructify, a sustenance plan was prepared. Under the plan, a modest investment of around ₹340 crore was to be made at Burnpur Works including the mines and collieries. The operation at Kulti Works, which engaged in the production of castings and pipes, and contributed disproportionately to the losses of IISCO was to be stopped, and the manpower offered VR. Substantial downsizing of the manpower was planned also at Burnpur Works.

Before submitting the plan for IISCO to BIFR (Board of Financial and Industrial Reconstruction), a meeting was organized at Kolkata, where representatives of IISCO from Burnpur, Kulti and Mines & Collieries were invited. The meeting was also attended by leaders of National trade unions active in IISCO. A detailed presentation was made on IISCO's survival plan to the unions.

From the SAIL management side, the team comprised Chairman SAIL, Arvind Pande, (who was also Chairman of IISCO), Executive Director in charge (IISCO), A K Jaiswal, and Sanjay Kumar from Business Planning, Corporate office, who was involved in the formulation of the survival plan. All questions asked by unions were answered with openness and a willingness to accommodate suggestions for improvement. In the end, the IISCO collective was more or less convinced of the sincerity of SAIL's approach in formulating the survival plan.

Whenever roadblocks to implementing the restructuring plan were encountered, the top management of SAIL took the initiative of reaching out to the opinion makers and thought leaders amongst the stakeholders. Hiving of the captive power plants posed a challenge when the visit of the NTPC team to the steel plant for due diligence was opposed by the DSP unions. Mr M. K. Moitra, Director Restructuring and Corporate Planning, wrote to the leaders of all unions active in DSP, Dr M. K. Pandhe, General Secretary, CITU, Shri S. B. Debroy, Joint Secretary, Hindustan Steel Employees Union, CITU, Shri Nirmal Routh, Secretary, All India Steel Workers Federation and Shri Subrato Mookerjee, President, Hindustan Steel Workers Union, INTUC.

Mr Moitra made an impassioned appeal that the future of the workers could only be ensured by protecting the future of the company. The funds generated by divesting the captive power plant were needed for upgradation of DSP's blast furnace number three, which was under capital repair. He appealed for the wholehearted support of the union leaders as the implications of missing out on restructuring were too grave to allow it to happen. Mr Moitra along with Chairman Pande, also met Shri Jyoti Basu, the Chief Minister of West Bengal, to apprise him of the proposed divestment of the power plant of DSP and gain his support for the restructuring initiatives of SAIL.

Mr Moitra also wrote letters to the heads of trade unions at the other integrated steel plants—Shri S. C. Dubey, General Secretary, Bokaro Steel Workers' Union, Shri R. C. Arya, President, Steel Workers Union, Bhilai, and Dr M. D. N. Panicker, General Secretary, Rourkela Shramik Sangh, informing them about the restructuring package cleared by the Government of India. He sought their support in implementing the asset restructuring and other tasks for which SAIL had entered into an MoU with the Government of India, with agreed timelines.

Presentations were also made to the Officers Association to keep them apprised of the Company's plan for Turnaround and Transformation. A well-planned communication drive ensured coverage of all interest groups on the restructuring plan for the company. Dr Sanak Mishra, Executive Director, Corporate Planning, wrote to the president of the Officers Association Shri B. T. Vijaya Raghava Reddy and Shri H. G. Umapathy, General Secretary, Workers' Association of VISL, how the option of divesting the unit in a JV would protect the interest of the unit and its employees, and assuaged the concerns raised by the officers association and the workers' union.

SAIL also reached out to the investors. The Unit Trust of India (UTI), an investor in SAIL, was facing problems as its investments in a number of companies were underperforming. In December 1998, UTI invited the major companies in which it had invested to come to its headquarters in Mumbai and make a presentation on the company's performance and prospects. The SAIL team led by Chairman Arvind Pande made a presentation to UTI on the root cause of SAIL's poor business performance and the Turnaround and Transformation Plan formulated by the company.

SAIL's proposal for financial restructuring then was under the consideration of the Government of India. At the end of the presentation, Arvind Pande asked UTI to write to the government supporting SAIL's restructuring plan. UTI readily agreed to do so after seeing the proactive actions initiated by the company and the tough measures it planned to undertake to turn around.

Similar presentations were made to other financial institutions who were assured of the sincerity of the company in implementing effective measures. These interactions were very helpful in overcoming the acute liquidity shortage faced by the company, as a loss of confidence by the investors could have led to a run on the deposits, further aggravating the tight position of funds. What stood out in these interactions was the fact the company, unprompted by the Government of India or any external agency, had on its own developed a plan for chalking out its future course of action. This plan was self-driven and did not shy away from tough measures.

Meetings were also set up with the Members of Parliament under whose constituency SAIL's integrated steel plants were situated. To participate in these informal meetings, Chairman SAIL sent some of his younger officers who had contributed to developing the turnaround and transformation Plan. It was a unique communication strategy, which pre-empted any false or motivated information, influencing an important constituency, on the turnaround initiatives of the company.

A presentation was also made on SAIL's turnaround plan to the Secretary Expenditure and other Senior Officials at the Finance Ministry in September 1999. The SAIL team led by Chairman Pande clarified the assumptions and the basis for the plan and provided confidence that the biggest turnaround package before the Government of India was backed by a credible plan for implementation, thereby allaying apprehensions that after receiving the one time support, SAIL would come back seeking further support on a later date.

Internal Communication

Internal communication in SAIL over the years had depended on the directives given by the Chief Executives of the respective plants and units. There was a great divergence at the micro-level, as the plants and major units had their own magazines brought out by their PR departments, which differed in presentation, design, layout, and periodicity. Some units published more than one house magazine.

Other than the house magazines, the medium for internal communication in the plants and units comprised visual and audio-visual presentations such as hoardings, posters, and leaflets, shop floor media such as posters, billboards and cable TV at some major plants.

When the communication campaign for the turnaround plan was initiated, it was realized that its effectiveness would depend upon it being easily understood and identified with. Further, it should be accompanied by an action plan from the management and should come from sources that could be trusted.

The contents of the house magazines were revamped to project the change agenda in its entirety. Special features on specific areas of concern, especially those related to employee interest, were introduced and employee responses given wide coverage. Along with the shop floor interviews of the workers, opinions of the supervisory staff were published for a balanced spread of awareness. Achievements of individual employees and groups in different units, especially in the area of conservation of resources, were highlighted to increase awareness.

Wall sheets at the shop floor locations kept employees not only periodically updated on the progress of the restructuring program but also on the changes in the company's business environment. Specially designed posters put up at different vantage points sensitized the employee to the messages from the top management.

Recorded addresses of the SAIL Chairman were telecast through cable TV networks in the different plant townships, enabling even the family members of the employee to become aware of the benefits linked to the change process.

Mass Communication Drive

Internal communication had been SAIL's strength. It started at the time of former Chairman Dr V. Krishnamurthy who held a series of workshops to evolve 'Priorities for Action' in 1987 with a large cross-section of employees, cutting across hierarchies and levels and encouraging a free exchange of views to develop a shared vision. The Management Training Institute of SAIL at Ranchi provided an excellent venue for this.

In line with the tradition of interacting with a large number of employees, a Large Group Interactive Event (LGIE), was organized with the help of Mr George Koreth to enable sharing of ideas and a renewal of commitment at different levels. LGIE was then a commonly practised management tool in developed countries, used for organizational review and restructuring, based on consensus generated among the employees themselves.

LGIE, also known as real prime time strategic change, was considered invaluable for whole system transformation. Facilitating a long-term outlook, LGIE was expected to provide the foundation for long-term systemic changes, by bringing in a critical mass of the organization to focus on what needed to be changed. The fundamental principle for LGIE was that effective change comes from within and those working in the organization best understood the opportunities and obstacles.

In India, the LGIE concept had then been used in a limited way by some progressive companies in the private sector. SAIL was the first public sector enterprise in the country to conduct an LGIE, with about 200 senior executives, including the top management at the Taj Bengal in Kolkata from 4 to 6 September 1998. Planned to achieve continuous and vigorous communication as well as to gain prior involvement of the ultimate implementers, LGIE at Kolkata covered all Directors, Executive Directors, General Managers and select Deputy General Managers. Other than coverage of such a large group, LGIE provided functional anonymity and credibility with the full participation of all concerned. It also provided the participants with a unique platform to share information about the issues they faced, and work on relationships across functions and levels of the organization.

Subsequently, a major company-wide communication campaign was launched following a workshop at Sariska in August 1999, where the SAIL Directors met and deliberated on the challenges confronting the company. It was decided in the workshop to immediately set in motion an implementation plan for maximizing earnings in the short, medium and long terms, for the profitability and survival of the company through the restructuring plan.

It needed to be communicated that given the policy environment, support to the PSEs the way it existed in the pre-liberalization era, would not be forthcoming. The destiny of the company, therefore, was to be shaped by the force of its own actions. The envisaged change however required the single-minded commitment of employees at all levels and called for the involvement of a wide cross-section from different functions and locations in SAIL.

A three-day workshop was organized at MTI, Ranchi from 24 to 26 September 1999, to develop a communication plan to disseminate the outcome of the Sariska Workshop throughout the organization. Attended by around sixty internal resource persons (IRPs) from all the SAIL plants and units, the restructuring plan was discussed threadbare. The resource persons were equipped with the communication module—'Restructuring, its need and implications' and a set of documents containing the possible questions, concerns and doubts likely to be raised on various aspects of the restructuring plan. The answers framed after detailed deliberations were expected to provide a uniformity of response, approach and direction with regard to the restructuring initiatives.

The workshop helped the IRPs in internalizing the strategies presented and discussed during the workshop. The presentation to the IRPs was in three parts. The first part which summarized the sum and substance of SAIL's strategy was presented by Mr R. P. Singh, Additional Director Corporate Planning. He covered the principal causes of the crisis confronting SAIL and the fact that it could be overcome with collective effort. He emphasized that specific measures would be required to alter the way the company had traditionally conducted its business. These measures included redefining the business to concentrate on those areas in which the company either was internationally competitive or had the potential to become internationally competitive; move towards a focused product-market strategy as well as improved marketing processes; attack all potential areas for cost reduction and instead of measuring performance in terms of tonnes produced or tonnes sold, switch over to a system of cash earned and cash spent.

Covering the second part, Mr J. K. Gupta, Sr Manager (Finance), drew the attention of the participants to the financial projection of the company if nothing was done, and things continued the way they were. He drove forth the logic that this situation was not sustainable. The immediate remedy hence lay in restoring the financial foundation of the company through a process of financial restructuring, which while addressing the balance sheet concerns would enable necessary breathing time to undertake business restructuring without which the sustained viability of the company was not possible.

The last part of the presentation was made by Sanjay Kumar, Sr Economist, Corporate Planning. This module dealt with the projection of the market scenario in the immediate future and the fact that SAIL could not depend on the market alone to pull it out of losses. Precise and well-focused interventions in the form of Key Account Management Process, cost reduction through operational excellence, procurement of materials based on total cost of ownership (TCO) concept, and differentiated sourcing strategy needed to be followed for getting the desired results. SAIL had already initiated these processes in the previous six months, which now had to be rolled over to tap the full potential.

Following the workshop at MTI, Ranchi, a series of communication workshops were organized cutting across the hierarchy of the organization. There was direct participation of CEOs and senior officials in all plants and units to sensitize the employees on the need for restructuring and the strategies required for its successful implementation.

A complete briefing by SAIL Chairman on video was played at all communication workshops to have continuity in the message. It was designed to break mental blocks and develop wider acceptance of various measures to be implemented. It pointed to the SAIL employees the choice of either letting things continue the way they were or, work for a viable, competitive and resurgent SAIL. It also emphasized to the employee the scope of his/her own contribution in achieving the desired change.

As a part of a structured exercise, Head of Plant/Unit—right from the Managing Director on to the Executive Directors, Operational Heads, Supervisor and shop floor leaders set out to meet groups of employees under their control at regular short intervals and communicate to them the state of affairs and the remedial actions.

This mass contact exercise informed every worker about the difficulties being faced by the company and the organization's plan to address those. More important, it delineated to the workers how they individually and collectively, could play a critical role in addressing the issues at hand.

This open communication brought in transparency that enabled every worker to identify with the organization and its difficulties and motivated them to do their part. It fostered a feeling of ownership and responsibility enabling them to view themselves as team members ready to shoulder the burden of the bad times.

The plant/unit level workshops conducted by the IRPs (Internal Resource Persons) commenced in October 1999 and by the end of the year, 16000 employees had attended the workshops. With consecutive workshops, the IRPs grew more confident in fielding queries raised by the employees. Those who attended the workshop were expected to carry the message to their peer group and colleagues. The plant-level discussions were conducted under the guidance of the Chief Executives. Each of these workshops was presided over by a representative of the top management to clarify and respond to the queries raised by the participants. The communication exercise in all the plants and units was personally supported by the chief executives/managing directors and attained almost 100 per cent coverage. Being truly interactive, it was perhaps the biggest internal communication drive undertaken by any company then.

Apart from direct communication, auxiliary modes like house journals, leaflets and brochures, and other internal campaigns via multiple channels helped reinforce the message. An interesting initiative in the area of internal communication was steered by SAIL's Corporate Affairs Division (CAD). A wallpaper called 'SAIL Shakti', was introduced as Chairman's address to employees periodically on current topics of concern and also announcements of the company's achievements. 'SAIL Shakti' was printed in colour on double broadsheets and was pasted at carefully decided designated areas, public places, in every Shop floor and every department. Printed in different vernacular languages (Hindi, Marathi, Tamil, Odiya, Bengali and Hindi), it spoke to the employee in his own language.

Focused Workshops

Another major intervention was an excellent workshop in Ranchi organized by Director Finance, Mr V. S. Jain with the help of Mr R. K. Agarwal, a senior chartered accountant to raise awareness of costs and financial ratios against the old mind-set of only production-related ratios.

It was perhaps for the first time that a behavioural change was attempted in a large organization through a massive communication exercise. It attempted to reorient the organization as a commercial entity, by redefining business in financial rather than only physical terms. Its success was subsequently gauged by the massive cost-cutting the company was able to effect in its operations.

Media Relations

The country's media traditionally gave wide coverage to SAIL owing to its nationwide presence and inter-linkages with the national economy. The sheer variety of information covered by press and electronic media on SAIL made media relations central to the company's activity.

Earlier many arms of the media were receiving varied information from multiple sources. This had led to duplication of efforts and overlapping of interests, apart from lack of accountability and reliability. Also, it was not in line with the 'One organization One Voice' approach. As SAIL's stature in the corporate world attracted media attention on all issues related to the organization, one of the main tasks of the media relations group at CAD was to sensitize media representatives on the company's activities, achievements and improve the awareness among the public on SAIL.

Amongst the newspapers, the financial press carried maximum news about the industry and reached the target external audience such as opinion-makers and policymakers. The mainline dailies published from the metros, provided adequate coverage to SAIL and the steel industry, as all had specified space for business industry. They had the advantage of a wider reach, given the wider readership. The regional editions of mainline dailies or the regional newspapers covered SAIL widely wherever SAIL had a major presence and often had a regional bias reflected openly in their coverage of SAIL. The local and the regional newspapers covered SAIL prominently wherever the company had a major presence. The target groups for the local newspapers being SAIL employees, their families and friends. It was perceived that wherever internal communication systems were superficial or lacked credibility, the local newspapers gained enormous prominence.

Dr Shoeb Ahmed, Head of CAD, recalled, 'Handling media was a sensitive job especially when the organization was passing through a major transition. SAIL was on a downward cycle and there was no sympathy being shown by the media due to a lack of understanding of the company's problems. This led to the misrepresentation of facts in several instances. We were taken aback when a section of media conveyed an observation that SAIL lacked transparency. Our credibility was severely eroded. We also realized that the profile of media itself had changed and the new generation of dynamic journalists did not rely on press handouts or replies to questionnaires alone for information. Besides, some of them were not even aware of the enormity and complexity of SAIL's operations.'

'The major task before us was to reorient our media policy and make it more proactive and responsive. Continuous interactions and briefings based on concrete data and facts and the conducted visits of groups of journalists to the steel plants for the first-hand feel of the things helped to bridge the perception gap to a large extent.'

A new media relations policy was developed whereby all engagements with the national media were looked after by CAD at the Corporate Office, while CMO, Public Relations handled the Kolkata-based media, and the plant PR departments the regional and the local media. Engagement with the media ensured that the company's point of view was considered for publication as a part of any report portraying SAIL in a negative light. A proactive strategy to inform and educate, and a constant endeavour to keep an ear to the ground, helped kill many stories based on a misconception or provided by motivated sources.

SAILNews, a high-class in-house journal, was used for establishing a two-way channel of communication with employees. The chairman message in each issue captured the key concerns, achievements and action plan for the company. The employees on the other hand provided their perspective on different initiatives that could be taken up to shore up the performance of the company. Restructuring as a topic was very widely dealt with and extensively covered in various issues of SAILNews from 1997 to 2003. SAILNews also became the medium to reach external readership, viz., media persons, Government functionaries, opinion makers, financial institutions, investors, etc., on news related to SAIL.

The role of corporate communication in SAIL's transformation process cannot be overstated. Through a sound communication policy and a series of interventions such as LGIE, plant/unit level workshops, mass communication drives, media and stakeholders engagement, the company ensured transparency, credibility, and clarity of communication to multi-layered interest groups for effecting unprecedented changes in the organization.

Mr P. K. Niyogi, who held the office of Chief of Communication at IISCO, DSP and CMO, during his tenure at SAIL said about DSP, 'The turning point in the perception about DSP was brought about by vastly improved and enhanced internal communication. We did not hesitate to talk about failures and explained what we were trying to overcome. We had been given the liberty to publish the views of departmental trade union leaders criticizing management actions and policies. These were published alongside management versions. People read both and formed their own opinion.'

Acknowledging the role of communication in organizational transformation, Dr S. K. Bhattacharyya, Managing Director of DSP said, 'Communication played a big role in bringing awareness and enhancing motivation, at the same time it boosted the morale of the workforce.'

Dr Mishra, Managing Director, RSP was of the view that his mass contact campaign involving regular structured discussions with the group of workers on the shop floor, was instrumental in increased workers' participation in the company's objectives.

The communication process in SAIL gained a level of maturity as it reached out to all its stakeholders especially external, like never before. There was honesty in transmitting what was happening to the company; along with a well-thought-out strategy to become a vibrant organization again. It was this continuous and intensive thought-out journey, which helped SAIL establish credibility and enabled the implementation of many tough decisions without any backlash.

CHAPTER 15

The Sense of a New Dawn

'Steel Authority of India Limited has been reborn, it is back to its feet; that brings no joy?' thundered the Prime Minister of India Atal Bihari Vajpayee, in the parliament on 19 August 2003. It formed a part of the opening rebuttal of the Prime Minister as he rose to defend his government, which faced a 'No Confidence Motion' moved by the opposition. He was responding to allegations on his government's intent to finish off the public sector!

SAIL indeed had turned around. It had posted a profit of ₹242 crore in the fourth quarter of fiscal year ending March 2003, after a gap of nearly 5 years. It was followed by one of the most spectacular corporate transformations witnessed in India inc., when its annual profits (after tax) for the year 2003–2004 soared to a new high of ₹2,512 crore, surpassing the previous best of 1995–1996 by more than ₹1000 crore.

When the Upturn Came

All the efforts of the turnaround and the transformation process set in motion from 1997 to 2003 were to prepare the company for seizing the opportunity of the upturn in the business cycle, once it presented itself.

A robust, resilient, transformed SAIL grabbed the opportunity as never before. It had pared its weaknesses. A sustained campaign for cost reduction had kept the per tonne production cost of saleable steel virtually constant despite inflation in the input prices. Production, sales volume and turnover attained new peaks year after year. Inventory holding levels were trimmed down to the minimum. Total loans which had soared to ₹21,017 crore in 1998–1999, were cut down to ₹8,689 crore by 2003–2004. In fact, the company became virtually debt-free in 2004–2005 as its term deposits with the banks exceeded the loans in the balance sheet.

The company's transformation was reflected in the upsurge of its share price in the bourses. SAIL scrip which had traded below par in the stock exchanges for most of the period after March 1997, entered the premium zone beginning January 2003; and its market capitalization which had shrunk to ₹2,000 crore in March 2002, bounced back to ₹13,340 crore by March 2004.

Post restructuring SAIL acquired a very solid foundation by the virtue of which it became the leading profit earner amongst all steel companies in India for the rest of the decade. Its cash reserves swelled to more than ₹22,000 crore, providing the company the confidence and the wherewithal to embark on an ambitious modernization and expansion programme of ₹72,000 crore.

Records Are Meant to Be Broken

The restructuring initiatives saw a continual improvement in all business parameters of the company. Overall sales volume increased from a level of 9 million tonnes in 2000–2001 to an all-time high of 9.5 million tonnes in 2001–2002, which was exceeded by sales of 10 million tonnes in 2002–2003, only to be overtaken by a new record of 10.7 million tonnes in 2003–2004. Supplies of rails increased to 7.1 lakh tonnes, out of which 1.5 lakh tonnes were in a higher length of 26 meters. The closing stocks of saleable steel in 2003–2004 were the lowest recorded over the past 20 years.

Performance Trends 1997–1998 to 2003–2004

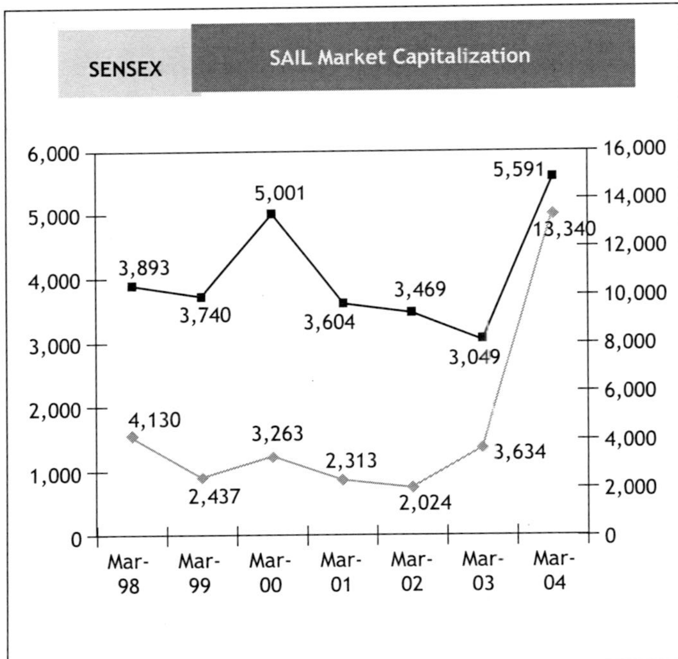

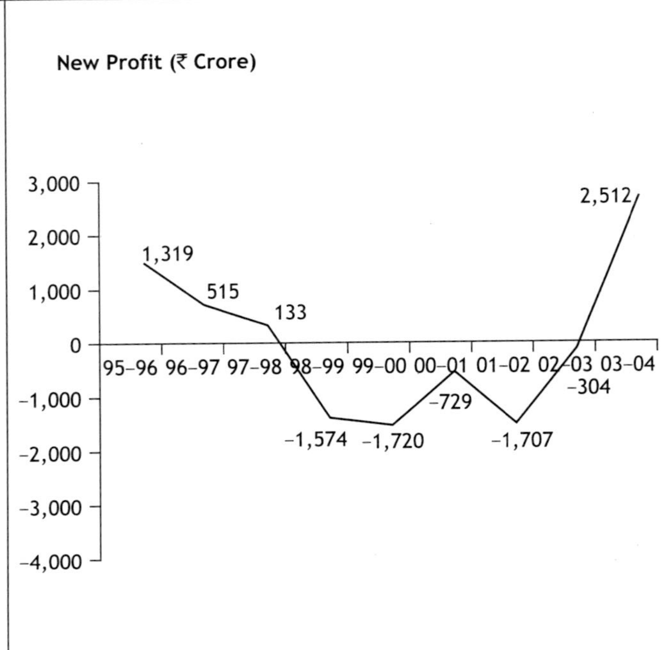

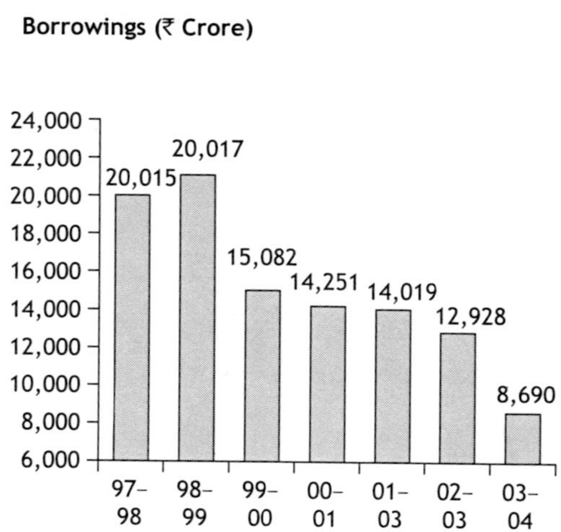

Borrowings (₹ Crore)
24,000
22,000
20,000
18,000
16,000
14,000
12,000
10,000
8,000
6,000
20,015
20,017
15,082
14,251
14,019
12,928
8,690
97–98
98–99
99–00
00–01
01–03
02–03
03–04

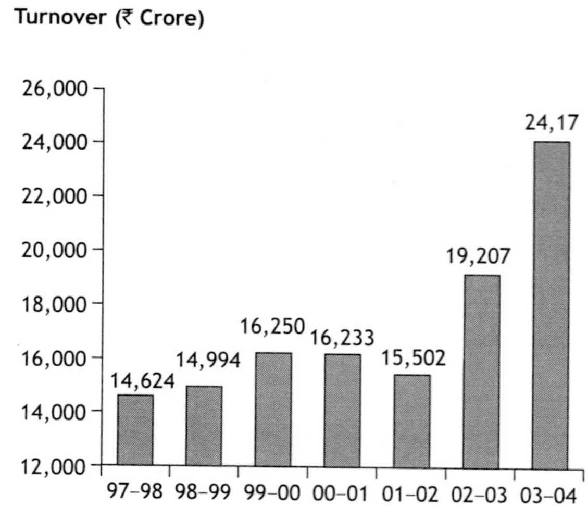

Turnover (₹ Crore)
26,000
24,000
22,000
20,000
18,000
16,000
14,000
12,000
14,624
14,994
16,250
16,233
15,502
19,207
24,17
97–98
98–99
99–00
00–01
01–02
02–03
03–04

Taking advantage of the improved market situation, SAIL shipped a record 1.17 million tonnes of steel in the foreign markets in 2003–2004. The main export destinations were China, South Korea, Thailand, Nepal, Myanmar, Sri Lanka and the Philippines. Inroads were also made in new markets by the export of wire rods and HR coils to Taiwan, Germany and the UK.

Record production of saleable steel at the plants provided the basis for record sales performance. Beginning 1999–2000 SAIL for the first time breached saleable steel production level of 9.5 million tonnes. Thereafter, each of the years up to 2003–2004 saw setting up a new record, culminating with a record production of 11 million tonnes of saleable steel in 2003–2004. The four main integrated steel plants at Bhilai, Bokaro, Durgapur and Rourkela operated at an average capacity utilization of 104 per cent for saleable steel in 2003–2004.

The company had invested significantly in the continuous casting facilities in the modernization program. By 2003–2004 almost 61 per cent of the total crude steel production was from BOF-CC route, with the rated capacity utilization of the continuous casting shops reaching a level of 120 per cent. SAIL's captive mines recorded the highest ever production of iron ore at 20.95 million tonnes in 2003–2004 and the entire requirement of iron ore was met from captive sources.

The operating efficiency of the production units also transformed. The blast furnaces operated at the highest ever productivity of 1.53 t/m^3/day in 2003–2004 overtaking the previous best of 1.51 t/m^3/day set just a year before. The energy consumption, lowest ever at 7.46 gcal/tcs for 2003–2004, followed the trend of setting a new benchmark every year from 1997–1998 to 2003–2004. This record was set at a time when the proportion of high energy-consuming value-added steel was expanding in the saleable steel production.

Manpower numbers had come down from a level of 183,000 in March 1997 to 132,000 in March 2004, a reduction of more than 50,000. The separations through VRS during this period accounted for around 34,000 numbers. The reduced employee strength and the increasing production boosted the labour productivity to 137 tonnes of crude steel/man/year, from a level of 96 tonnes of crude steel/man/year in 1996–1997.

The overall cost reduction measures in the operations area were supplemented by financial measures which reduced overall debt and curtailed the cost of finance. Substitution of high interest-bearing instruments by lower interest debt and reduction in overall debt saw a sharp reduction in interest charges to ₹899 crore in 2003–2004 from a peak of around ₹2000 crore in 1998–1999. The debt-equity ratio, which had risen to 6.5:1 due to the continuous losses, came down sharply to 1.86:1 at the close of fiscal 2003–2004.

The period of restructuring and transformation brought about an unprecedented improvement in the plant operations. For the first time in SAIL, the concept of rated capacity lost its meaning. Rated capacities were exceeded in each of the integrated steel plants of SAIL, billet caster and merchant mill at DSP, slab caster at BSL, SMS-II, rail and structural mill, wire rod mill, merchant mill and plate mill at BSP. Each of the integrated steel plants at Bhilai, Durgapur, Rourkela and Bokaro recorded their all-time best performance since inception during 2003–2004 for production of hot metal, crude steel and saleable steel.

In the area pertaining to operating efficiency, Bhilai Steel Plant set a new record converter lining life of 1788 blows; its BF productivity hit a record of 1.74 tonne/m^3/day. Durgapur Steel Plant attained the lowest ever coke rate of 560 kg/tonne hot metal, and lowest ever specific power consumption at 427 kwh/tcs, BSL attained the lowest ever energy consumption at 7.75 gcal/tcs, lowest ever refractory consumption of 13.68 kg/tcs and highest lining life of 2657 heats in its converter-1 in SMS-2. The energy consumption at RSP in 2003–2004 was best at 8.7 gcal/tcs and the yield at its silicon mill was the best since inception.

Closing down the shops which had outlived their utility was not an easy decision at SAIL. It required redeploying labour and engaging with the unions. In the years 1997 to 2003 many uneconomic units were shut down—the bar mill at ASP, the fish plate plant at DSP, the blooming and slabbing mill and the fertilizer plant at RSP. The rejuvenation was comprehensive as the new efficient units operated without having to carry the burden of shops that had outlived their utility.

In addition to improved productivity and new products, a welcome outcome was the sharp improvement in some of the key environment indices. Water consumption in SAIL plants steadily reduced from a level of 15.9 m^3/tcs in 1996–1997 to 6.3 m^3/tcs in 2003–2004. This significant reduction in specific water consumption was achieved through a combination of measures such as curbing leakages, up-gradation of existing and installation of new water circulation systems, reuse of treated water, etc. Conscious of the steadily deteriorating air quality, SAIL invested in efficient air pollution control equipment such as scrubbers, cyclones, ESP, bag filters, etc., which brought down specific particulate matter (PM) emission from 9.34 in 1996–1997 to 3.12 in 2003–2004.

The Summing Up

In the MoU signed with the Government of India on Financial and Business Restructuring, 17 tasks were identified for which targets were set. An additional task was added when captive power plant-2 of Bhilai Steel Plant was put in the list of the assets for divestment, taking the total number of tasks for SAIL to 18.

By March 2004, SAIL had accomplished 12 of the 18 tasks. Of the remaining six, the one related to manpower rightsizing was to continue, while the rest comprised divestment of the three special steel plants, IISCO and the Rourkela Fertilizer Plant.

Asset Restructuring

Due to lack of interest by prospective bidders for ASP, VISL and ISP, and resistance by employees in case of SSP, SAIL decided to handover the plants to the Ministry of Disinvestment (MoD) for further

Business and Financial Restructuring of SAIL

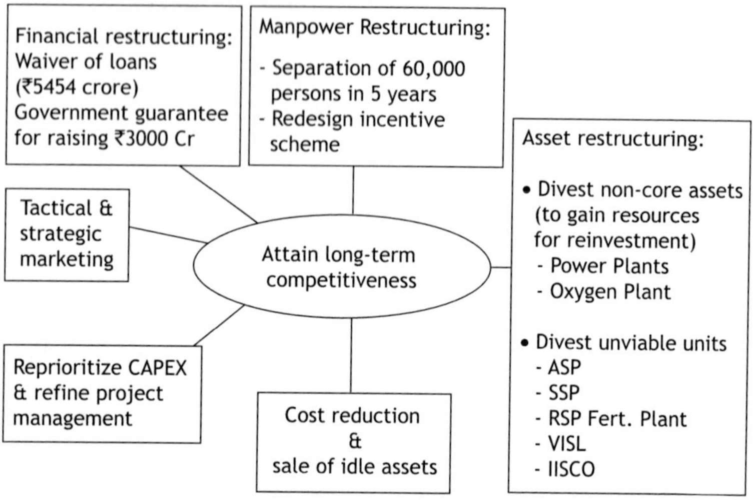

continuation of the divestment process. The MoD however took a view that divestment of the units fell in the nature of asset sales as no disinvestment of shares of the Government of India was taking place with regard to the above units.

MoD was willing to take up the process of induction of a JV partner, who would have the management control in IISCO, after obtaining permission from BIFR. As regards the disinvestment of ASP and VISL, these units needed to be demerged into separate companies for MoD to take them up for disinvestment. MoD wanted SAIL to continue with their process of disinvestment of SSP and Rourkela Fertiliser Plant.

With the coming of the new Government in May 2004, the stance of the authorities on asset disinvestment underwent a change. For the special steel plants, the focus shifted to improving the performance and to bring them to black. To a great extent, the three ailing special steel plans SSP, VISL and ASP reduced their loss and earned marginal profits for some time. SSP was first to come in black and earned a marginal profit in 2003–2004 and 2004–2005, and improved on it further to earn profits of ₹118 and ₹102 crore in 2006–2007 and 2007–2008, respectively. ASP too came in black and earned marginal profits in 2005–2006, 2006–2007 and 2007–2008. VISL earned marginal profit once in 2005–2006.

The divestment of the Rourkela Fertilizer Plant did not appear to be headed towards a desirable outcome, which made the second-best option of closure increasingly appealing. A decision, therefore, was taken to shut down the fertilizer plant, redeploy the labour and sell off the assets.

As regards IISCO, a proposal of reviving the company was already under implementation as approved by the government in June 2002 and cleared by BIFR in November 2003. SAIL's finances had started shoring up from the last quarter on 2002–2003. The iron ore mines of IISCO had great strategic relevance for SAIL for providing iron ore security in its future growth plans. So it was decided that SAIL would merge IISCO as its unit and undertake its modernization as part of its Corporate Plan 2012.

So far as divestment of oxygen plant-2 of Bhilai Steel Plant was concerned, a decision was taken that all new oxygen plants in SAIL would be set up on BOO basis, given that divestment of existing oxygen plant under a JV had not found favour with the prospective bidders.

SAIL was successful in divesting power plants at DSP, RSP, BSL and BSP. An assessment of the power plants under the JV power companies formed with NTPC and DVC (NTPC SAIL Power Company Limited and Bokaro Power Supply Company Limited), after a few years of operations showed that the cost of the power for each of the steel plants had come down due to efficient functioning of the units under the JV, despite an increase in the input costs of the power plants.

There was a significant improvement in the plant load factor (PLF) of each of the captive JV power units. In fact, the physical performance of the captive power plants under the JV, within a period of 4 years became better than the best ever prior to JV formation.

Physical and Financial Targets

As a part of the restructuring, MoU signed with the MoS, Government of India in March 2000, certain physical and financial parameters were set to be achieved by SAIL 2003–2004. Given the strong physical performance and the uptick in the market, SAIL was able to achieve almost all the targets set for the company for 2003–2004 as shown below:

		2003-2004	
Parameters	*Unit*	*Target*	*Actual*
Production (4 ISPs)	’000 T	10,753	10,727
Sales quantity	’000 T	10,633	10,710
Sales turnover	₹ crore	21,541	24,178
Gross margin	₹ crore	4,231	4,650
Net profit (after tax)	₹ crore	1,376	2,512
Coke rate	Kg/thm	540	542
Energy consumption	Gcal/tcs	7.83	7.46

This performance was but an outcome of the numerous initiatives covering operating and purchase cost reduction, redesigning incentive systems, improving sales force effectiveness, initiating key account management process, organizational restructuring and redesigning key corporate processes such as redesigning of promotion policy, redesigning business performance review, etc.

The targets set for operating cost reduction was around ₹1,000 crore over a period of 3 years and for purchase cost reduction approximately ₹350 crore. The cost reduction initiatives in operating and purchase costs starting 2000–2001 enabled SAIL to realize more than ₹1,500 crore over a period of 4 years.

SAIL was also able to adhere to its plan of rationalization of capital expenditure and earnings from the sale of idle assets. In fact, the monetization of its surplus flats and houses provided it liquidity that had not been envisaged.

What Was Unique in SAIL Restructuring

SAIL restructuring had several fascinating aspects, of which the first and foremost was 'being proactive'. SAIL had started working on a Turnaround Plan in 1997–1998 before the company came into red. It could foresee that given the market conditions, the company could not sustain itself under a 'business as usual' approach.

Once a decision for transforming the company was taken, its strengths and weaknesses of SAIL were ruthlessly analysed. Each of the production units was assessed on its ability to stay afloat and no easy options were entertained. Other than seeking a guarantee for loans to mobilize funds at a competitive rate, no other support from the Government of India was sought. The relief from SDF loans did not have any cash flow implications. Its advantage lay in improving the balance sheet by extinguishing a part of liability in the books of SAIL, which in fact, was created from its own contribution to the fund.

The tough decisions of asset restructuring, divestment of power plants, divestment of special steel units, etc., were all an outcome of SAIL's internal decision making. The Government of India played the role of an owner to monitor the performance of the company against a target that the company had set for itself.

Another unique feature of SAIL restructuring was its human dimension. It is normally observed that when a company gets into the phase of financial distress, the employees are the first to bear the brunt. Delay in salary and wages and the delay in payment of terminal benefits to the separating employees are commonly observed phenomenon.

SAIL however kept the interest of its employees foremost. The mass contact exercise gave confidence to the employees that the restructuring measures were for the survival of the company and thereby for the survival of every individual. Importantly, the management was very sensitive not to push employees to the wall by harsh decisions. There was no delay in payment of monthly salary to the employees and there were no compulsory separations. In one instance a plant deliberately delayed the payment of salary to its employees by a week, to impress upon them the liquidity crunch faced by the company. When Chairman Pande came to know this, he was furious, and a stern message was passed to the errant plant.

Another important aspect of SAIL's restructuring was its total transparency. The management did not hide anything from its employees. The condition of the company, the measures required for transformation, the process by which the turnaround was to be effected—everything was shared with the Unions, Officers Association and the employees through numerous structured interactions and mass contact programs. As a consequence, the employees developed an implicit faith in the genuineness of the transformation program. It goes to the credit of SAIL that such a huge transformation in one of the largest public sector companies in India happened without any labour strife.

Another interesting dimension of SAIL turnaround was the all-encompassing nature of the improvement in the company. Not limited to select plants or a handful of shops, all production units migrated to a higher performance level. New records were consistently set, new records were consistently broken. Instead of disheartening, the Turnaround Plan galvanized SAIL manpower as never before. It gave the organization a unity of purpose. It enabled SAIL to take the bold step of a wage revision when the company was still in the red!

The outcome of the Transformation Plan was unprecedented. It imparted to SAIL a momentum that last more than a decade. From 2004–2005, all four integrated steel plants of SAIL came into black, something that had never happened in the past, and a status that was maintained for the next 10 years without a break. The company could brave the meltdown of 2008 to emerge as the most profitable steel company at a global level in the first half of 2009. World Steel Dynamics in 2009 ranked SAIL second after POSCO in the list of world-class steel makers based on a 23 parameters index.

Under the leadership of Chairman Pande, who owned the environmental responsibility of SAIL as the steel industry leader, the first ever Charter on Corporate Responsibility for Environment Protection (CREP) was launched in 2000. The purpose was to go beyond compliance with regulatory norms for prevention and control of pollution through various measures including waste minimization, in-plant process control and adoption of clean technologies. The Charter set targets for conservation of water, energy, recovery of chemicals, reduction in pollution, elimination of toxic pollutants and process and management of waste residues in an environmentally sound manner for 17 categories of highly polluting industries including Steel.

SAIL was amongst the first public sector Indian companies to participate in these discussions at MOEF and affirm their commitment to the initiative of the Ministry of Environment and Forests. The action plans drawn by SAIL for CREP are in implementation even today and truly reflect the aspirations of all stakeholders to voluntarily go beyond compliance, nearly 20 years after the charter was launched.

What SAIL Means to Its Communities

In 2001, SAIL adopted a new vision and credo statement. One of the core values, which formed a part of the Credo read 'we value the opportunity and responsibility to make a meaningful difference in people's life'. Articulated for the first time in 2001, it had been a guiding philosophy for the company since its inception.

Seen from a wider perspective, SAIL restructuring had significance much bigger than the turnaround of a steel company. It was not only a revival of an economic unit but the survival of an ecosystem. This would be apparent, if one were to trace the way SAIL nurtured its neighbourhood communities.

The townships set up and managed by SAIL, thrived as modern, vibrant, cosmopolitan centres of mini India. Ranked amongst the best cities in the states they were set up, they also had a significantly positive impact on the neighbourhood communities. In fulfilling its social obligations over the years, the SAIL had focused on achieving critical thresholds in areas of education, health, infrastructure, and community development. At the time SAIL was fighting a battle of survival, it continued to have a huge engagement in the socio-economic arena.

The total number of schools run by SAIL numbered 152, which imparted education to around 1 lakh children. Education to children from disadvantaged communities was free. Other than education facilities in form of primary and secondary schools; infrastructure support was provided to the private bodies to run educational institutions in the township. Some of the interesting features of SAIL run schools were achieving a ratio of 1:1 for girls and boys for all levels of education, and a very high survival rate (retention of enrolled students) of more than 93 per cent in primary and more than 90 per cent in secondary schools.

In the area of health, SAIL provided medical treatment facilities in the form of hospitals and primary health centres, catering to the population of Plant Township and the peripheral areas, resulting in access to improved health care infrastructure to over 22 million people. The beginning was modest, but after three decades of perseverance SAIL's efforts resulted in establishing 39 primary health centres, 18 reproductive and child health centres, and 4 super-specialty hospitals.

Its other social initiatives included making provisions for access to potable water and electricity in the areas adjoining plants/townships and building and maintaining roads in townships and peripheral areas.

Moreover, SAIL set up sports academies at all the Plant locations for encouraging local sporting talent. The company set up six sports academies—an Athletics Academy for boys at Bhilai, a Hockey

Academy at Rourkela, a Football Academy at Bokaro, an Athletics Academy for girls at Durgapur, an Archery Academy at Kiriburu mines and a Football Academy at Burnpur. By basing sports at the grassroots level in the steel townships/company-run schools, SAIL helped embrace sports as a way of life.

A hugely successful cooperative movement in form of Durgapur Steel Peoples' Co-operative Bank Ltd. (earlier known as DSP Employees' Co-operative Credit Society) formed by SAIL, DSP employees, provided easy credit and transformed from a credit society to a licensed co-operative bank. Its particular significance lay in the fact that this initiative was conceptualized and implemented six years before the world-renowned experiments of Grameen Bank in Bangladesh.

It Is Sobering to be a Winner

The auditorium was jam-packed as the company gathered to bid goodbye to Chairman Pande on 30 September 2002.

At the end of a tightly packed program, the master of ceremonies Mr U. P. Singh, Executive Director (Operations) at SAIL Corporate Office, invited from the audience anyone who wished to speak very briefly on the occasion.

Girish Tuli who had earlier been an office-bearer in the Employees' Union at SAIL Corporate Office went to the dais. As he started exceeding his time limit, Mr U. P. Singh intervened. 'It is difficult to keep track of the time when emotions are high,' retorted Tuli. He concluded his speech by saying that no one other than Chairman Pande would have given the employees a wage revision at the time it was implemented.

Arvind Pande in his last communication to SAIL collective recalled how after taking over the charge in 1997 he had remarked, 'We have no choice but to be decisive, daring and different, take calculated risks and not seek refuge in conventional alibis.'

Facing real competition for the first time in the latter half of the nineties, SAIL embarked on a restructuring programme, the first of its kind in any PSU, which made the company stronger as never before, while addressing a widely felt need to operate as a commercial entity irrespective of the nature of ownership.

The entire focus of the restructuring initiatives had been to bring about a change—in thinking, in working and in aspirations; and it was satisfying that the company had travelled quite a distance on the chosen path.

He drew attention to how SAIL had transformed. There was a realization that an aggressive, proactive approach formed an essential ingredient for success, based on which SAIL had met competition headlong, outsmarting the competitors on many occasions. Its activities had become customer-centric and the end objective-enhancing value to the customers. Financial awareness encompassed every aspect of operations. The whole company, across functions and units, worked towards a greater goal, unleashing the power of synergized working.

When Arvind Pande rose to leave, the incumbent Chairman V. S. Jain whispered 'Let's give him a standing ovation'! As if on a cue, the entire house stood up and broke into thunderous applause, which continued to reverberate as Pande exited the auditorium and SAIL.

Back to the Present

As this book comes to a close, the world is in the midst of a worldwide pandemic (COVID 19), and there is uncertainty about how and when the economy, and the steel industry, and SAIL will revive. It promises to be a challenge bigger than ever faced before. However, in a small way, the experience of restructuring and turnaround described in this book can provide some pointers.

There were in subsequent years, other attempts to revive industries suffering from a cyclical downturn, or overtaken by technological changes, which made their products unviable. Many such cases came before the BRPSE (Board for Reconstruction of Public Sector Enterprises, Govt of India), of which Arvind Pande was a Member from 2004 to 2014. Most requested only for financial restructuring or debt waivers. The companies were always advised to come back with a more detailed and comprehensive plan, but few managed to do so. In many cases, the debt restructuring was recommended and approved by the Government but always proved to be a short-term relief. The experience in SAIL, on the other hand, was one in which the management was able to plan and implement a comprehensive Turnaround Plan, which revived the company and maintained it in a strong position for many years.

In one of the reforms announced as a response to the pandemic, the Government of India plans privatization of all non-strategic PSUs, which will probably include SAIL. There have been many earlier thoughts of privatizing SAIL or parts thereof. In fact, the privatization of steel companies across the world started in 1985 with British Steel, followed by others and by the Soviet plants after its break up. Today, only China and India have state owned steel plants. The urge to privatize comes from the need to raise resources for the State Exchequer, and a feeling that the private sector may manage the resources more efficiently. The efficiency argument is not well established as not all privately owned steel companies have proven to be more efficient.

PSUs do, however, complain of excessive interference and misguided oversight by the three Cs—CVC, CAG and CBI. These can become a tool in the hands of unscrupulous politicians to harass and extract illegal benefits from PSU management. Many believe privatization would free management from this handicap. Attempts were made in the past, including recommendations by a Committee headed by Arvind Pande in 2004, on Vigilance Administration in PSUs, for the CVC. Several measures were suggested which could ensure that fraud is prevented by a review of procedures and various other actions, without becoming an excuse for harassment. Unfortunately, these recommendations were never implemented. Hence, a continued argument in favour of privatization.

BRPSE had also suggested a restructuring of the interface between Govt and PSUs. The argument was that a large structure of Ministries had developed over the years to enable close monitoring, supervision, policy guidance with independent Ministries for Coal, Steel, Textiles, etc. After 1991, reforms and increasing delegation of powers to PSUs, there was no need for such Ministries which became overstaffed and underworked, leading them to create work for themselves by unnecessary interference in the affairs of the PSUs. BRPSE's suggestion was to bring all PSUs under one Central Ministry for ownership functions to be performed. This is the model being followed by SASAC in China (State-owned Assets Supervision and Administration Commission of the State Council), Temasek in Singapore and similar organizations in Malaysia, Italy and France (Government Shareholding Agency).

Soon after divestment of government shares in SAIL began, Arvind Pande met Mr L. N. Mittal in Mexico City in 1999 at a meeting of the International Iron and Steel Institute. Mr Mittal was willing to consider investing in 10 per cent of SAIL equity with a seat on the Board and felt he could contribute to improving SAIL's operations. The government, at that time, was however not willing to consider a strategic sale of shares. The policy is now different and strategic sale may be an option for SAIL. McKinsey in their report had also suggested privatization. Earlier chapters have described unsuccessful attempts to privatize IISCO, ASP, SSP and VISL. Divesting the special steel plants is an activity which again has been revived in recent years.

Looking back on the SAIL experience of restructuring and turnaround during this period, what are striking are the commitment and participation of the employees. Management theorists have for some time been talking of the primacy of stakeholder value vis-à-vis shareholder value. In a way, SAIL management was the first to consciously look at enhancing the stakeholder value. Mr Narayanamurthy once said that good corporate governance means that no one stakeholder benefits at the cost of another stakeholder. All stakeholders—shareholder, investor, banker, employee, customer, supplier and communities—must benefit. Today many management gurus talk of creating and maximizing value for an enterprise by doing so for all its participants, especially employees. The strength of SAIL today remains its employees, to the thousands of whom this book is dedicated.

SAIL Board of Directors
(As on 31 July, 2000)

Shri Arvind Pande
Chairman

Shri V. Gujral
MD, BSP

Shri S.B. Singh
MD, DSP

Shri B.K. Singh
MD, BSL

Shri R.C. Jha
MD, RSP

Shri V.S. Jain
Director, Finance

Shri M.K. Moitra
Director, Restructuring & CP

Shri S.C.K. Patne
Director, Projects

Shri A.K. Singh
Director, Commercial

Dr. S.K. Bhattacharyya
Director, R&D

Shri S. Pandey
Director, Operations

Dr. Atul Sharma
Independent Director

Shri D. Basu
Independent Director

Dr. Y.R.K. Reddy
Independent Director

Shri D.V. Singh
GoI Nominee Director

Shri C.S. Rao
GoI Nominee Director

Steel Production Process Flow Chart

BF-BOF and EAF/IF Routes

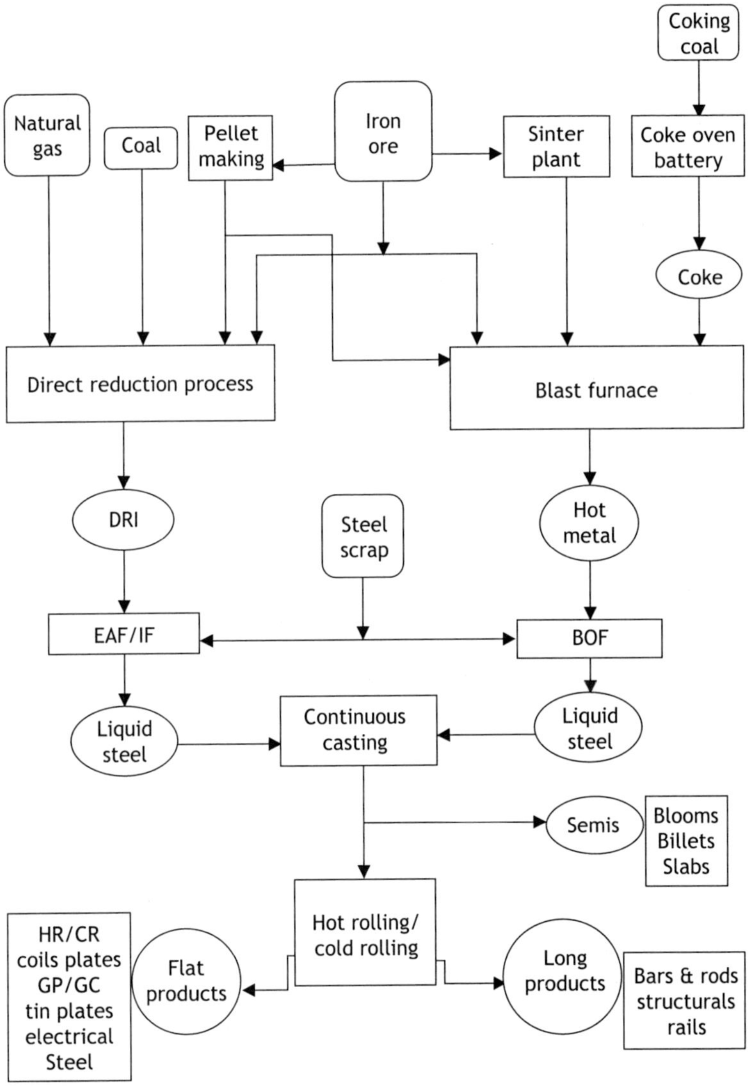

Bibliography

Bandopadhyay, M. (1987, December). *Story of public sector steel.* Publications Division, Ministry of Information and Broadcasting, GoI.

Business Standard. (1998, April 30). RSP cutting costs to save Rs.140 crore. *Business Standard.*

Business Standard. (2000, February 16). SAIL Gets Rs.8454 Cr Package. *Business Standard.*

Cooney, C. (2003, November 10). *The American steel industry: A changing profile.* CRS Report for Congress Congressional Research Service.

Dalal, S. (2002, November 24). Another steel plan. *Indian Express.*

Das, S., Krishna, K., Lychagin, S., & Somanathan, R. (2013). *Back on the rails: Competition and productivity in state-owned industry. American Economic Journal.* http://econdse.org/wp-content/uploads/2012/08/rails.pdf

Financial Express. (2002, October 25). SAIL banks on Rourkela Steel Plant for turnaround. *Financial Express.*

Government of India. (1989). *Metals in India's development—The vision of Jawahar Lal Nehru.* Ministry of Steel and Mines, GoI.

Government of India. (1991, July 24). *Statement of industrial policy.* Ministry of Industries, GoI.

Government of India. (1996–1997). *Economic survey.* GoI.

Government of India. (1997–1998). *Economic survey.* GoI.

Hindu Business Line. (2000, June 13). SAIL sets up office of restructuring. *Hindu Business Line.*

Indian Express. (2002, November 22). CCEA to review restructuring at SAIL on Friday. *Indian Express.*

Induction melting. *Encyclopedia Britannica.* https://www.britannica.com/technology/steel/Open-hearth-steelmaking

Industrial Development Bank of India. (1998, August). *SAIL financial restructuring report.* IDBI.

International Iron and Steel Institute. (1978). A hand book of World Steel Statistics. IISI.

International Iron and Steel Institute. (1996). *World steel in figures.* IISI.

International Iron and Steel Institute. (1997). *World steel in figures.* IISI.

International Iron and Steel Institute. (1998). *World steel in figures.* IISI.

Jayaswal, R., & Mukherjee, R. (2001, November 8). US threatens safeguard duty on flat steel products. *Indian Express.*

Kumar, R. (2014). *Intrapreneurs@mjunction. The making of an e-commerce giant.* Rupa Publications India Pvt Ltd.

Mathew, G. (2002, November 27). Crisil seeks another steel sector bailout. *Indian Express.*

McKinsey & Co. (1999, March). The Competitiveness Plan for SAIL. Mckinsey & Co.

Ministry of Industry. (March, 1998). Disinvestment Commission (Report VII). Ministry of Industry.

Ministry of Steel, Rajya Sabha Sectt. (2003, May). *Implementation status of modernisation expansion and financial cum business restructuring program of SAIL at a glance.* Ministry of Steel, Rajya Sabha Sectt.

Mukherjee, A. (1998, 6 April). Sail or sink it's a Titanic job. *Outlook.* https://magazine.outlookindia.com/story/sail-or-sink-its-a-titanic-job/205316

National Council of Applied Economic Research. (2015, September). *The Indian steel industry: Key reforms for a bright future.* NCAER.

Organisation for Economic Co-operation and Development. (1999, October). A North American steel industry perspective on steel in the CIS and other major markets. OECD.

Organisation for Economic Co-operation and Development. (2004, June). *Recent steel market development.* OECD.

Organisation for Economic Co-operation and Development. (2009, June). *Policy response to steel crisis.* OECD.

Radelet, S., & Sachs, J. (January, 2000). *The onset of the East Asian financial crisis.* NBER.

Rohini, S. (2004, April 17). Steel Industry, A Performance Analysis. *Economic and Political Weekly, 39*(16).

Sachitanand, N. N. (2003, December 5). Bhilai Steel contributes to safer rail travel. *The Hindu.*

Sarkar, R. (1999, July 22). Can SAIL rapidly (Re)Steel its Future. *Business Today.* http://archives.digitaltoday.in/businesstoday/22071999/cf4.html#

Schwartz, S. K. (1998, November 4). Steel industry faces meltdown. *CNNmoney.com.* https://money.cnn.com/1998/11/04/companies/steel/

Sengupta, S. (1998, May 15). SAIL Plans to Convert SDF Loans into Equity. *Business Standard.*

Srinivasan, N. R. (1990, March). The Corporate Story of SAIL. SAIL.

Steel Authority of India (1996–2004). *SAIL annual reports, 1996-97, 1997–1998, 1998–1999, 1999-00, 2000–2001, 2001–2002, 2002–2003, 2003–2004.* SAIL.

Steel Authority of India. (1997, August). SAILNews—Special Commemorative Issue (Vol. 25, Issue 6–8). SAIL.

Steel Authority of India. (1998, July). *Path to turnaround and transformation.* SAIL.

Steel Authority of India. (1999, Jan-Feb to 2004, March-May). SAILNews (Vol. 27–31). SAIL.

Steel Authority of India. (2004, December). *Statistics for iron and steel industry in India.* SAIL.

Steel Authority of India. (2008, February). A golden era, 50th year of production in SAIL. SAIL.
Suroor, S. (2001, November 8). Call to privatise India's steel industry. *The Hindu.*
The Hindu. (2000, February 21). Move for privatization of steel plant flayed. The Hindu.
The Hindu. (2000, February 28). Salem steel plant issue: bandh on March 4. *The Hindu.*
The Hindu. (2000, March 5). Halt Salem steel plant privatisation. *The Hindu.*
The Hindu. (2000, March 9). Centre urged not to privatize steel plant. *The Hindu.*
The Hindu. (2000, May 29). Panel voices concern over SAIL move. *The Hindu.*
The Hindu. (2000, June 3). Separate setups to market SAIL's long, flat products. https://www.thehindu.com/todays-paper/tp-miscellaneous/tp-others/separate-setups-to-market-sails-long-flat-products/article28019176.ece
The Hindu. (2000, September 12). Opposition plans dharna on steel plant issue. *The Hindu.*
The Hindu. (2001, April 16). Steel majors hit by dumping. *The Hindu.*
The Hindu. (2001, August 5). India may take steel issue to WTO. *The Hindu.*
The Hindu. (2001, March 17). SAIL sells two captive plants to JV. *The Hindu.*
The Hindu. (2001, September 21). Steel majors' agenda for revival. *The Hindu.*
The Hindu. (2002, December 7). SAIL may close RSP's fertilizer unit. *The Hindu.*
The Hindu. (2002, July 18). How long will the steel price rise last? *The Hindu.*
The Hindu. (2002, March 7). U.S. curbs on steel imports. *The Hindu,*
The Hindu. (2002, May 12). Salem Steel Plant: Centre seeks T.N. cooperation. *The Hindu.*
The Hindu. (2002, May 18). CR steel: U.S. levy not to affect India. *The Hindu.*
The Hindu. (2002, September 10). SAIL to divest fertilizer unit soon. *The Hindu.*
The Hindu. (2002, September 12). SAIL revamp sent to back burner. *The Hindu.*
The Hindu. (2003, April 2). SAIL salable steel output touches 10 m tonnes. *The Hindu.*
The Hindu. (2003, January 10). Steel units toil to get out of debt trap. *The Hindu.*
The Hindu. (2003, January 23). Steel cos. get new lease of life. *The Hindu.*
The Hindu. (2003, January 29). SAIL makes cash profit in Q3. *The Hindu.*
The Hindu. (2003, June 3). SAIL upbeat after turnaround. *The Hindu.*
The Times of India. (2004, May 28). SAIL books highest-ever net profit. *The Times of India.*
Vinayak, M. (2000, June 15). Corrosion within SAIL. *The Hindu.*
World Steel Association. (2012). *The white book of steel.* World Steel Association.
World Steel Dynamics. (1996, May). *Steel strategist* (Issue no. 22). World Steel Dynamics.
World Steel Dynamics. (2002, July). *Steel strategist* (Issue no. 28). World Steel Dynamics.
World Trade Organization. (2001). *First written submission of India* (Report No. WT/DS206/R). https://www.wto.org/english/tratop_e/dispu_e/206r_b_e.pdf

About the Authors

Sanjay Kumar superannuated from Steel Authority of India Limited (SAIL) in September 2019, as Chief General Manager, after serving it for more than 30 years, in various capacities.

After joining SAIL in 1988 as an economist in the Business Planning Directorate, at its Corporate Office, he rose to head the business planning function of the company. In his tenure at SAIL, he was actively involved in tasks pertaining to strategic planning, joint ventures and business development. He was also a part of the investors relations team that regularly interacted with the investors, merchant bankers and equity analysts on the performance and prospects of the company and the steel sector.

Some of the key assignments he handled included formulating long-term strategy for the company—SAIL Vision 2030, Corporate Plan 2012 and Corporate Plan 2005. He developed the demand module for India Vision 2020 for the World Steel Association. He was also a part of the team that prepared the 'Investor Relations Guidelines' for the central PSUs in 2011.

Mr Kumar was a key member of the team that formulated and implemented SAIL's Turnaround Strategy in the years 1997–2003. Subsequently, in the chairman's secretariat, he dealt with the issues related to the company's special steels business, cost reduction strategies, business environment analysis and contemporary issues concerning the industry.

He holds a master's degree in economics and business administration from the University of Delhi.

An avid sports fan, Sanjay Kumar has diverse interests encompassing music, reading and watching movies.

Arvind Pande has worked as the chairman and CEO of SAIL from January 1997 to September 2002. During this period as chairman, he led the company in a major transformation and turnaround, facing challenges after decontrol of the steel industry and entry of new private players and supplies from overseas players. He joined the Board of SAIL as a full time functional director in August 1986, in different areas such as corporate planning, personnel, finance, Rourkela Steel Plant, and special steel plants. He worked as a vice chairman from 1992 to 1997.

After superannuation, he was an independent director in several private and public sector companies such as HDFC Bank, Coal India Ltd, Sandhar Technologies Ltd and Visa Steel. He chaired the Board of Bengal Aerotropolis Projects Ltd which, along with Changi Airport of Singapore, have built the first private greenfield airport at Durgapur in West Bengal.

He advised POSCO (South Korean steel company) for several years and chaired J-PAL South Asia (2009–2012). He was the member of Government of India Board for Reconstruction of Public Sector Enterprises (2004–2014) and member of conciliation board for ONGC, NTPC, NBCC.

Arvind Pande had joined the Indian Administrative Service in 1965 and has had varied experience in different districts.